SECRETS OF SUCCESSFUL COACHING

WINNING TIPS & ADVICE FROM 50 OF AMERICA'S MOST SUCCESSFUL COACHES

GREG BACH

SQUAREONE
PUBLISHERS

EDITOR: Allison Cirruzzo
COVER DESIGNER: Jeannie Tudor
TYPESETTER: Gary A. Rosenberg (InDesign)

Square One Publishers
115 Herricks Road
Garden City Park, NY 11040
(516) 535-2010 • (877) 900-BOOK
www.squareonepublishers.com

ISBN 978-0-7570-0468-1 (pb)
ISBN 978-0-7570-5468-6 (eb)

Library of Congress Cataloging-in-Publication Data

Names: Bach, Greg, author.
Title: Secrets of successful coaching / Greg Bach.
Description: Garden City Park, NY : Square One Publishers, [2019]
Identifiers: LCCN 2018034135 (print) | LCCN 2018040355 (ebook) | ISBN
  9780757054686 (ebook) | ISBN 0757004687 | ISBN 0757004687q(paperback)
Subjects: LCSH: Sports for children--Coaching.
Classification: LCC GV709.24 (ebook) | LCC GV709.24 .B33 2019 (print) | DDC
  796.083--dc23
LC record available at https://lccn.loc.gov/2018034135

Printed in India

10   9   8   7   6   5   4   3   2   1

Contents

For
Mom and Dad

Acknowledgments

In the fall of 1993, while working as a sports editor at a daily newspaper in Michigan, I sent my resume and some writing samples to Fred Engh, who was listed as the president of an organization called the National Youth Sports Coaches Association in a book I had checked out from my local library. There was no internet at that time, so I knew nothing about the company—or even if they were hiring. I assumed they did something with sports, and with the mailing address of West Palm Beach, Florida, year-round sunshine sounded pretty good to a life-long Michigan resident who was bracing for another season of covering high school football games in frigid conditions, where post-game interviews were conducted with chattering teeth and fingers covered in heavy gloves, unable to hold a notepad.

Some weeks later, I got the call that would change my life. Fred received my materials, we arranged for me to fly down for a weekend interview, and before I returned home from my twenty-one hours in South Florida, I had a job offer to weigh—and soon accept. And ever since that trip, I have been lucky to be a part of this amazing organization—now known as the National Alliance for Youth Sports —for twenty-five years. Fred gave me a chance, and I'm grateful.

Now, it's an impossible task to acknowledge everyone who has helped me along the way, but there are certainly a few that stand out, who, without their guidance, wisdom, and influence, I certainly wouldn't have ever had the confidence and courage to move across the country and change careers, or even entertain the thought of tackling a book. There is my first college journalism professor, Cy Leder, whose restaurant reviews in *The Flint Journal* were must-reads for anyone who appreciated great writing. He taught me so much about structuring sentences, grabbing readers, and conducting interviews—and he made learning the craft of writing fun. He was a special man who touched lives.

I also owe big-time gratitude to Ron Mason, the legendary hockey coach at Michigan State University, who also later served as the school's athletic director. While pursuing my degree in Journalism there, I worked for *The State News*, the campus newspaper, and somehow landed the glorious job of covering the Spartan hockey team. Coach Mason, who ranks second all-time in NCAA history with 924 wins, gave me near-limitless access to one of the nation's premier programs. I rode on the team bus to every away game, including places like Chicago and Columbus; I stayed in the team hotel; and win or lose, he always answered every single one of my questions. As a twenty-year-old who had no idea what he was doing, I know without a doubt that most of those questions were likely bad ones. But he never hesitated in providing a response. The man was pure class, and because of him, that season ranks as one of the greatest times in my life.

A big thank you goes to John Engh, the executive director of NAYS, who gave the green light for this project when I presented the idea to him. As NAYS continues to be a national leader in providing the best training and resources for those involved in youth sports—and this book is just one small piece of our many outstanding efforts and initiatives—it's exciting to consider what awaits in the coming years under his leadership and vision. He has a genuine passion for youth sports and giving kids positive experiences, so it's exciting to walk through these doors every day and be a part of something special.

I'd also like to thank Rudy Shur at Square One Publishers, for believing in this idea when I presented it to him, and for his incredible insight and guidance through the years. A phone call with this man produces lots of laughs, and I always end up with pages of notes as I scribble down golden nuggets on the writing process that he shares with me. Through the years, he has spent a lot of hours on the phone with me on different projects, and his guidance is greatly appreciated. Ally Cirruzzo has also been a huge asset on this project, as her special touch is on every one of these pages, making this book a true team effort.

Of course, the biggest reason why this book is in your hands is because fifty incredible coaches with calendars packed with obligations and responsibilities took the time to speak with me. They carved out time because they genuinely care about kids and coaching them the right way.

There was University of Miami basketball coach Jim Larranaga, who made a special trip to the team's facility in Coral Gables on a mid-week summer morning to sit down and talk youth sports for more than half an hour.

New Orleans Saints coach Sean Payton made time at the NFL's annual league meeting to connect on a second-floor balcony in Boca Raton, Florida. World Series champion Joe Maddon, manager of the Chicago Cubs, spoke with me outside the team's dugout two hours before a game at Marlins Park. I drove four hours—one way—for a powerful six-and-a-half minute conversation with former Tampa Bay Buccaneer head coach and current Ohio State University defensive coordinator Greg Schiano that was worth every mile.

There was volleyball legend and U.S. Women's Olympic coach Karch Kiraly, who spoke passionately for nearly thirty minutes while driving to the team's practice facility in the months leading up to the 2016 Summer Olympics. St. Louis Cardinals manager Mike Matheny and Baltimore Orioles manager Buck Showalter shared their insights with me during interviews at their teams' spring training facilities in Jupiter, Florida and Sarasota, respectively. Doug Bruno, the long-time and hugely successful head women's basketball coach at DePaul University, and assistant coach on the 2016 U.S. Women's Olympic basketball team, spoke to me while driving during an out-of-state recruiting visit.

Plus, there were so many early morning and late evening phone calls with coaches who were kind enough to squeeze me in, like Stanford football coach David Shaw, Northwestern basketball coach Chris Collins, and Sacramento Kings assistant coach Jenny Boucek, just the third woman to hold an assistant coaching position in NBA history. There were Olympic softball greats Cat Osterman and Leah O'Brien-Amico, soccer standout Yael Averbuch, and University of Loyola Chicago basketball coach Porter Moser, who spoke with me from his car just two months after shocking the nation by leading his Ramblers to the Final Four.

There were former championship basketball players turned coaches, like Wake Forest's Danny Manning, Elon University's Charlotte Smith, and Pepperdine's DeLisha Milton-Jones. There were Olympic swimming medalists Caroline Burckle, Misty Hyman and Kara Lynn Joyce, who all work with young athletes these days. And there's Olympic track great and current Golden West College track coach Monique Henderson and former NHL coach Ken Hitchcock, the third most winningest coach in the history of the league, who gave willingly of his time following a morning skate to talk coaching kids, and so many more. Every one of them is terrific.

And, to my amazing mom and dad, there aren't enough words or pages to describe how much their love and support has shaped my life. They are simply the best. Early on in this project, I lost my dad, so it's painful that he's no longer around and that he didn't get to see the finished product. Sports was a bond we shared, where teams, coaches, and players provided endless hours of conversation that I cherish. I think he would have enjoyed reading what these wonderful men and women shared with me.

Foreword

In 1981, my dad, Fred Engh, started the National Alliance for Youth Sports (NAYS). Back then, it was called the National Youth Sports Coaches Association. The organization was focused on providing volunteer coaches with training and information to help them handle their roles and responsibilities and have a positive influence on their young players. As time went by, programs were created to address all aspects of youth sports, but the organization's major focus has always been on helping those who volunteer to coach kids' sports succeed. Whether they willingly stepped forward to coach or were persuaded to do so because no one else would, we wanted to make sure that a NAYS coach would provide all their players with life-changing experiences that they will remember for all the right reasons.

I signed on in 1988 and now, as the executive director of this organization, I sit in the chair that my dad occupied for more than three decades. I am proud of the incredible work our organization has done. And I'm even more excited about the future. We have the honor and privilege of working with some incredible organizations and people who are committed to providing the very best sports experiences for the boys and girls in their communities. It's what makes walking through the doors to our building every day so rewarding— these are some truly special people doing amazing work. And I'm thankful that we have been a part of these efforts for all these years and will continue to do so. Through the remarkable work of these dedicated organizations and individuals across the country, and on U.S. military bases worldwide, we have trained more than 4 million volunteer coaches. And those coaches, in turn, have impacted millions of children who show up at fields, courts, and rinks to play the sports they love.

Now, the youth sports landscape has changed dramatically through the years. And it is certainly a different atmosphere than what existed when we first arrived on the scene in '81. There are more opportunities for kids to play these days: there are all sorts of beginner level programs, countless recreational programs, and a dizzying array of travel teams that crisscross the country, competing all year long. But through the years, what hasn't changed when it comes to kids playing sports is the need for coaches to fully understand their roles and responsibilities so that they can make a positive difference in the lives of every player on their roster. Learning those all-important life skills like teamwork, respect, always doing your best, handling wins and losses with grace, and so many others, doesn't just magically happen. It requires adults knowing how to teach those aspects—and being a model of them all season long, too.

Coaching kids is hard. I know, I've done it for several sports. It doesn't matter if you have played sports all your life, like I have, or never had the opportunity to wear a colorful uniform and take the field. Regardless of a volunteer's playing experience in a sport, being on the sidelines in charge of motivating, encouraging, and correcting kids is challenging. Delegating playing time minutes, communicating with parents, and keeping all the kids safe is stressful. Conducting action-packed practices that grab kids' attention while also fueling their development is much more difficult than it sounds. And all of that is barely scratching the surface of what coaching kids is all about.

That was the driving force behind my dad starting this organization when he did. As the father of seven kids with a background in recreation and coaching, he began seeing too many volunteers in youth sports who, despite the best intentions, were causing emotional and physical harm to players—often, without even realizing what was happening. My father's drive to fix the problem formed the foundation of our volunteer coach training program from the beginning. He set out to gather insight from experts that could be passed on to moms and dads who were coaching kids, and ever since, we have strived to enhance and improve both the insight collected and how it is passed on to coaches.

Today, our volunteer coach training program, which is available at our website, nays.org, and can be completed from the comfort of home at an individual's own pace or onsite at thousands of recreation agencies, features insight from some of the top professional and collegiate coaches in the game. And our SportingKid Live site—nays.org/sklive—features free content updated daily on different aspects of coaching kids, parenting young athletes, and so much more. NAYS has never wavered in its commitment to provide the latest and best information to help those involved in any aspect of youth sports—from coaching to parenting to administering to officiating—fulfill their responsibilities to the best of their abilities.

Speaking of our SportingKid website, the author of this book, Greg Bach, is the person who manages it. Greg has been with NAYS for twenty-five years.

I remember when we first hired him. I had a sense early on that we had hired a lifer. His passion for sports goes far beyond that of a participant or a fan. He has always understood the positive impact that sports' inherent life lessons can have on a person—because they helped him in his own personal development. The ideas that hard work is rewarded, and that you will experience both failure and success and learn lessons from each, are the kinds of things any employer would love to have from a new employee coming to work on day one.

Greg started as our communications director with the responsibility to promote not only what we were doing on a national level, but to also help get press for the thousands of organizations that NAYS has been involved with over the years and to highlight the great work that they were doing on the local level. When Greg started, NAYS was mainly a training organization with the mission of educating volunteers who had signed up to coach their children in youth sports. As an organization, we learned along the way that there are way more needs than just training for these coaches. The idea that professional administrators of youth sports programs—those people who work at agencies that administer youth programs all over the country—had no formal training was a real eye opener. So back in the '90s, we created our Academy for Youth Sports Administrators with a professional certification to go along with it. Over the years, through so many different programs, from Hook A Kid On Golf, which gives kids who likely would never have had the opportunity otherwise to play golf, to Start Smart, a series of motor skill development programs to help parents teach their children sports skills before signing them up for organized leagues, Greg has been there along the way.

At some point, Greg went from communications director to a researcher and author. He helped our founder, my dad, write his own book about how and why he started the organization. And then, all of a sudden, in what seemed like no time at all, Greg had written eight instructional books for coaches, including six in the *Coaching for Dummies* series. Greg has become a valuable asset for NAYS and a true expert on youth sports, and specifically coaching children. We still rely on his ability to get experts from many different fields to provide content, but he has also become one of those experts himself.

With this new book, you, the reader, will benefit from what has taken Greg years to gather. Over the years, he has interviewed hundreds of the high-profile athletes and coaches that we see every day. They all have different philosophies and life experiences, but almost every one of them has a memory from their early days playing sports—and the valuable lessons that they learned have stuck with them. Can you imagine the value of this scenario to a parent just starting out with a child in youth sports? Let's set this up. You have 200 or so Olympic athletes, NCAA coaches, Super Bowl winning coaches, World Series participants, WNBA stars, and many others lined up to answer these important questions: what do you remember from your youth sports experience, and what do you want to pass on to the thousands of future participants, parents, and coaches that are coming after you? Then you take the fifty or so best answers and put them together in one place. That would be some pretty valuable information—and that's what you are getting with this book!

As a life-long and mega-passionate Baltimore Orioles fan, I accompanied Greg when we traveled to Sarasota to sit down and talk coaching and impacting kids with Orioles manager Buck Showalter during spring training a few years ago. He shared eye-opening insight on how he goes about connecting with the players at his level, and what coaches of children should be doing to forge those special bonds with their young players. It was fascinating to listen to, and inspiring to see firsthand. Here was one of the game's most respected leaders, with the pressure and responsibility of running a Major League baseball team, who carved time out of his schedule to talk about coaching kids. He cares. He wants youngsters having fun and learning skills—and that can only happen when volunteer coaches know how to go about their roles. Knowing that what Buck shared that afternoon comprises just one chapter in this book, it's easy to see how this can be such a valuable resource for coaches as they navigate their seasons. As you read, you will find so much more advice, tips, and insight from some amazing people who made time to share a few of their coaching secrets.

I am proud of the work our organization has done through the years, and continues to do every day, to be a leading voice and resource for helping provide safe and positive sports for kids. This book represents just one small piece of our wide-ranging efforts, but it provides significant insight on the challenges and complexities that accompany coaching youth sports—and being an effective leader. Coaching youth sports is a privilege, and it's a role that can have a life-long impact on kids. Use the incredible wealth of knowledge shared in these pages by some of the most respected coaches in all of sports to be that volunteer coach that kids love playing for and learning from.

John Engh
Executive Director of the National Alliance for Youth Sports (NAYS)

Introduction

I'll remember the conversation I had with a particular Super Bowl winning coach on a warm spring afternoon in Owings Mills, Maryland, forever. It is the reason you are holding this book. I had traveled to this Baltimore suburb a few years ago, which is the home of the spectacular practice facility of the NFL's Baltimore Ravens, to interview long-time Ravens head coach John Harbaugh. He is one of fewer than three dozen men in the history-rich NFL to guide a team to a Super Bowl win. He's also the only one who had to beat his brother to get his hands on that coveted Lombardi Trophy. In that drama-filled Super Bowl XLVII that was contested in the Superdome in New Orleans, the Ravens nipped the Jim Harbaugh-coached San Francisco 49ers 34–31.

As the Senior Director of Communications for the National Alliance for Youth Sports (NAYS), an organization I'm proud to say I have been a part of for a quarter-century now, part of my job involves gaining the insights of coaches, athletes, and various experts that we use in our trainings and feature in stories we share on our free SportingKid Live website, nays.org/sklive, to help volunteer coaches, parents, administrators, and officials make youth sports the best they can be for all kids. This particular springtime trip to Baltimore evolved as we were putting together a new video for our volunteer coach training program, which more than 4 million coaches have completed through the years.

Earlier that year, I had reached out to the Ravens to inquire if Harbaugh, one of the game's most respected leaders, would be interested in sharing his thoughts on some key aspects of coaching, such as teaching sportsmanship, cultivating teamwork, and winning and losing with grace, among others, that would help volunteers in all sports teach these important components to their young athletes. When I later heard back from the Ravens' media relations department that he was on board with this project, there was also an interesting request that accompanied the note: They asked that I send over the questions we wanted to ask in advance. I was happy to accommodate, never imagining even for a moment that an insanely busy NFL head coach—a *Super Bowl winning* coach—would ever see them by the time we sat down with him.

About two months later, I was at the Ravens compound, which sits on thirty-two acres and features three full-sized and immaculately maintained football fields situated behind a gorgeous 200,000 square foot training facility. I was accompanied by Patrick Engh, our long-time NAYS videographer. The Ravens were conducting their Optional Team Activities, OTAs in football jargon, which is just a fancy phrase for practices held for a few days during the offseason. Position groups were scattered across the three fields. Pads popped, whistles blew, coaches yelled, and trash-talking among the players punctuated the late morning air.

We were part of the media contingent numbering in the double figures, awaiting our chance to speak with Coach Harbaugh. The roughly two-hour practice ended with assistant coaches running wind sprints with the players across the width of the field, to cheers, jeers, and laughter as good-natured jabs and jokes were thrown around. Once players slowly began heading for the locker-room, the flurry of post-practice interviews began with Coach Harbaugh. He was swarmed by cameramen and reporters. Microphones and tape recorders jabbed in front of him. The NFL Network was there. So were local television crews, an Associated Press writer, a national magazine writer, photographers, local reporters, and many others. We watched the whirlwind of activity enveloping him while we set up for the interview that we had flown more than 1,000 miles for.

We were experimenting with the positioning of the chairs to ensure the proper angle to the sun when the Ravens' media relations director came over and stuck a dagger in our plans. She began with "I'm sorry," and my stomach flipped. What followed was catastrophic. She informed us that some of Coach Harbaugh's other interviews were running long, compromising his schedule, and that we would only be able to ask a couple of questions from our list of more than a dozen. A *couple.* Translation: I was in big trouble. My stomach burned. And my heart hammered. We had spent a lot of money—well, a lot of the company's money—flying to Baltimore, staying overnight in a motel, renting a car, and now we'd only be coming back with a couple of abbreviated responses. That's not exactly a message you want to deliver to the boss.

I felt my career disintegrating on the spot and would rather have been run over by a Ravens linebacker at that moment than return to the office and relive what was becoming a disastrous expedition. So, I began nervously pacing back and forth, meandering along the sidelines of the practice field where we had set up the chairs, wondering just how much we were going to be able to squeeze out of what was rapidly shaping up to be one colossal failure of a trip. I began scanning my list of questions, trying to determine which would be the most important ones to ask, since we were only going to be able to get Harbaugh's insight on a couple of them.

Eventually, he made his way over to where we were set up, greeted us with a warm smile, and shocked me with what he said next. He asked one of the media relations staffers to run up to his office and grab the questions we had sent over roughly sixty days ago. Why? Because he had made notes on points he wanted to make. He had no intention of giving us generic responses, or to throw out answers on the fly. He took this interview seriously because of the impact it could have on volunteer coaches who saw it. It's a moment that is seared in my memory. He not only made time for us, but he was fully committed to giving us his very best on every single question. He truly cared.

And man, did he deliver. Every question I tossed at him, he responded with insight and passion. He never glanced at his watch, looked at the media relations director hovering steps away to bail him out, or cut an answer short to move onto the rest of his day. His responses oozed enthusiasm. He even shared personal experiences from his days as a young athlete, as well as those involving his own daughter in youth sports, that provided a special touch. It was a fascinating conversation. I kept asking, he kept answering, and we got to ask every question on our list. And every response was pure coaching gold.

Through the years, I've interviewed thousands of coaches and athletes, and that exchange ranks as one of my all-time favorites. It also brings us back to what I shared at the beginning of this book. If John Harbaugh, son of a coach, a Super Bowl champion, and a parent of a child involved in youth sports, cared *this much* about helping volunteer coaches be the best they can possibly be for the young athletes they are working with, then there had to be other coaches in the professional and collegiate ranks who were just as passionate and caring about the best ways to coach kids and impact young lives as he was. So, my pursuit began to track down the very best insight from some of the most respected male and female coaches around.

And the response to my efforts was amazing. The coaches who made time in their mega-busy schedules to talk coaching young athletes have won Super Bowls, World Series, NCAA Championships, Olympic medals, WNBA titles, a Stanley Cup—and many are Hall of Fame inductees in their respective sports. They are some of the greatest leaders their sports have known, and what they have to share can change lives at every level of sport. So, regardless if you are new to coaching and will be taking on a team for the first time soon, or if you are a long-time coach who has spent many seasons on the sidelines, the incredible insight these coaching greats share will help anyone enhance their coaching skills at any level, and in any sport.

Consider this: as coaches, we expect athletes to embrace opportunities to learn, improve, and grow, and to use the feedback they get to fuel their pursuit of improvement and raise their performance. And the same mind-set applies to those who take on the role of a coach. To be a high-quality coach, one who molds character and impacts lives, requires being a life-long learner and grabbing every chance available for using new ways to motivate players, run more engaging practices, be a more influential leader, and so on. One of the many fascinating characteristics that all the coaches featured in this book share is their unquenchable thirst for knowledge. They never stop searching for new and better ways to perform their responsibilities. They see every day as a chance to help not only their athletes improve, but to become better and more well-rounded coaches, as well.

In these pages, you will discover the powers of coaching with a growth mindset and helping young athletes embrace the process. The wisdom imparted by these coaches includes the importance of bringing the juice— meaning high energy and enthusiasm to every practice; innovative techniques for encouraging and inspiring young athletes; and creative approaches for cultivating teamwork. You will learn the right ways to correct and motivate young athletes, and how to use visualization to help them operate in a positive frame of mind. You will also learn how to overcome obstacles that can undermine confidence and sabotage work ethics, and move past setbacks so they don't affect future performances.

The coaches in this book foster a genuine love and bond amongst teammates and truly care about their performances and experiences with the team. They share the best ways for handling pressure so that it doesn't disrupt focus and hinder an athlete's ability to perform at their best. And they teach the importance of being a great sport in victory and defeat.

All the amazing individuals featured in this book fell in love with sports as children, played them throughout their childhoods (many even collegiately and professionally), have coached at numerous levels, have achieved enormous success and, most important of all, have impacted countless lives in a positive manner. What is so impressive is what they all have in common: that deep reservoir of knowledge and insight that they enjoy sharing to help others help young athletes. They truly *care*. And they want you—no matter what age level or sport you coach—to be a positive influence on every athlete on your roster.

Coaching young athletes is a privilege, and with it comes huge responsibilities. Your coaching philosophy and how you choose to approach a season will have far-reaching and long-lasting implications on players for years to come. Your ability to communicate, innovate, inspire, build confidence, mold character, instill sportsmanship, plan practices, manage game day, be a terrific role model, and so much more, impacts whether your players improve, have fun competing, and develop an unquenchable passion for the sport; or if they have a negative experience and you sabotage their interest in playing the sport in the future. Use the advice shared by these amazing women and men, and you will be headed on the right track to being one of those special coaches that athletes remember for all the right reasons—for the rest of their lives.

Yael Averbuch

Professional soccer player with Seattle Reign FC ▪ Two-time national champion at the University of North Carolina ▪ Former member of the United States Women's National Team ▪ Youth soccer coach and trainer ▪ Founder of Techne Futbol, a training app for soccer players

When Yael Averbuch embarked on her youth sports adventures while growing up in Montclair, New Jersey, she cared about what most kids her age generally focused on—being with her friends and having lots of fun. She wasn't concerned about the coaching resume of the volunteer coach of the Orange Bullets, the first soccer team she joined at the age of seven. She didn't wonder if her coach had lots of experience playing the game, nor was she the least bit worried about how knowledgeable he happened to be in the sport. She was simply excited to be a part of the action and to step on that big patch of green grass on game day wearing a cool uniform. It was here, years before she would emerge as one of the country's top players, that her love of the sport was forged, thanks to caring coaches who put a heavy emphasis on having fun throughout the season—and delivered. That's something she has never forgotten while her career has taken her across the globe.

"Players can feel your passion for what you are doing as a leader and a coach, and it doesn't matter how much you know about the game or not," says Averbuch, who won two national championships at the University of North Carolina. "Volunteer coaches need to be passionate and fun-loving. That rubs off on players more than anything."

That passion for the sport, and for teaching skills and impacting lives, needs to be evident at all times. It can't be check in, run the practice, and check out for coaches. There's too much at stake. Young athletes' attitudes and interests are shaped by coaches, and their love for continuing with the sport can sizzle, or fizzle, depending in large part on the coach overseeing them.

"That's the thing I remember about my coaches," Averbuch says. "During water breaks, if they were messing around with the soccer ball and trying different things with it, I remember thinking, 'That looks really fun,

I've got to do that.' If they were excited to be out there, I was excited to be out there, too."

Ponder those words for a moment. Here's a world class player who has competed and succeeded at the highest levels of the sport. She was a dominant performer during her collegiate days in Chapel Hill. She played for one of the most storied soccer programs in the country, where she set a record by starting 105 consecutive games, and was later honored by having her number seventeen jersey retired. She was good enough to play on the United States national soccer team, and all these years later, remains a talented performer in the National Women's Soccer League. So, through the thousands of games and practices she has laced up spikes for, conducted everywhere from Washington to Seattle, and from Russia to Sweden, she recalls the *water breaks* during her youth practices with clarity. And a smile. That highlights just how powerful youth sports experiences are in a child's life, and reminds coaches of all sports how significant their responsibilities really are every second that they are working with players.

"Volunteer coaches need to be passionate and fun-loving. That rubs off on players more than anything."

Foremost, it's showing up at every practice and game with large doses of enthusiasm. It simply has to be there every time out. "The worst thing as a kid is to show up excited to play, and the coach looks miserable and doesn't want to be there," Averbuch says. "Volunteer coaches really just need to share that joy of being active and learning a sport together. Even if they admit to the players that they are learning it with them, that's fine."

By age nine, Averbuch had already made the decision that she wanted to be a professional soccer player. Her parents, Paul and Gloria, were both high-level long distance runners, so she learned from an early age not only the value of being disciplined and diligent with your training, but being passionate about something and then aligning yourself with coaches who matched that passion.

"The older I get, the more I realize how influential my parents were," she says. "I remember waking up to go to school and both my parents would have already done their workout for the day, showered, and were eating breakfast. So in my mind, it was just a normal part of life that every day you did some sort of physical activity or chipped away at something that was important to you or you were passionate about."

Soccer had grabbed her heart and wasn't letting go, and that passion for playing it has never wavered. By age eleven, she was already searching for new challenges on the field, so for the next few years, she was the only girl on a boys' team. Then she spent her high school years playing for a U18 girls' club team while also traveling and competing with youth national teams. She savored the competition, and she loved coaches who ran practices that dialed up the intensity level and pushed everyone to perform the best they could.

"If you're able as a coach to develop some type of competitive structure where everyone feels like they have a chance and can engage in the competition at whatever level they are—from a beginning player to the most elite player on the team—that's where you make it really fun," she says.

She also appreciated, and has some fond memories, of her coaches inserting themselves into the practices. It presented new and exciting challenges for players; it was a great way to prevent practice boredom from having a chance to creep into a mid-season session; and what young player doesn't relish the opportunity to out-perform the coach in a drill?

"I remember I would always look forward to going to my team's practices because I knew it was going to be really competitive, and our coach would play with us," Averbuch says. "And I always wanted to beat him and take the ball from him."

There are numerous ways coaches can spice up their practices by being a part of drills. It can be something as simple as being the goalkeeper while a group of young players go through a shooting drill; or during one-on-one drills, the coach can work his or her way around the field so each player has a chance to try to steal the ball from the coach, and vice versa. One thing is for certain: Any time a coach steps on the field and becomes involved in the drills, the practice energy skyrockets, enthusiasm flourishes, and players' focus becomes laser-intense.

During her offseason from the National Women's Soccer League, where Averbuch plays for the Seattle Reign FC, she spends a lot of time working with young players at camps and clinics across the country. She's gained tremendous insight from her years in the sport, from the youth playing fields to some of the biggest stages, and she relishes the opportunity to share what she has learned to help the next generation. She's grateful for the impact her coaches have had on her throughout her journey in the sport, and she's passionate about impacting young lives through a game she loves.

"A big thing that I try to relay in every event I do is putting the responsibility in the hands of the athletes. Every time I talk to youth players, I empower them to take control of whatever they want soccer to be for them," Averbuch says. "Whether if they just want to play for fun, or if they really want to take their game to the highest level."

It's an interesting, and effective, approach that helps youngsters really put some thought into what they want to gain from the sport and then savor and fully enjoy their journey. "If they feel like that's their responsibility and they're in control somewhat, that becomes enjoyable and empowering to them," she says. "I always tell them that I'll show them a ton of ideas that they can do with the ball, but they don't need me, and they don't need their coach, to do these things. As players, they have the control to go out and work on their own and develop into whatever they envision for themselves. You can make yourself as good as you want to be, and that's fun."

Opening young athletes' eyes to opportunities they can seize on their own to work on their skills, and the best ways to be efficient with that work, is part of being a true leader. Averbuch learned lessons in leadership from legendary North Carolina soccer coach Anson Dorrance, and what she says about playing for him rings true as the ultimate compliment any coach at any level should strive to achieve: "He really does genuinely care about every single player who plays for him as a person, even more than as a soccer player. He's a very classy person, and his goal is to leave every player with an experience that will make them their absolute best on the field and give them the tools to succeed in life."

Averbuch had an opportunity to be a captain at North Carolina, a huge responsibility that matches what all volunteer coaches take on when they work with a group of young athletes. "The biggest thing I learned was that being a leader really is about serving other people," she says. "It's not just delegating and demanding of other people, but being a wonderful example." Now, that's what coaching any sport is all about.

Jennie Baranczyk

Drake University women's basketball coach ▪ 2018 and
2017 Missouri Valley Conference Coach of the Year
▪ Recipient of Big Ten's Medal of Honor for academic
and athletic excellence in 2004 ▪ First Team All-Big
Ten selection in 2003 at the University of Iowa

 The post-practice scenario for youth sports teams around the country is chaotically similar: players scurrying around, grabbing water bottles, checking text messages, chatting with teammates, and heading for their rides. This whirlwind of activity is usually preceded by the coach gathering players for a quick rundown of the practice or game schedule for the coming days, and then everyone scatters. It's a valuable chunk of time that coaches of young athletes can actually put to much better and more profound use, just like what unfolds in Des Moines, Iowa, when the Drake University women's basketball team concludes its practices.

Jennie Baranczyk, an All-Big Ten performer during her playing days at Iowa, where she averaged sixteen points a game as a senior, has been the head coach at Drake since 2012. Baranczyk has long recognized the enormous value of feedback, but her perspective is uniquely different—and incredibly refreshing. When it comes to feedback, she doesn't travel one-way streets, only dispensing it to her players as the leader of the team. At Drake, her players are *required* to give feedback, too. Every day.

"One of the things that we have learned to focus on at the end of our practices is having our players give feedback," says Baranczyk, the 2018 and 2017 Missouri Valley Conference Coach of the Year. "Some days, we say, 'Okay, just give feedback if you have it,' and then other days, everyone is required to give feedback."

That's right, players have a voice. And what they share matters. Consider the message that sends to every player on the roster: the coach cares about me; the coach cares about what I am feeling about this practice; and the coach genuinely cares about our team and our thoughts on how everything is going. That's pretty powerful, and Baranczyk's approach has applications at all levels of sports.

"It's relatable at any level," says the mom of three. "I have a five-year-old, and after he plays in a baseball game, we ask him what was really fun, and what is he going to try to work on. You can do the same things with your kids that you are coaching, and then you can do the same things with players at our level, too."

As you head into your respective seasons with your teams, work this into your post-practice routines from the outset. Just recognize, especially if you are coaching older athletes in their teens who have been competing for many years, that this may take some time to gain traction with the team. Many young athletes are accustomed to listening to their coaches, and then working to live up to what has been said to them. Being asked for their input, or to dig deep into their feelings about how everything is going, will be unfamiliar territory for them. But if coaches keep at it, it can be a pretty cool turning point in the season when that feedback starts to flow and kids are comfortable—and appreciative—of the opportunity to share their thoughts and be respected for what they have to say.

When she first asked for her players to share any feedback they had, Baranczyk says, "We had a lot of crickets for a long time." Gradually, players became receptive to the opportunity to speak, and now it's simply a normal part of the daily practice flow. "It just became part of what we do, and I don't really even have to ask for it," she says.

It all starts with a couple of simple questions, too. "One of the things that we ask them every day is to name one thing that went really well, and one thing that we need to be better at tomorrow," she says. "Sometimes they have to write it down, sometimes they have to say it out loud in front of everybody, and sometimes they just have to think about it."

For coaches with several players who may be quiet and shy, or even new to the sport or competition, having everyone write down their thoughts is a great way to get things rolling. Then gradually, as the season moves on and players become more comfortable with their teammates and coaches and their personalities begin to emerge, they will become more open to sharing their thoughts in front of the team.

"It is so valuable when you can make people self-reflect," Baranczyk says. "The things they say and are held accountable for at practice are what they're going to say when they go home, too. So the more self-reflection they do and feedback they receive, the better."

Baranczyk finds enormous value in her players providing post-game feedback too, so that's another area coaches can make note of as they navigate their seasons. What athletes have to share about the game can be terrific feedback that helps shape the course of the upcoming practices, and can even serve to help coaches with specific aspects going into the next game.

"After games, I have them write how they felt and their reflection of the game before I talk with them, just so I can get their thoughts before my opinion becomes theirs," Baranczyk says. "I want their opinions and thoughts to become their own. It's typically just between me and the player, and if there's a lot of common threads in something, then I can share the next day with the entire team that 'a lot of you shared this,' or that kind of thing. But I just want them to be thoughtful, and I want them to be self-reflective. Self-awareness is important. We have to know when we are on our A game, and we have to know when we weren't really on our A game and need to do better next time. Those are just life lessons for all of us."

"We have to know when we are on our A game, and we have to know when we weren't really on our A game and need to do better next time."

Of course, athletes at any level bump into days where, for whatever reason, they just don't have it. The spark isn't there, or the execution is a step slow. That's sports; it happens. Baranczyk also doesn't hide from the fact that players aren't the only ones who under-perform or make bad decisions. Those off-days can strike coaches, too.

"As coaches, we're not always great either," she says. "We make bad decisions, too. And sometimes we're not decisive enough, or we're not direct enough, or we've got to be better in other areas too, and our players see that. Even in my feedback, it's not always about what the players didn't do well, it's also got to be about the things that I didn't do well."

And by establishing open lines of communication between coaches and players—where they are encouraged to speak freely and openly—coaches can gain incredible insight on areas that they could have performed better in for the benefit of the team. Just like coaches want young athletes to digest their feedback that is intended to help them perform better in the sport, they also have to be receptive to getting feedback in return that can be utilized to enhance their coaching skills.

"Your role as a coach is very significant," she says. "Players really want to know the why and the how, and they want to know that you're a real person and that real people make mistakes."

Of course, some practices will be spot on. Those are the days that coaches love as players perform with energy and enthusiasm, executing at high levels and savoring the hard work it takes for getting better. And then there will be those sessions that flop, with players who aren't engaged and drills that are messy and unproductive.

"You can be positive without saying everything was great and fantastic," Baranczyk says of those practices that fail to meet everyone's expectations. "You can still be positive and constructive at the same time." And then you take the feedback of players, listen and note their comments, and prepare for the next time you practice together.

Doug Bruno

DePaul University women's basketball coach ▪
Winner of more than 700 games ▪ Assistant coach
for the USA women's national basketball team ▪
Played college basketball at DePaul University

Doug Bruno is quite the multi-tasker. The legendary women's basketball coach at DePaul University, who has won more than 700 games, doesn't attain this staggering success without being able to skillfully navigate numerous tasks with laser focus, and get the results he covets. On a Friday afternoon in late April, the Chicago native, whose Lady Blue Demons play at McGrath Arena on the Doug Bruno Court named in his honor, is multi-tasking from a rental car somewhere in north Florida. While on a recruiting trip, listening to his GPS spit out left and right turns, he's passionately speaking over the driving instructions about a topic that he cares deeply about—and that's coaching young athletes the right way. His wisdom will help you navigate your seasons, too.

You see, Bruno loves basketball. He's an enthusiastic teacher who cherishes opportunities to work with young athletes on all elements of the game—everything from the proper way to release a shot to the right way to behave on the court. He's a huge proponent of coaching all the nuances of the sport in the proper fashion. It all matters. And he's a true master at it. During his girls' basketball camp, which has been running for more than forty years, he's not a casual observer patrolling the sidelines. He's out there among all the players, dispensing wisdom, applauding effort, and remedying miscues.

"I'm on the floor of our camps seven to eight hours every day," he says. "And I do know how hard it is coaching kids, and that's what I tell my coaches: If you can teach a ten-year-old how to execute a fundamental, then it should be a lot easier to teach an eighteen-year-old that same fundamental."

One of the notable challenges that coaches of all young athletes face is delivering the constructive feedback that is crucial for learning how to perform fundamental skills correctly, but which is often so unpleasant for young players to hear and digest. Nobody enjoys criticism, so when young athletes are in a group setting during a practice session and are drawing attention for doing something incorrectly, that discomfort only multiplies when a coach addresses it. Being called out in a lay-up drill for releasing the ball wrong, or using poor footwork on defense, can be traumatic moments in a young athlete's life. They want to please coaches and be successful athletes, but many aren't aware of the long process involved and all the coaching that is required to take them where they want to go.

Those interactions between coach and player, where critiques and corrections are made, can define the season and set the course for that athlete's journey through the sport. It can't be avoided—use of improper techniques while performing fundamental skills must be addressed right away, as well as continually worked on at every practice. So it's important to handle these exchanges with care, as they'll occur at practices all season long.

"It's very important to play to the players' strengths while you are working on their deficiencies or weaknesses," says Bruno, who played college basketball at DePaul under Hall of Fame coach Ray Meyer. He advises pitching to young athletes that any comments directed their way are all about helping to make the team the best it can be. So if critiques are framed in that manner—that this is all about building and developing the team, and players have a responsibility to their teammates to listen and learn from the feedback—it can make the process of teaching and coaching operate much more smoothly.

Bruno also recommends that coaches talk about accountability to both the individual athletes and the team as a whole. "And encourage them to talk to each other as well," he adds. "That makes the critique not just about the players, but about their responsibility to the team."

His approach to teaching skills goes back to his childhood. "I use a teaching method I learned from my seventh grade nun, Sister Raphael Mary, who was a member of the Adrian Dominicans," he recalls. "It's instruction, demonstration, imitation, and repetition. A teaching method of instruction is the coach talking; demonstration is showing visually what to do with the coach demonstrating, or having players demonstrate; imitation is getting the athlete to execute slowly and correctly; and repetition builds to game speed."

Bruno has added another component to the mix: constructive critique.

"If you can communicate to your players what every drill is going to be, explaining to them that 'This is going to be instruction, so we're going to be in a talking mode now,' the players aren't going to be frustrated because you are talking," he says. "If we're in a demonstration mode, everybody is in a position to be observing the correct demonstration. Imitation is teaching slow, slower, and slowest and getting the athlete to execute correctly; and then repetition is building to game speed, where you are letting them go and letting them make some mistakes on the fly. They know that they're going to make mistakes and that you're not going to stop them."

After working through all those stages, Bruno and his staff dive into the feedback and help work through all the challenges that accompany learning new skills and plays. If coaches present this entire platform to players, and explain the purpose of each phase, players will be more receptive to the process. They will recognize the feedback they receive as valuable information intended to help the team operate at a higher level, as it raises the level of play of each athlete.

"If you prepare players for adversity, they are going to be more equipped to handle it, as opposed to being surprised by it."

"The constructive critique comes after the fact," Bruno says. "It's a method that we use, and that helps us. If you can have your players understand the rest of the teaching model, then the constructive critique just doesn't become what the entire practice is all about. Often when receiving constructive criticism, players, specifically young players, can develop a feeling that they cannot 'do anything right.' It is so important to meet with your entire team before practice ever begins and carefully discuss where these interpretations and feelings are truly rooted. It is vital that players know they are doing 'so much right;' however, the constructive critique process tends to focus on what they need to improve."

Bruno recommends the "sandwich method" of critique: "Positive comments, followed by what needs to improve, followed by more positive comments. However, even when a coach uses the sandwich method, a young player can still feel overwhelmed and believe they 'can't do anything right.' It is our job as teachers and coaches to meet these potential feelings head-on, before they ever occur. It is also very important that we continue to be in touch with these inner feelings athletes have of, 'I can't do anything right,' and constantly communicate to our players outside of practice all of the great things they are doing right."

When players transition to game day and are ready to put those skills to use, Bruno notes that it is important for coaches to address with the team the fact that adversity will occur during games. After all, there will be shots missed, perhaps several in succession at different junctures of the contest. Your team may play great defense, but simply encounter a hot-shooting team that is draining shots from all over the court. Or maybe some close calls will go the other team's way. Adversity strikes in many different forms, and it can show up at any time during a game. The more young athletes are aware of it, and how to work through it, the less likely these moments will disrupt their confidence or wreak havoc with their execution.

"You have to teach players how to handle adversity and talk about what it's about," Bruno says. "If you prepare players for adversity, they are going to be more equipped to handle it, as opposed to being surprised by it. You let players know where it's going to come from in a game: a referee may make a call you don't like, an opponent may scratch you or trash talk you or do something of that nature; or I, as a coach, might say something to you in a way that you don't necessarily like—that's adversity. If you've gone seven trips without scoring—that's adversity. If the other team gets on a roll—that's adversity. But if you are teaching them these aspects of the game, because adversity is a part of every game, you are helping them with life skills. We'll make adversity our best friend—we'll strive to play the perfect game and embrace anything that comes our way. That's what you are supposed to do as a coach."

Jenny Boucek

Assistant basketball coach with the Sacramento Kings ▪
Former head coach of the Seattle Storm of the WNBA ▪
Played college basketball at the University of Virginia

 During the 1980s, the state of Tennessee churned out big-time women's basketball players at an assembly line rate. "Tennessee was the best high school state for girls basketball at that time," says Jenny Boucek, a good authority on these matters because she *was* one of those special players that countless college coaches wanted on their campus. Growing up in the shadows of the state capital in Nashville, Boucek was a gifted multi-sport high school athlete who excelled at basketball, volleyball, and tennis—though it was the basketball court where she did her best work and would later help others do so under her leadership. As a teen, she shredded defenses, scoring more than 2,000 points during an illustrious career as the state's top scorer. Her exploits put her on the radar of top women's collegiate basketball coaches, and she eventually signed a letter of intent to play for Debbie Ryan at the University of Virginia. But then there was the *almost* phone call that sent a strong message that forever changed her thinking—and her approach to the game.

"I came home after a game, and I was beating myself up," Boucek says. "We had won, and I had scored a lot of points, but I was becoming a little bit of a perfectionist. My mom came into my room, picked up the phone, and said she would call Debbie right now and tell her that I'm not playing in college, 'because the second you stop having fun playing sports is the second we won't let you do this anymore.' She really left an impression on me that this is for fun, and I still have that deep inside of me. It has never left."

Moms know best, and Boucek grabbed onto that message and carried it with her to Charlottesville, where she did get to play for the Cavaliers and Coach Ryan—and boy, did she ever *play:* the four-year starter helped lead the team to four regular-season ACC titles and three NCAA Elite Eight appearances, twice earned team Defensive Player of the Year honors, and finished her career as a member of the 1,000-point club. From there, she took Mom's message to the professional ranks, where she was a long-time head coach in the Women's National Basketball Association (WNBA) and now has the distinction of being just the third woman in National Basketball Association (NBA) history to serve as a coach, where she's on the Sacramento Kings staff as an assistant coach.

"If we can have fun on the pro level, there's no excuse for not being able to do that on every level," says Boucek, with an oh-so-important reminder for coaches of young athletes to weave that crucial fun element throughout their season. During her tenure as head coach of the WNBA's Seattle Storm, it was common for music to play during practices.

"We make competing fun," she said from her Seattle office during her final season with the Storm. "We don't make it an environment where they are afraid to make mistakes. There's a time and a place for more goofy fun, and that's not practice. But we make competing fun for them. If they've lost the love for the game along the way, we want to rekindle. We want to stir the flames and passion inside of them, so that even though it's technically a job for us, I want their primary motivation to be their love for the game. Basketball is our first love for all of us, and I don't want that to change. And if it has changed, I want to get it back, so we prioritize that. We prioritize having fun."

The word *fun* gets tossed around a lot when the topic is youth sports. But it simply can't be stressed enough. Think about your own job or activities that you participate in. When you're having fun, you feel good and you feel invigorated. When you are focused and engaged in the process, your mood elevates, your worries evaporate, and you can't wait to do it all again. That's the type of atmosphere that transforms young athletes into life-long participants. So, when coaches can fill kids' emotional tanks with those same good vibes, they will respond accordingly: you'll notice energy levels rise, effort multiplying, and enthusiasm skyrocketing.

"Players, coaches, and people perform their best when they're having fun," Boucek says. "And it's understanding that it's not mutually exclusive. The ha-ha fun when you're at parties is different than the type of fun of working hard with a group of people and getting better and accomplishing goals and embracing challenge and embracing failure. You can make all that fun."

When coaches can turn something like learning a basic fundamental skill of the sport into an interesting and fun pursuit, players will be more receptive to feedback; they won't be devastated by the numerous mistakes that will certainly happen along the way; and they'll look forward to learning other skills in the same fashion because they know the experience won't be filled with peril at every turn.

"The point is to make competition fun and to celebrate making mistakes when we try something new," Boucek says. "To make it fun, to celebrate your teammates' success, and to experience how gratifying it is to be focused on somebody else. And I always tell them, if you're a real team, then all the blessings that we experience are multiplied, and all the challenges are divided. And that's when you can get through anything. Every little victory that a single player has, the whole team gets to celebrate, so it makes it fun."

That approach, accompanied by a growth mindset, is a wonderful platform for teaching, molding, and building skills. And enjoying the work that goes into it. But it has to be genuine, otherwise there is little chance of success. "Every coach should study the difference between a growth mindset and a fixed mindset," Boucek says. "And look in the mirror and see which one that they live by, believe in, and ascribe to. Because if it's not who you are as a coach, then you're not going to be able to impart that to your team. So you have to buy into it first. If you buy into a growth mindset, it comes out pretty naturally, because you know that that's what brings out the genius in young players. The greatness in young players is not being afraid to get outside of their comfort zones—not too far out, but just past that threshold, where they are getting better."

"The greatness in a young player is not being afraid to get outside of his or her comfort zone."

That's the real beauty of a growth mindset in action. It's nudging young players into that uncomfortable terrain just a step or two beyond what they are capable of doing at that juncture in their development. It's where mistakes are going to happen, and they are going to happen frequently. But when coaches know and help players understand that this is territory where, with patience and hard work, skills are learned, developed, and honed, incredible learning can take place. And they are recognized and applauded.

"Getting better should be the thing that we celebrate way more than performance," Boucek says. "That's relative to every player and every team, but when it's your measurement of success, then every player can experience it. And that's something that can be celebrated continually, and should be celebrated continually. You have to be very careful to not overhype players who are naturally better, or players who things come naturally easier to, and really stay focused on trying to be consistent in celebrating improvement and growth and taking steps that will lead to improvement, and not just results."

To help young athletes navigate the ups and downs of competing and learning requires plenty of resilience, which has been one of Boucek's core values since she began coaching. It's one that—when learned—can help young athletes, both in sports and life. "When it comes to resilience, there's an epidemic nowadays of just an obsession with results, and quick results at that," Boucek says. "It's about performance, and a lot of reinforcement to talent. You want resilience on your team, and a culture where they are free to fail, and you're encouraging that—you're teaching and encouraging that making mistakes is how you get better. And you don't just say it, you live it."

A coach's words and messages are important, but young athletes are going to observe a coach's actions as well, and those will resonate more than anything. Messages must be tied to behavior. Actions must relate to a coach's philosophy. "If resilience is one of your core values, then you have to create a culture that reinforces that," Boucek says. "The biggest thing with coaching is that your actions have to align with your messaging."

Players will notice if you really mean what you are saying. If you don't back up your messages with the appropriate actions, you'll sabotage opportunities for learning and growth. "For example, if you say you prioritize defense, and defense is the most important thing to you, but you don't take your best offensive player out when he's not playing defense, or you say that attitude is really important, but then your best player is copping an attitude after missing a shot and you don't discipline her, then you're going to get nowhere," Boucek says. "And so whatever it is that you value, or you say that you value, you have to be consistent in valuing that."

Caroline Burckle

Olympic swimming medalist ▪ Personal development coach ▪ 2008 NCAA Female Swimmer of the Year ▪ Competed on the University of Florida swim team

 Long before Caroline Burckle emerged as one of the nation's elite swimmers, and later an Olympic medalist, the door to the mental side of competing was nudged open by her father. It happened during post-race conversations with him during her childhood, which gave the young swimmer her first peek at how vital it was to manage those mental aspects and not get tangled up in some of the negative thoughts that lurk in the shadows. Those chats also proved to mark the start of a fascinating trip for her: They led to competing at the University of Florida, winning SEC and NCAA titles, capturing a bronze medal at the 2008 Summer Olympics in Beijing, and now helping others manage the mental challenges that can snuff out dreams and ruin the chase of delivering when the big moments arrive.

All young athletes must learn to confront disappointing performances, which requires self-reflection, analysis, and having coaches or parents help them sort through the debris that can collect on the fringes of one's subconscious, stymieing future performances if they aren't handled correctly. Burckle recalls the disappointment she felt after a number of youth swim meets she competed in growing up.

"My dad said, 'Hey, I know you weren't super happy with that outcome, but I'm really proud of you. What is it that you feel you can do better?' His questions made me think on my own more than being told what I was doing wrong or right," she explains from her home in Hermosa Beach, California. "It was really great being asked questions and supported in that way. It's interesting because I felt more pressure from myself than I did from anybody. My parents were the most supportive individuals when it came to sports, and they were the kind of parents who were like, 'Well, if you don't want to do it for yourself, then you don't need to do it.' Of course, hearing that from your parents kind of tells a child something; it gave me the power of choice. I also realized, 'Oh man, I'm going to prove them wrong. I do want to do it.'"

Burckle was a fast swimmer—and an equally fast learner, too. The first time she qualified for Junior Nationals, she chose not to compete because she recognized it wasn't quite her time yet.

"I wasn't ready," says Burckle, who won two NCAA individual championships in the 200- and 500-yard freestyle events in 2008. "And so I just really needed some time to understand that it wasn't about places and times and being super-competitive, but it was more about the journey and doing things when I was personally ready. So I felt the pressure mainly from myself, but I really didn't have anybody who pushed me in a negative way other than to tell me, 'Hey, we're here for you when you're ready.'"

As Burckle went deeper into her career, the pressure of the meets intensified, and the stakes grew higher. She felt it. That weight of expectation, of trying to please others and prove herself every time she hit the water, was as difficult as ever. Coaches of young athletes in all sports must recognize that athletes have to fight these internal struggles, but if they don't have your helping hand to pull them through it, they may not ever discover their true potential or, even worse, bail out on the sport and miss out on a lifetime of enjoying it recreationally. It's what drove Burckle and Olympic gold medalist swimmer Rebecca Soni to create RISE Elite Athletes, a sports psychology-based approach to mindfulness and personal success in both sports and life. From competing in the glare of the Olympic spotlight, where the cauldron of pressure boils, to now working with athletes, Burckle has a unique perspective that can help you help your young athletes win that oh-so-complex battle of the mind.

"We created our program for that reason," Burckle says. "To be able to develop the Olympic mindset, which is a holistic approach to empowering yourself and knowing who you are as a person first. That helps control and calm the nerves, because the broad perspective is not making it all about, 'Oh my God, if I don't do this, then I'm a failure.' You know who you are; you have that self-confidence that when you go into a race, even if you didn't perform as well as you had hoped, you have something you're striving for regardless."

She explains that when it comes to performance pressure, "Something we talk to our athletes about is just knowing that the work is already done, and turning it on is the same thing as turning it off. Turning your brain on and clicking it into performance gear is the same thing as turning it off, because you get into autopilot, you get into a flow, and you learn that getting rid of distractions, zoning in on your focus, tuning the bad stuff out, and concentrating on what it is that you can control lets you turn off all of the things that you don't need to be focusing on."

Burckle helps young athletes develop that powerful laser focus by teaching them to center on those aspects that they can control, and ridding themselves of the baggage of what they can't control. "It's kind of this trick," she says. "We think we need to think harder, harder, and harder, but really it's just about trusting yourself, focusing on what you can control, and tuning everything else out. That's something that I learned probably later than I should have, but that's the beauty of what we have going now with society and sports psychology."

When game days, tournaments, or meets roll around, the competitors are going to bring an incredibly mixed bag of thoughts and emotions to the contest. For many, their confidence may be razor-thin if they failed to deliver their last time out or if they endured one of those weeks of practice where nothing seemed to be clicking for them. It's natural for young athletes to harbor fears of failing; fears of disappointing their parents; fears of letting down their teammates; or even fears of not fulfilling their private aspirations. Anyone who has ever competed in any sport at any level has experienced these anxieties, so as coaches, it serves no purpose to pretend they don't exist.

> ## *"It's important to acknowledge that your feelings are valid, but you don't live in that state of mind. You move forward."*

"For starters, I think that we're a society of, 'Get rid of it, get rid of it, stop thinking that,'" Burckle says. "And while it's true that you can snap out of things, you also have to be aware of your thoughts and where they are coming from. In my opinion, that is the biggest area for growth right now. We've got to change the culture surrounding, 'Stop thinking that.' Because the second somebody hears *stop*, they think of something negative."

Instead, fire up conversations about it with your athletes. If you can explore those thoughts and have open dialogue about them, guess what happens? Athletes will most likely become less fearful; they'll recognize their fears for what they are, and won't allow them to affect them as negatively as they may have in the past.

"What are you thinking and why are you thinking it?" Burckle says. "It's acknowledging that it's okay that people have those thoughts and fears, instead of trying to push them out so quickly. It's the thing that is on my mind the most: yes, athletes are taught to flip the switch and get rid of those thoughts, but are they not allowed to feel anything at all? It's important to acknowledge that your feelings are valid, but you don't live in that state of mind. You move forward."

As athletes go through the ups and downs of a season, coaches can highlight the process, that constant pursuit of improvement. And it's pointing out that there doesn't always have to be a hurdle that needs to be cleared, either. It's about getting athletes to operate in a consistent fashion.

"It's a learning process," Burckle says. "Things don't have to be broken for you to fix them, and things aren't always going to be peachy keen either, so it's about helping athletes learn from their fears and focus as much as they can on consistency with their emotions surrounding the ups and downs."

Jillian Carroll

Long-time youth soccer coach ▪ Former collegiate
soccer player at Northern Iowa University ▪ Sideline
reporter and broadcast host, Fox Sports Midwest

Some of sports' greatest lessons can be delivered by the unlikeliest of sources, and at the most unexpected times. And they can take on a far-reaching, life-changing legacy of their own. Jillian Carroll knows all about these moments. She was on the receiving end of one of them, which took place on a soccer field in her freshman year at St. Thomas Aquinas High School in Overland Park, Kansas. The moment was so powerful that she's never forgotten it; and so special that it has helped fuel her drive to have that same type of impact on the young soccer players she works with as a long-time volunteer coach in the Kansas City area.

Carroll's childhood was filled with activity, as she grew up playing all sports. "I played everything under the sun, including tackle football with the boys," she says. "But I didn't really ever find something I fell in love with until I had a ball at my foot. It was probably around fourth or fifth grade when something just clicked with me, and I found real success and enjoyment in soccer. Those two things go hand-in-hand—when you find something you're really good at, you enjoy it more."

She relied on a fierce work ethic to counter her small size at the time, and has never forgotten how important her club coach was in her development. "He is the reason why I was successful," Carroll says. "He stayed after practices with me and worked with me, just helping me learn as a student of the game. I was really lucky to have such a great relationship with him. I just admired him for teaching me the game that I fell in love with, and it took me very far."

Which brings us to a certain soccer field in Kansas during that fateful freshman year of high school. "I will never forget this memory. We had to do these shuttle sprints, and if you couldn't finish them, you weren't dressing that weekend for the game," Carroll says. "I could make five out of six of them, but you had to make all six or you could not play. I remember I kept trying and failing, and I was so blessed to have an older teammate stay after and run extra with me until I completed the time. Having a teammate stay and push through those sprints with me not only had a positive impact because I got to play, but also because of the character she showed by doing so. The way that she was so selfless and determined to help me achieve my goals, which would therefore better the team, is something I will never forget."

Carroll went on to have a stellar high school career and earned a scholarship to play collegiately as a midfielder at Northern Iowa University. But that moment, which occurred after one of countless practices conducted during her high school days, still shines bright.

"She was a senior at the time, so we only played that one season together," Carroll says. "That one training session, which felt like twenty-four hours but realistically was only about thirty minutes, had an invaluable impact on my life. Just the fact that she ran with me. Everybody hated those shuttle runs, and when you were done with them you were done, you wanted to get out of there. But my teammate stuck around with me, and I easily ran at least five extra times without making the time, so therefore it didn't count. I was exhausted, but I had to run it again and again until I finally succeeded. Her selfless act of putting the team first and helping her teammate is a life lesson that I learned and continue to use in my coaching career today. She's fantastic and I'm lucky enough to still have a relationship with her in my adult life."

"Having a teammate stay and push through those sprints with me not only had a positive impact because I got to play, but also because of the character she showed by doing so."

There is an ever-growing group of young soccer players in the Kansas City area who would apply that same wonderful tag to Carroll. She brings a special vibe to the field. A former elementary school teacher who now works as a sports broadcaster, she cares deeply and passionately about her players becoming a true team, one that genuinely cares for each other, supports each other, and enjoys working in unison. And, thanks in large part to the ultimate gesture by a high school teammate long ago, one of her focal points is getting players to wrap their arms around the true power of being part of a team and being there for each other.

Teamwork is one of those coaching concepts that gets tossed around a lot, but unless coaches are really putting in the time and effort to make it happen, young athletes will miss out on some golden life lessons. And some life-long friendships, too. Teamwork means much more than simply teaching players to deliver a pass to an open teammate. It's about cultivating a team-first culture, where athletes are working hard to improve their own skills and working just as hard to help a teammate improve theirs, too.

"It's a big challenge," Carroll says. "It's really about teaching the power of the team. What I've been able to really do with my kids is to teach them to find joy in being a student of the game, and being competitive with one another with the spirit of making a teammate better to make our team better." When young players stay after practice to help a teammate—because they *want* to—that's the ultimate sign that players care for each other and are willing to invest whatever they can to help the team grow. Coaches can't force friendships and caring, but what they can do is follow Carroll's lead by finding creative ways to blend team-focused activities into the season.

When players get to spend time around each other, they get to know one another better, the seeds of relationships are planted, and they have an opportunity to grow and flourish throughout the season. "We do a lot of things off the field, but as a team," Carroll says. "For example, we will go run a 5K together, because when I was young I did not like running, so I try to make it an enjoyable event with my players. We also do community service; we'll donate books, or help out at food kitchens. So we do things that are team-oriented, but not game-oriented. When we go to travel tournaments, we'll always do something crazy, like paint each other's nails or braid each other's hair, just to have some lighthearted moments where we can enjoy each other's company and still be a team away from the game. It's important that when you are coaching young players, it just becomes their norm, and then they learn that it feels good to give back. Or even if they want to do a 5K, they are thinking, 'Let me ask my teammates to see if they are interested,' and then it just becomes the culture."

It's that type of culture that coaches of all sports should have on their pre-season to-do list. It's no different than college basketball teams that take a summer trip to Europe. Sure, it's a chance to play some games, but the driving force behind those trips is building team camaraderie. Because when it doesn't exist, it's difficult for the team to operate at top efficiency. When those player bonds begin to form, team chemistry emerges, and that's a huge part of what makes participating in sports so special.

The young players on Carroll's teams, competitive as they may be, aren't going to remember the scores of all their games during the season, but you can bet they will remember gathering as a team for a road race, helping out together in the community, or just being goofy with one another before a game. Carroll bonded with her high school teammate after a practice, and their relationship is unbreakable today. "It's important to instill the values of a team," Carroll says, "and make it a team effort to pull each other along."

Patrick Chambers

Penn State University basketball coach ▪ Played college
basketball at Philadelphia University ▪ Father of four

 When it comes to fears, roller coasters twisting and plunging from the sky, snakes hissing in the grass, and receiving an unexpected call from the IRS all certainly qualify. These tend to bump the blood pressure up in most of us. But in sports, there is no room for players harboring fears of any kind if you want to lead your team to fulfilling its maximum potential. Because when players allow fears—of making mistakes, underperforming, losing, or doing something embarrassing during the game—to wedge into their minds, then disappointment and lackluster performances usually aren't far behind.

"I talk about being fearless and not worrying about what you look like," says Patrick Chambers, the head men's basketball coach at Penn State University, and a father of four. "Especially with the younger generation today. I have kids, and I'm trying to teach them not to be afraid. I tell them to be the first one on the dance floor. It's kind of a funny line that my father used to use, but it builds confidence. Who cares what you look like?"

In today's social media-crazed world, mistakes and mishaps bring an extra layer of discomfort for athletes, as errors can be captured and distributed on a variety of platforms before the game has even concluded. So it's to be expected that coaches will come across athletes who may approach games with a lot of trepidation. There may be basketball players reluctant to loft shots simply because they are afraid of missing in front of family, friends, and all those strangers in the stands on game day; there may be a quarterback who doesn't zip the pass to a receiver like he does in practice because he doesn't want to risk an interception; or there could be a softball player who begs out of the line-up when it's her turn to step up to the plate because it's the last inning of a close game and she dreads making the final out. These types of fears are everywhere, and a lot of young athletes have them. It's just that some are better at hiding them than others. It's the coach's job to spot them and help young athletes conquer them before they become so overwhelming that they kill kids' interests in continuing on with the sport.

31

Chambers understands that mistakes are part of the game; it's impossible to navigate a contest without teams making them. He's clear about them with his team, too. "It doesn't matter if you dribbled the ball off your foot," he says. "Nobody is perfect. Steph Curry does it, too. We're all going to have some type of adversity in our lives. Just focus on the next play, keep moving forward, and stay the course. But do it with great confidence." The moment a player's confidence begins to waver, an avalanche of negativity can flood positive thoughts.

"Sure, our confidence gets rattled at some point, but understand if you keep working at this, you are going to be okay, and there are going to be more positives than negatives," Chambers says. "And don't dwell on that negative. In society today, we dwell on that negative and enlarge it until it becomes 95 percent of the day. It happened. We've got to learn from it and move on from it."

To help counteract those negative vibes that can consume players' bodies and sabotage their minds, Chambers opts to blow up the positive. His voice reverberates through the Bryce Jordan Center during a Penn State practice when good things happen. "I'm going to applaud and make sure the entire gym knows when they do something well," he says. And what about those teaching moments that arise when a player doesn't have a handle on what is being worked on? "I'm going to pull him aside when I have to and give what I call 'constructive feedback.'"

So, by piling attention and praise on the good stuff, and addressing mistakes without acting as though they are catastrophic, coaches free players up to perform. Players don't feel shackled; they understand mistakes are part of the game because the coach treats them as such. So they end up taking shots when they are available, without their mind swirling with thoughts about missing. And they play aggressively, without constantly glancing to the sidelines thinking they're going to be yanked out of the game for delivering an errant pass or committing a turnover.

"If somebody is open, I tell them to shoot," Chambers says. "I don't tell anybody not to shoot. I try to give my guys on the collegiate level as much confidence as possible. They know I have confidence in them; I never pull them out for a bad shot. I want them to shoot open shots, and I want them to never look over their shoulder. If you can teach that at a young age, we're going to have better leaders, and I firmly believe we're going to have more confident kids."

Now that's a message to take to your practices all season long. It's got to be the approach during practice—every practice—for it to have a chance to translate to game day, too. When young athletes get a real sense of how coaches respond to those mistakes and miscues during practice, and then see that same mindset playing out on game days, opportunities for growth and strong performances flourish. Plus, athletes will be free to play without the burden of worrying that every missed shot or turnover is going to land them on the bench and cut into those playing time minutes that are like gold to players. Just be sure not to deviate from your practice personality once the scoreboard turns on. If coaches suddenly start treating mistakes on game day in front of everyone differently than they did during practices when no one was around, players will notice it immediately, and their play will suffer.

"If you're not goal-oriented at a younger age, you're just wandering in the woods. . . . You need some type of direction."

Chambers, who grew up the youngest of twelve children, is high-octane, full-time. He learned about the importance of playing hard and respecting the game from his grade school coach, who he still speaks with. "He really set the tone and taught me the foundation and the discipline of basketball," Chambers says. "I wish every young kid could have the type of impact that he had on me at that age."

That love of the game was seared into his heart, and he took it to Philadelphia University. He walked onto the Division II school's basketball team, started at point guard, and left as the school's all-time assist leader. So when it comes to leadership and directing players, Chambers is that guy.

"For me, it's all about passion," he says. "I wake up every morning and I can't wait to tackle the day. I can't wait to change lives and impact young adults and watch the progression of them becoming men. For me, it's the passion of running practice and the passion of helping kids. And they send the energy right back in return. They are the ones bringing the juice. Our practices are high energy, high intensity, and a lot of communication."

Establishing that vibrant practice atmosphere requires a genuine love of coaching, teaching, and inspiring young athletes. Chambers has it, and when coaches are genuine with that same passion, players devour it and respond accordingly.

"Positive thoughts equal positive outcomes, I live by that," Chambers says. "If you have a negative thought, you're never going to get a positive outcome. So be upbeat, be positive, bring energy, bring juice, and make it fun for the kids. If you make it fun, they are going to approach it differently, and they are going to want to practice hard for you and give you their best effort."

It's spoken about all the time in coaching circles, but it really does start with the fundamentals. Yes, young athletes see their idols performing at incredibly high levels on television, and of course they want to be lofting step-back, long-range three-pointers, or dribbling between their legs and behind their back on drives to the basket. But if they don't have a handle on the fundamental elements of the game first, they will develop bad habits that become increasingly difficult to break the deeper they go into their playing careers.

"I just think coaches on the youth level need to teach the basics, and they also need to be patient," Chambers says. "We all need to teach the basics so kids have a great understanding and they continue to get better. Simplify it; it's not about the Xs and Os on that level. The foundation of the game and the basics are more important than the Xs and Os."

Chambers offers coaches this bit of advice: "Develop a good relationship with the members of your team. Give them something to think about and strive for every day. Help them set goals. I'm very goal-oriented. I give my athletes goals all the time. If you're not goal-oriented at a younger age, you're just wandering in the woods. You're a ship in the middle of the ocean without a captain. You need some type of direction."

Chris Collins

Northwestern University men's basketball coach ▪
Played college basketball at Duke University ▪ Team
captain and MVP of Duke his senior season ▪ Named
Illinois Mr. Basketball as a high school senior

Growing up with a four-time NBA All-Star father who played alongside Julius Erving in Philadelphia, and later coached Michael Jordan in Chicago, it's no wonder that Chris Collins fell in love with basketball at an early age. He watched his father, Doug, average nearly eighteen points a game during a spectacular professional career that later resulted in several NBA head coaching jobs, and along with that, memorable access to practices and games for Chris. Though he tried all sorts of team and individual sports early on, sports such as tennis and golf didn't trigger much excitement due to the slower pace and individual aspects of them. But once he stepped on a basketball court, the speed of the game and all the components of working together as a team flooded him with excitement. And there was no doubt this was the sport that he was going to be immersed in for a lifetime.

"From a very young age, I just fell in love with the sport," says Collins, who starred at Duke during his college playing days and now is the head men's basketball coach at Northwestern University in Evanston, Illinois. "I just loved the game from the start. I loved the competition and I loved being on a team. I didn't like individual sports because I liked having teammates. I liked sharing things with teammates—both the good things and bad things. I played tennis for a little bit growing up and I played a little golf, but for me, those weren't as fulfilling as being a part of a team. I loved that basketball was non-stop action, it was back and forth. You went from one play to the next. It was just love at first sight for me. Obviously, I was around it a lot as a kid, having a father who played, so I was always tagging along with him as much as I could."

Those trips with his dad to practices and game-day shootarounds kindled that love for the game, fueled his work ethic, and focused his desire to elevate his game to elite levels. During his senior year of high school at Glenbrook North in Illinois, he averaged thirty-two points a game, shot a sizzling 47 percent from three-point territory, and was named Mr. Basketball in the state.

From there, he played for coach Mike Krzyzewski at Duke, where lessons on basketball and life were dispensed by the legendary Hall of Fame coach every day. Following his playing days, Collins later returned to the Blue Devils campus in Durham, North Carolina, to spend thirteen years as an assistant coach on Krzyzewski's staff.

"The best advice my dad and Coach K gave me, and they both told it to me on separate occasions, was that you always want to learn," Collins says. "Those guys are always striving to learn and know more and study great coaches in all different sports, and that's something I do. I watch the great coaches and I try to learn different things that they do. But the best advice that I ever got from both my dad and Coach K was that you have to take the things that you have learned from your mentors and others that you have learned from, and you have to put your own spin on things. You have to use your own personality. You have to be yourself."

> ### "[Y]ou have to put your own spin on things. You have to use your own personality. You have to be yourself."

That's an important point to remember for all coaches of young athletes, regardless of how long you have been involved in sports. Sometimes it's easy to get caught up wanting to be like coaches that we see on television, or act like the coaches we admire of our favorite professional and collegiate teams. But that's an ill-advised move not likely to get favorable results. Yes, it's terrific to want to emulate the best, but each individual has to find what approach fits best with their personality. Go ahead and identify qualities and characteristics that great coaching role models like Chris Collins or Mike Krzyzewski exhibit, and work those into your teachings. Just don't get caught up in trying to copy them. You've got to be yourself, and young athletes will respond to a genuine you far better than you trying to walk in someone else's footsteps.

"I can't try to be Coach K or Doug Collins. I have to be Chris Collins," he says. "I have to be myself. I have my own personality and my own beliefs, and I have to take the things they taught me and put my own spin on it and my own personality into it. That's the way you can get the best results."

Collins listened to that insight. And boy, did he ever learn. Besides soaking up the knowledge shared by his father and Krzyzewski, he also spent time as an assistant coach on the great Nancy Lieberman's staff with the WNBA's Detroit Shock; and on former Duke guard Tommy Amaker's staff at Seton Hall, so he knows as well as anyone the life-defining impact coaches can have on young lives. He's experienced it and seen it with countless athletes through the years. So after he was hired to resurrect the Northwestern basketball program in 2013, guess who he turned to? His high school basketball coach. That relationship all those years ago still resonated with him.

"When I got the job here at Northwestern, the first guy I hired to be my assistant was my high school basketball coach, Brian James, who is now my top assistant," Collins says. "So that kind of tells you a little bit about the way I feel about him and the impact that he had on my life and the time we spent together."

Sure, Collins recalls how James helped him hone his skills on the court, but even more impactful were all the lessons he learned that are used to navigate life. "He had a big impact on my life," Collins says. "Not only did he help me learn the game, but also how to act, how to be a good teammate, and how to be a good person."

After taking over the Northwestern program just three seasons later, in 2013, he guided them into the NCAA tournament for the first time in school history, ending seventy-eight years of heartbreak. But simply making an appearance wasn't enough; the Wildcats beat Vanderbilt in an opening round game in Salt Lake City and then put a scare into top-seeded Gonzaga two days later. Collins has turned the program around quickly for lots of reasons, one certainly being that the players he inherited, and those he has recruited, believe in him as much as he believes in them. It's about navigating that two-way street of showing players that you care about them as people, and that you are fully invested in helping them reach levels that they may not have even considered attainable before interacting with you. When belief and trust is established, and it's an everyday building process and not simply token words sprinkled on occasion at practice, it's powerful to see the connections that are born and the development that emerges.

"To get the most out of a young person and to really see him flourish, the kid has to believe in you, trust in you, and trust that you have his best interests at heart," Collins says. "To me, the best way to do that is to build relationships by spending time, by putting your arm around him, and by pushing him when he needs to be pushed. Those are things the best youth coaches do in order to really get the most out of young people and help them grow in each and every area."

It starts during practices. Connections aren't going to be formed during the course of an hour-long practice, and trust isn't going to be established by the end of the season's first week. It's—and here's that word—a *process*. But if it's a genuine focal point, players will recognize it, and those relationships will begin to grow.

"Ultimately, young kids want to be taught and they want to be coached," Collins says. "Certainly, times change, generations change, and kids have different interests. There are different ways that you have to get to young people today. You have to talk to kids differently. To me, the best coaches and the best mentors are the ones who understand that all kids are different, and you have to figure out how you can get to that kid and really get the best out of him—and the only way you can do that is to build a relationship. Obviously, that's something even at my level that I try to do. Relationships are key."

Plus, how those practices are run and the exchanges that take place between coach and player will help cultivate those connections. When practice sessions feature those key elements of variety, learning, and fun, then productivity thrives. Collins has been known on occasion to run practice sessions without a basketball as a way to help the squad dial in on how important it is to play strong defense. And other times, he'll have music piped in during practice to help loosen the players up. Every practice can't be the same, otherwise you risk your team becoming lost and ineffective in a haze of boredom. Collins employs a variety of practice methods to keep energy levels and engagement high, and it's a must at the younger levels of sports where kids' attention spans are sparse and sporadic to begin with.

"Try to always integrate new ideas and new practices in your teaching," he says. "All young kids want to be excited, they want to be stimulated. If you just do the same things all the time, the same drills, if you don't mix in different things, new ideas, new competitions, or new ways to keep it fun and exciting, it can get stale, and then young people are going to lose interest. Coaches who use their creativity and imagination to come up with new ideas, maybe to teach the same footwork or the same fundamentals in different ways make it more fun for the kids. It keeps them excited and interested and coming to practices. There has to be a complement of games with fundamentals. The more that youth coaches can mix that in and continue to teach the game and show these young people how to play the right way and not just rely on athletic ability, it will help set them up as they move up into junior high and high school, and for some of the lucky ones, eventually college."

Ty Detmer

1990 Heisman Trophy winner ▪ Played fourteen
seasons in the NFL ▪ Two-time Consensus All-
American quarterback at Brigham Young University
▪ Former college and high school football coach

Ty Detmer's record-smashing, Heisman Award-winning college
football career at Brigham Young University began with the most
unlikely of performances: four interceptions, five sacks, and a fumble. The man whose name would later reside next to sixty-two NCAA records;
who threw for more than 15,000 yards and 121 touchdowns; and who piled up
enough mindboggling numbers to make an accountant cringe looked like
anything but a quarterbacking great on this particular Saturday afternoon in
Laramie, Wyoming. The redshirt freshman missed on seventeen of the twen-
ty-six passes he attempted in his college debut that day, playing in front of
more than 28,000 fans at the University of Wyoming's War Memorial Stadium, and four of those misses wound up in the hands of Wyoming defenders
on their way to beating Detmer and his Cougars 24–14.

Yet Detmer, the son of a high school football coach, didn't sulk when he
misfired on a throw, pout when he came to the sidelines, or even allow that
performance to dissolve his confidence, compromise his attitude, or sabotage
his work ethic moving forward. His love for the game never flickered, and his
competitive spirit never weakened. Instead, he used the harsh lessons learned
that day—difficult ones for a young player to digest, for sure—to begin the
never-ending process of growing and developing as an athlete and person.
It was just one game among hundreds he played during his stellar collegiate
and fourteen-year NFL career, but it's one Detmer recalls with clarity more
than a quarter-century later because it really was a difference maker, and not a
confidence crusher, in his development.

"My first game at BYU, I threw a touchdown pass and then threw four
picks and fumbled in the second half," he says. "I learned more from that game.
I learned that I needed to work harder, and all those things that made me a
better person and eventually a better player just from having that experience."

Ironically, it's those types of experiences that many volunteer coaches often try to protect their young players from these days. Though the reality is that they just happen to provide the biggest boosts in helping young athletes evolve and, in many cases, later thrive in the sport. Detmer, the 1990 Heisman Trophy winner, is a shining example of that.

"We all need to fail in order to get better at some point," notes Detmer, who still holds school records for passing yards, touchdowns, and total offense, among others, and is a College Football Hall of Fame inductee. Granted, the life lessons that are woven into the setbacks and disappointments young athletes experience aren't easily extracted. It takes a concerted effort on a coach's behalf to dig underneath the surface and help kids embrace this part of the process.

Let's be clear, too: It's rocky terrain that volunteer coaches will be traversing. The journey will no doubt be filled with stumbles and missteps along the way, as there's no shortcut to leading players through the process. But good things await, like improved skills and renewed confidence, when coaches get their players to commit to the process and accept that every practice and game will not be filled with perfect execution. Far from it. Detmer saw firsthand the new vibe that surrounds much of youth sports while coaching a private high school in Austin, Texas, several years ago. Many players were genuinely afraid of making mistakes. Also adding to the complexity of the issue, mistakes were viewed in many of the kids' eyes as catastrophic events that weighed them down all game long.

"One of our mottos has always been, 'Play the next play.' You can't go back and change what just happened."

"I've had some cases where I coached kids at the high school level where they would come off the field in a game after making a mistake, and they're looking in the stands at their parents," Detmer says. "I'm telling them 'Just focus, go play the next one. Don't worry about the last one.' A lot of times, these guys beat themselves up to where they can't even play the next play. You talk through the play with them and what happened. One of our mottos has always been, 'Play the next play.' You can't go back and change what just happened. You can learn from it, but you can't change it, so play the next play."

Following mistakes, a coach's response to them is just as significant as the player's. Detmer advises coaches to avoid falling into the trap of staying away from the play that didn't turn out well. For example, if a young quarterback throws an interception on a slant pattern, coaches will tend to scrap that call from the playbook the remainder of the game.

"Sometimes, when a kid makes a mistake, we as coaches kind of get it in our heads to say, 'Oh man, don't run that play again,'" he says. "Well, that's probably the time to run it again, because he knows now what he did wrong and how to fix it. You put that kid back in that situation and let him learn from it. Sometimes we kind of go away from it, or we put another player in without allowing kids to learn from their mistakes."

Plus, young athletes take note of the play calls, too. When a coach stays away from a play that didn't go well, the player recognizes that, and it can be a jolt to his or her confidence. But, when coaches do what Detmer suggests and go right back to that call, that sends a strong message that the coach believes in and trusts the player. Regardless of how the play turns out, the coach has made a statement, and the player has noticed. During practices, coaches can lay the framework for building resilient athletes, ones who grab that play-the-next-play mentality and aren't hindered by the results of the previous play.

"You can't be too high after a good play, and you can't be too low after a bad play," Detmer says. "So when you are doing drill work and they make a poor throw, you just get back in line and do it again, or repeat it, and not give them time to beat themselves up." Along with that, it is important for coaches to maintain a calm demeanor in the wake of a mistake.

"I don't think yelling at a kid for messing up does anybody any good," Detmer says. "There are times when we are all emotional, but it's about stopping and taking the time to tell players what they could have done differently, instead of just yelling 'Catch the ball' at a receiver when he drops it. You have to coach them. What could he have done differently to have caught the ball? Was his hand placement wrong? Did he take his eyes off of it? Figure out what caused him to drop it, and then try to coach him on that. I've been around a lot of coaches who are that way. The kid already knows he messed up, so it doesn't do any good to just berate him—go help him learn how to not make the same mistake again."

Detmer's journey certainly gives credence to the power of taking those experiences that don't go well and using them as platforms for growth, learning, and development. That rough collegiate debut back in Laramie didn't shred his confidence or push him into a dark place that he never recovered from. It simply inspired him to work harder, so the next time he took the field he would be better prepared and more confident to execute plays. And that's exactly what he did.

By season's end, he had ratcheted up his level of play and was beginning to display the ability and wits that would have him holding the Heisman Trophy just two seasons later. At the conclusion of his freshman season, the Cougars were in Anaheim, California to play the University of Colorado in the Freedom Bowl. Trailing at the half 14-7, legendary BYU Coach LaVell Edwards summoned Detmer to start the third quarter in place of junior quarterback Sean Covey and resurrect its sputtering offense. Detmer didn't take the field burdened by that disappointing season-opening performance against Wyoming. Instead, he confidently took over behind center. He promptly took the team on a 65-yard scoring drive on their second possession of the second half that he capped by throwing a 15-yard touchdown pass; and he played splendidly in helping BYU to a comeback victory. Plus, he earned the game's Most Valuable Player award.

The rest of Detmer's journey is well-documented and on full display in the entryway of the BYU football facility that he entered every day during his tenure as an assistant coach for the Cougars: the jersey, action photos, various mementos, and the Heisman Trophy from an illustrious career that later led to fourteen NFL seasons and becoming the co-founder of Quarterback Elite, which works with young players from the youth, high school, college and professional ranks to help enhance their skills. Certainly, one of the messages delivered during the camp is trusting the process and understanding that development takes time, and it requires a big dose of patience on the part of both coaches and young athletes.

"We're not the most patient society, so we have to allow kids to make mistakes," Detmer says. "Some of the best learning experiences I had were from making mistakes."

Terry Fair

Assistant football coach at the University of Tennessee
■ First round selection in the 1998 NFL Draft ■
Two-time All-Southeastern Conference selection
as a player at Tennessee ■ Named to the 1998
NFL All-Rookie Team by *The Sporting News*

 The distance from Phoenix, Arizona to Knoxville, Tennessee is 1,814 miles and covers six states, but for Terry Fair, that journey never materializes if not for a passionate and caring group of volunteer coaches who left their imprint on his life. Born and raised in Arizona's state capital of Phoenix, Fair was on the move as a child. He dabbled—and excelled—at a variety of sports. A talented athlete, it was the messages that he received throughout his participation that were drenched in positivity that helped inspire and drive him in ways he never could have imagined at the time.

"They had an unbelievable impact," Fair says of his youth coaches. "To this day, I still keep in touch with a lot of those coaches, and outside of my family and the support that I had, it was huge how they just kept pushing me and driving me each and every day, giving me that motivation and determination to go out and be the best. And just them saying that I could accomplish anything, and do anything, if I put my mind to it."

Those words struck a chord with Fair and forever altered the course of his life. "One of the biggest things they got across to me is that you have to work at everything that you want to do," he says. "It doesn't matter how big you are, and it doesn't matter if you're not the most gifted athlete, but if you work at it, you can be that guy. Just having those words said to me and just being able to listen and hang on every word that was taught to me at a young age about perseverance and having the right attitude and work ethic did wonders for myself in terms of where I ended up."

Where Fair ended up was in Knoxville, playing college football at the University of Tennessee after a spectacular high school career at South Mountain High School in his native Phoenix. During those high school days, you could find him playing running back, wide receiver and quarterback on offense, and defensive back when his team didn't have the ball. He starred as a defensive back and punt returner for the Volunteers, helping them win the Southeastern Conference title during his senior season. Grabbed in the first round of the 1998 NFL Draft by the Detroit Lions, he played eight productive seasons, and these days serves as the defensive backs coach at Tennessee. Now, that's a career *round-trip.*

While Fair works with players competing in arguably the nation's premier football conference, he's never forgotten the lessons that were imparted to him by his coaches along the way. No matter the sport or the talent level of the athletes, coaching is teaching. It's teaching skills, life lessons, and more.

"You have to be a great teacher," Fair says. "You always have to teach the *why. Why* are we doing this? *Why* are we doing that? *Why* don't I want you doing it like this? You have to show them, you have to correct them, and you have to teach them. The biggest thing we do is we coach, critique, and correct on a daily basis."

"First of all, as a coach, you've got to love what you're doing, and it has to be a great learning environment."

How those critiques and corrections are addressed and sorted through can have major ramifications on a young athlete's psyche and competitive desires moving forward. Being too harsh and overly critical can wreck confidence and enthusiasm, but choosing the right words and tone can drive development and foster a real love for the sport and striving to improve in it.

"It's a two-way street," Fair says. "It just can't be the negative things all the time. There has to be recognition when there is marked improvement in what they're doing." It's the ultimate balancing act that all coaches must perform: delivering praise and encouragement, but also tackling when corrections need to be made to perform specific skills as effectively and efficiently as possible.

"There are always going to be times where you coach guys up as you want to influence and teach and build," Fair says. "As you are coaching them, you have to be able to also put your arms around them and be calm and talk about the mistakes that are being made, while also pointing out what they are doing well. There has to be some positive as well, so they can see the progress that they are making."

Essentially, what it comes down to is the environment that coaches are creating for their players to learn and grow. Fair recalls his physical education teacher back in Phoenix, who would hang newspaper articles on her wall in school of teams and athletes who had performed well. Fair, and all the other student-athletes, were inspired by that, and it gave them that extra dose of motivation to work harder and do their best for the team because they wanted to get on that special wall. It was a teacher who cared, and she's never been forgotten because of it. That same mentality applies to sports and coaching, too.

"First of all, as a coach, you have to love what you are doing, and it has to be a great learning environment," Fair says. "For us, as coaches, we're just like that teacher that, when you go into that class, you excel because that teacher communicates well with you, and it's a fun environment for learning. You're not just being told that you're the greatest all the time, and you're not being told that you are the worst. You're being corrected and you're being taught. You're getting that arm put around you every now and then, and also being loved up. So, it's just about the environment and the coaching that you create, so that kids continue to take pride in playing the sport and learn to love the game because of how it was taught to them."

As an NFL and collegiate defensive back, Fair performed at one of the most challenging positions on the field, one where a missed tackle or blown coverage could result in a quick six points for the opposition. So he learned the value of what it means to be a team player. When mistakes were made and tackles were missed—which happens to all players at all levels—he understood that there wasn't time to dwell on those. If he did, he would hurt his team even more by not concentrating on the next play, which would open the door to additional mistakes. So he points out that when coaches are working with their players on recovering from mistakes and moving on, they should share that it's a selfish move to dwell on that one bad play, because it hurts the team when everyone isn't focused on the upcoming snap.

"As the coach, you have to help players understand that their focus has to be on the guys around them, their accountability to their teammates, and really going out and being that ultimate competitor," Fair says. "You want to instill in them that drive and will to succeed on each and every play. It's not just sometimes, it has to be consistent."

Getting that message to resonate with players requires them wanting to play well not only for themselves, but for the benefit of the team. In any team sport, athletes must recognize and understand that the more in sync they are with each other, and the harder they play for one another, the better the team will perform.

"It starts with practice," Fair says. "It's helping kids learn to want to play for each other, knowing that if they go out there and they don't have that focus, one play can be detrimental, and they really don't want to let their teammates down. It's got to come from within a little bit, but coaches are there to encourage it as well."

Of course, everyone is going to make mistakes, commit penalties, and fail to perform in the big moments, but the more coaches can help players work through and move on from those experiences, the better. During practices, be aware of when a player shows any signs of lingering frustration over a previous play—head down, shoulders slumped—and address it right away. Bad body language screams trouble, and good teams will spot players who are down on themselves and go after that player right away again. So if they are not fully engaged in the moment, the previous bad play can tailspin into another one. So while addressing this tricky component of competing with young players, it's about helping instill in them that competitive mindset to want to come back stronger and make a play to help the team, instead of focusing all their energy and attention on a play that is already over and done with.

"You teach players to never feel sorry for themselves," Fair says. "If you do get beat, you have to get back up and continue to play and get it out of your mind, because it's all about making a positive impact on the game any way you can. That game is four quarters and you're going to be given another opportunity to get back out there and do your job, and when you get back out there, you have to focus on the task at hand. I don't think it's ever too early to learn those lessons."

P.J. Fleck

Head football coach at the University of Minnesota ▪
Two-time Mid-American Conference Coach of the Year ▪
Ranks third in career receptions at Northern Illinois University

P.J. Fleck spent his childhood in perpetual motion. Encouraged by his parents to be active, he played everything from baseball and football to basketball and soccer. He even gave gymnastics a try. When organized games weren't on the schedule, you could find him kicking a soccer ball in the front yard or throwing tennis balls off the garage.

Fleck carried that love of sports into his teen years. He led his high school football team to back-to-back undefeated state championships, but despite recording more than 3,000 receiving yards in his career, recruiters weren't exactly crowding on his doorstep with scholarship offers in hand for the skinny five-foot-nine receiver. He eventually landed at Northern Illinois University, where he quickly stamped himself as a leader, as well as a receiver with hands as smooth as a pickpocket, capable of grabbing anything in sight. He caught 179 passes during his collegiate days at NIU, which ranks third in school history; and his seventy-seven receptions during his senior year ranks second in school history for single-season catches. But it's a pass he didn't haul in—interestingly, the first pass of his college football career—that impacted him in ways that he never could have imagined at the time.

Today, Fleck is the incredibly energetic, mega-charismatic, fast-talking, ultra-likable head football coach at the University of Minnesota, who delivers rapid-fire sentences drenched in positivity. As head coach of the Broncos at Western Michigan University, he took the team on a magical 13-1 ride in 2016 and parlayed that success into the Golden Gophers gig. Yes, the barometer used to judge Fleck will be the team's win-loss record in the talent-laden, hard-hitting Big Ten Conference. But there's so much more to him, his program, and what he's aiming to achieve. It also happens to be one heck of a good blueprint for coaches of young athletes in any sport to follow.

"My job is way bigger than Xs and Os," Fleck says. "My job is to develop the person. It all comes down to relationship building. Period." Fleck has captured what coaching kids is all about in about 1.5 seconds. Remember, he talks fast—but he makes points that matter. That brings us back to Fleck's first college football game, and that first pass thrown in his direction. The one he wasn't able to corral.

"I dropped my first pass ever at Northern Illinois," he says. "We were in the red zone, and the ball went right through my hands, and the guy went ninety-five yards all the way down and scored. I'm this true freshman and Joe Novak, our head coach, walked over to me when I came to the sideline, and I'm thinking I'm going to get ripped."

It's understandable that those thoughts were charging through the young receiver's mind at that moment. Mistakes that result in big plays or, even worse, points for the opposing team, generally result in the decibel level of the coach's voice rising several notches and the player forced to the bench to reflect on his transgression. But that's not the path Novak took with Fleck, and it resonated with the young player. And still does all these years later. You can still hear the admiration in Fleck's voice for what Novak did at that moment. He didn't choose to berate Fleck or question why he didn't come up with the ball. And he didn't send the freshman to the bench and replace him with somebody else. Instead, he did what great coaches do.

"He came over and put his hand on my shoulder and said, 'Don't worry, youngster, we're going to come right back to you,'" Fleck says.

Now take a minute to let that soak in and consider how that brief exchange enabled Fleck to keep his head up, his morale high, and his confidence intact when he returned to the field for the next series. Plus, examine how crucial those initial seconds are following a mistake made by a young player on your team and how what you choose to say—and *how* you say it—in that small window of opportunity can really have life-long consequences. Fleck knows, because he has experienced both extremes: the "boost the player up" approach, and "the tear the athlete to shreds and stomp on his confidence" method. He knows which style fueled his development and influenced how he chooses to handle mistakes with his players these days.

"I had a wide receivers coach who was yelling at me to catch the ball, but never taught me how to catch it without dropping it," he says. "That stuck with me as a negative thing. One coach was just yelling at me for the sake of it, and the other was really working to develop me into a better person and to create that 'never give up' mantra. And from that day forward, those were the two things that have influenced me."

No young athlete finds any joy in committing a mistake, and they certainly don't occur on purpose. But when they do happen—and they most certainly will in every game, no matter what the level of competition—coaches must rein in their emotions and refrain from doing the obvious, which is pointing out the mistake. The young player knows he made a mistake; his teammates know; and so does everyone in the stands. So when a ball is dropped, for example, ridiculous phrases like "Catch the ball," or absurd questions like "Why didn't you catch the ball?" serve zero purpose, except for carving up confidence and embarrassing the player.

"The biggest thing as a coach is that you learn how to teach," Fleck says. "If you're pointing out that a player is dropping the football, that's the first mistake you are making. No young person likes to make mistakes or drop passes. So it's dissecting the catch and figuring out *why* he is dropping them." Then coaches can proceed to help him overcome whatever the issue happens to be.

"The biggest thing young people want to know is *why*," Fleck says. "If you're teaching me this, *why* are you teaching it? If you're making me do this, *why* are you making me do it? That's where we start—we always start with the word *why*."

> **"The biggest thing young people want to know is why. If you're teaching me this, why are you teaching it? . . . That's where we start—we always start with the word why."**

Along with that *why*, coaches blend in heavy doses of genuine affection for their players. They don't just do it when the cameras are rolling on game days; it's an all-day, every-day approach to establishing coach-player relationships that have real substance. Ones that will stand the test of time and mean something years down the road. Of course, Fleck wants to develop great football players and have a team that performs at a high level on Saturday afternoons. But the man who sleeps with a stack of index cards by his night table in case an idea strikes in the middle of the night cares about the overall player.

Coach Novak cared about a young P.J. Fleck many years ago, and now it's Fleck's turn. And for every young athlete that you come across in your coaching endeavors, it's your turn, too. It has to be evident, sincere, and on full display—during practices, when few people are usually around, to game days, when the stands are full. There's simply no room, or time, for caring to get dumped in the backseat if you want to be a coach of impact like Fleck, who helps individuals become not only good football players, but great people, too.

"Our coaches have incredible energy, and energy is love," Fleck says. "And love is everything. So we create energy in our practice because we love what we do. It's pretty amazing to watch how fast it goes and how energetic it is, but it doesn't just happen—it has to be taught. But I absolutely think that is what you need to do when coaching kids."

Fleck is well-known for his "Row the Boat" saying. He uses it to show that when you are rowing a boat, you're facing the opposite direction the boat is going. You can see the past and where you have come from, but you are unable to see what awaits in the future, whether it's choppy water or a beautiful sunset. But everyone is on this special journey together, rowing together, working through the rough patches together, and savoring the good times as one group, too. It's a powerful perspective, an outlook that certainly applies for coaches of younger athletes.

It's about getting a group of players to buy into the pursuit of common goals, and doing it with a strong work ethic, respect for their teammates and coaches, and with a genuine love of competing and enjoying all the moments— the good and not-so-good—that occur along the way. In short, it's prepping people for life and the ups and downs that make every day so unique.

"This program is about developing people," Fleck says. "That's why our kids really trust us, they like playing for us, and we like having them as our players, because they are real people. It's pretty amazing."

David Fulcher

Former college football coach
■ Played eight seasons in the NFL ■ Three-time
All-American at Arizona State University

Most NFL players can recall in striking detail their first professional game. Much like that first kiss or first car for those of us who didn't play professional sports, these special moments are stashed away in our memory banks, where they can be revisited and savored for a lifetime. And so it is with those who take the field for their first NFL game: the stadium, the sounds, the fans, and the ferocious speed of play. All of that, and so much more, stays with them forever. Eight-year NFL veteran David Fulcher remembers it all from his professional debut. He can rewind the plays of that day in his mind. He recalls that feeling of fulfilling a dream. And something else of particular interest lingers in the shadows of his memory on that special day, too. The yelling. And the criticism. Because there was *a lot* of it. It came in flurries from Hall of Fame defensive coordinator Dick LeBeau, and it never relented all game long.

Fulcher was the Cincinnati Bengals' third-round pick in the 1986 NFL Draft. Growing up in South Central Los Angeles, he dodged the gangs, drugs, and violence that wrecked the lives of so many around him and was all-in on sports. Athletically gifted and a tenacious worker—a must-have combo for success in sports at the highest level—he was good enough to have played professional baseball, if he had wanted to go that route. But his love of hitting running backs and receivers as a defensive back carried more appeal than hitting curveballs, so he chose football at Arizona State.

A three-time All-American known for delivering bone-rattling hits and big plays, the Bengals immediately plugged him in as a starter in their secondary. Which brings us back to the aforementioned NFL debut of Fulcher, which took place on a September Sunday afternoon against Kansas City. The Chiefs ran more than sixty offensive plays that day, and on one particular play early in the first half, Fulcher did what all rookies are known for doing: he made a mistake. He read a play wrong, which resulted in a touchdown for the Chiefs. And plenty of criticism awaited him when he came to the sidelines.

"It's my first NFL game against the Kansas City Chiefs, and it's a running play, and I came up to take on the fullback," Fulcher says. "There was the running back behind him, and I jumped inside the fullback, and thought I could make the tackle because that's what I did so much of in college. But the fullback blocked me, and that running back ran right down the sideline eighty yards for a touchdown. So I got to the sideline, and there is Dick LeBeau saying to me, 'Hey kid, if you jump inside like that again, you're going to be on the sideline with me holding a clipboard, and you will not play. Your job is to turn that thing back inside, because there are ten football players inside of you that can make the play.'"

They were harsh words delivered with volume. "This was my first game as a professional football player, and I was doing great, but LeBeau mentioned that play to me at least ten times throughout that game," Fulcher says. "He kept saying, 'I cannot believe that you jumped inside. Why would you do something like that?'"

So how did we arrive at this story, and this particular play, being told more than twenty-five years later by a three-time Pro Bowler and former head football coach at Cincinnati Christian University, an NAIA Division II college? Because the topic on the table is coaching kids. Fulcher, speaking from the Queen City, is tackling the dynamics of complimenting and criticizing. The words coaches choose—and the decibel level they use when delivering them—can either propel young athletes to greater levels of play, or crush their confidence and enthusiasm.

> ## *"[These young men are] going to be asking, 'How am I doing, Coach? Am I doing this right?' And that's what you want when a kid comes to you, because that means they're listening to you and they believe in you."*

Fulcher isn't sharing this story because he's sensitive to criticism, because he's not. And he hasn't dug up the details of this play against the Chiefs because of any lingering animosity toward LeBeau, of which there isn't any. Instead, he's chosen to lay it out to make a point about the mindset of coaches when they see mistakes being made by young players and their responses to them. It's easy to let loose a torrent of criticism on a young player when he commits a mistake during his Saturday morning game. But one of the real skills of coaching young players is maintaining a calm demeanor and communicating with the athlete in a respectful manner, while ideally providing some feedback and insight that proves beneficial moving forward.

"His only response to every great tackle and interception that I got would be, 'good job,'" Fulcher says of playing for LeBeau. "And it's not because he was being cruel to me, but every time we do something wrong, we're always after that person and harping on them. We've got to be able to give more praises than we give the negative stuff to kids, especially today."

In youth sports, coaches have a tendency to yell and criticize when a mistake is made because, well, it seems like the most natural of reactions. Something is done wrong and the coach's voice automatically rises. They see coaches at the professional and collegiate ranks doing so on television, and it's easy to copy those same behaviors while forgetting that these are younger players, not elite-level scholarship athletes or professionals being paid hefty sums of cash to perform at a high level.

But what's the impact on a child's psyche? What does that do to their self-esteem? How are they going to feel about themselves, when they lay their head on their pillow that night after being verbally accosted and embarrassed by their coach in front of their teammates and family members over a missed tackle? Or a fumble? Or a dropped pass? Consider this: if a fifty-three-year-old man who has played in a Super Bowl can recall this one particular play among the thousands he was involved in during a productive NFL career—and the coach's harsh words that followed in the aftermath—think for a moment about the effect a volunteer coach's words can have on young athletes who are fairly new to the world of sports and competition, whose confidence is often as fragile as porcelain. Plus, young athletes are going to make a ton of mistakes, because they're kids and they're learning. And that's what kids do. So, if every mistake is going to be accompanied by an avalanche of criticism, where's the fun in continuing to show up? What's the incentive to do their best?

"Think about this just in everyday life," Fulcher says. "Every time we do something wrong, we're going to hear about it more than once. So we've got to make it fun for these young men to come out and play football, and we've got to compliment them. They want to hear how good they are doing. They're going to be asking, 'How am I doing, Coach? Am I doing this right?' And that's what you want when a kid comes to you, because that means they're listening to you and they believe in you. But you've got to stay off the negative stuff with young men today."

Fulcher leans heavily on the positive when communicating with his players, which frees them up to play to the best of their ability. And have fun doing so, too.

"When I talk to my players, I try to get them to play physical, to play fast, to play smart, and to have fun doing what they are doing," he says. "I had fun doing what I was doing. Even in the losses I had fun, because I can't control wins and losses. I can only control what David Fulcher does. I try to tell my kids to do their job, and they will be okay. I tell them to just go out and let it go and don't worry about making mistakes. I'm not going to take them out of the game because they make a mistake. Now, if they constantly keep making that mistake over and over again, then they will have to come and talk to me about it. But if you play the game with passion and to the best of your ability, you probably won't make a whole lot of mistakes if you play with that mindset."

When volunteer coaches don't have to reach for the throat lozenges following games—because they're operating with the mindset that mistakes are simply a part of youth sports and there's no need to yell every time one occurs—the kids will play hard. They'll play with passion. And they'll play fearlessly. They'll play like David Fulcher did. And that's a pretty good model to emulate.

Jerod Haase

Stanford University basketball coach ▪ 2016 Conference USA Coach of the Year ▪ Played college basketball at the University of Kansas ▪ Big Eight Newcomer of the Year

During the latter part of the 1990s, the University of Kansas basketball roster was crammed with talent. On a team that would spend the final fifteen weeks of the regular season ranked number one in the country, and with four starters—Jacque Vaughn, Scot Pollard, Raef LaFrentz, and Paul Pierce—who would all go on to being first-round NBA draft picks, there weren't many opportunities for other players on the roster to contribute as far as scoring and rebounding goes. So Jerod Haase, a co-captain of the squad, would do *anything* to help the team any way he could. And he didn't mind surrendering skin or collecting bruises in the process.

"At Kansas, I played with a bunch of future NBA players, so the only way I could get noticed was just to work as hard as I possibly could," says Haase, the head men's basketball coach at Stanford University. "I was known for diving on the floor."

Was he ever. During his junior season, he got his hands on so many loose balls by diving for them that the staff added a new stat that they tracked: floor burns. "Every time I dove on the floor, or anybody on the team would dive on the floor, they would keep track of that throughout the year," Haase says. Of course, you-know-who led the team that year with 167 of them.

Now, those types of plays aren't as glamorous as sinking a three-point shot, or driving to the basket and delivering a thundering dunk that raises fans out of their seats, but they are important and valuable to the team's success. Just consider how many extra possessions the Jayhawks got that season as the result of Haase's willingness to throw his body on the court, and how many additional attempts to score that translated into. Or think about how his passionate play energized his teammates who saw the sacrifices he was willing to make for the good of the team. Players don't have to be sinking shots from all over the court or grabbing all the rebounds to be valuable to the team, or to feel good about their play. Regardless of the sport, there are so many nuances to competing in them that there are countless opportunities to be a contributor. It's just up to the coach to help young athletes identify those roles, embrace them, and be encouraged and acknowledged when they deliver.

"I always took great pride in controlling the things you can control," Haase says. "I'm not six-foot-ten, and I had some limitations as a player, but I was taught that if the work ethic was there, good things would happen."

Haase's work ethic was forged during his youth, where growing up in South Lake Tahoe, California, he didn't allow even Mother Nature to disrupt his free-throw shooting practice sessions. During the winter months, he would shovel snow off portions of the family's half-court so he could get his work in. When he attended Kansas and had the chance to play for the legendary Roy Williams, hard work in all facets of the game was of course emphasized, as well as noted and applauded.

"The foundation of the program was very clear, and he was reiterating all those things that my mom and dad were teaching me," Haase says. "The work ethic and doing things the right way were always at the forefront." Talk about a guy who played the game the right way. This is how much he loved the sport and wanted to help his team enjoy success: during his senior season, he broke the wrist on his shooting hand in the season-opening game against Santa Clara, but even broken bones didn't slow him down or dampen his love for the game and competing. He still managed to average twelve points a game and make it through the season. Once the season ended, he had surgery.

"I'm not six-foot-ten, and I had some limitations as a player, but I was taught that if the work ethic was there, good things would happen."

Haase has carried that same approach with him wherever he's gone. In just his fourth season coaching at the University of Alabama-Birmingham, he led the Blazers to a 26-5 record and the school's first regular season Conference USA title in several seasons. How he approached games as a player, and how he connects with young players, drew the attention of Stanford, where he is in charge of leading the Cardinal back to prominence. When it comes to relationships, feeling a genuine part of the team and understanding the most effective ways to contribute, many of the same facets that Haase focuses on with his players relate to working with younger players in any team sport, too. It's finding ways for kids to be engaged in the process and legitimately contribute. Players will see right through false accolades; they must feel a genuine connection to what is going on, otherwise they will be lost.

"It's important as a coach to make sure you are rewarding everybody on the team for doing a good job," Haase says. "And that includes the kids at the end of the bench. I talk with my team now about playing well and—whatever your part is—to play that well. If it's not a lot of minutes, there's still an important aspect to that of being a great teammate, being great on the bench, and being a great practice player as well. So it's about making sure that every player throughout the program *knows* that they are appreciated—and that they *are* appreciated."

It's easy for the team's top players to recognize their contributions and see how valuable their performances are, but for those who play fewer minutes or perhaps aren't as talented, it requires more effort on the coach's part. That's where it's important to come up with some other categories that you can recognize players in, such as the "floor burn" category that Haase both inspired and dominated during his days in Lawrence. Or you can create a category for taking charges, for example. It's also not all about numbers: you can recognize your best display of good sportsmanship from the past week of action among your players; or how about the player who worked really hard in practice and whose effort really forced other players on the team to pick up their intensity level, too. Bottom line: when young athletes go home after practices and games, or conclude seasons, you've got to ask yourself if you did everything possible to help every one of them be a genuine part of the team and a real part of everything. You don't want to be one of the reasons why a young athlete gives up on a sport, or lets their interest fizzle because they never really felt a part of the process.

"Invest in the kids," Haase says. "The role of youth coaches is huge. It's there to supplement the teachers, the parents, and the families, and so delivering the same kind of messages is important. At the end of the day, the players really consider their coaches their role models, and so doing things the right way is hugely important, and it'll be a major impact on those kids. Having the coaches and support system that I had growing up was huge in my success and getting to where I am now. There's not a day that goes by that I don't think back and appreciate what those people did for me."

When coaches work hard, and players can see the intense commitment level, a lot of good can result. "You can't ask players to work any harder than you are working," he says. "You also have to earn the respect of the kids by working hard and doing things the right way. Once you have the respect of the kids, they'll listen to you and believe in what you say. If you put in the time and the effort, you'll make a great impact on the kids you coach."

John Harbaugh

Head coach of the Baltimore Ravens ▪
Winner of Super Bowl XLVII

One of the endlessly fascinating qualities kids possess is their story-telling skills when sharing a special experience. Whether it's a stomach-flipping amusement park ride they braved, a thrilling movie they saw, or an action-packed new video game they played, the glow in their eyes and the smile spread across their faces while delivering the rundown is memorable for so many reasons. So when it comes to coaching kids, a great goal to aim for is to be a part of a child's post-practice story sharing. That's right, when coaches have players so excited to share a story that occurred, it's a terrific sign that the session was memorable and impactful for all the right reasons.

"When that child goes home and they've got something to brag to their mom or dad or brother or sister about, you've been successful as a youth coach," says John Harbaugh, the long-time coach of the Baltimore Ravens, a Super Bowl champion, and one of the game's most respected leaders. Harbaugh has spent a lifetime in sports, playing everything growing up, and is now part of an elite group that has led a team to a Super Bowl title. He's seated on the sidelines on one of the immaculately manicured practice fields at the Ravens' facility following a spring practice, and he's fired up, engaging, and passionate—because the topic is coaching kids. Harbaugh, son of a coach, knows how influential sports are in a young person's life. He's one of those guys who genuinely cares about sharing knowledge and insight to help coaches at lower rungs on the competitive ladder have a positive impact with their players.

"I remember my coaches more than anything," Harbaugh says. "I think you remember the encouraging coaches, the coach that tells you one time one thing that you do well that kind of defines you a little bit as a kid. All kids are looking for what they are all about, who they are, and something they can be good at. And then, all of a sudden, a coach tells you that you *are* good at something, whether it's throwing or batting or tackling or hitting a tennis ball—whatever it is that makes you feel like, 'I'm good at this. The coach thinks I'm a little bit special.'"

Harbaugh is a high-profile, high-character coach. He works with multi-million dollar athletes. But when you turn back the pages on his journey to his childhood, he was a kid who loved sports, competing and—just like everyone else—performing something well on the field or court, and being praised for it. So when coaches are planning practices, Harbaugh urges them to make note of the importance of finding skills or attributes that can be highlighted. In short, as you are navigating practice sessions, consider what these kids are going to be able to share with their family and friends afterward. Are you giving them top-notch storytelling material, or are you failing to give them a post-practice conversation starter?

Keep in mind that it's important that practices feature time devoted to athletes working on the core fundamentals of their craft, and adding layers of confidence for performing them in game settings. Additionally, there will be portions of a practice where more difficult skills will be introduced and worked on, which typically will result in a lot of mistakes and frustration as players work through them. As long as coaches keep the atmosphere positive during these more difficult moments, these experiences can often be good material for athletes to talk about afterward, when they are excited to dissect the new skill being added to their repertoire.

"When that child goes home and they've got something to brag to their mom or dad or brother or sister about, you've been successful as a youth coach."

"Probably the biggest challenge for youth coaches is making everybody a part of it and getting everybody involved," Harbaugh says. "Over the years, we've been involved in a lot of camps, and that has always kind of been the motto: short lines, everybody is involved, everybody is throwing, everybody is catching, everybody is running, and you're making it competitive. You set up drills where there are no lines, where everybody is going against somebody, and you have a chance to kind of encourage and impact every single player at every single moment."

Harbaugh continues, "The minute you see a young kid, a boy or girl, standing around losing interest, to me that's a disaster, because that child is going to lose interest in sports or activities really for the rest of their life. But if you can take that hour, hour and a half, two hours, however long you have them, and keep them engaged, keep them doing something where it's them going against somebody else, then you have a chance to have a special drill for them." By making competitive drills a defining element of practice, the path of opportunity widens for exposing athletes to special moments that will be revisited and recapped on the ride home.

Just like writers who outline chapters and develop a plan for where the story is going to go, or when directors are constantly tweaking scripts and exploring different camera angles to get that special shot, coaches need to adopt that same mentality when designing practices. The drills have to be engaging; there needs to be a competitive element that hooks the participants, and the atmosphere surrounding the session needs to be encouraging.

"Building confidence in kids, whether it's your own kids or whether it's someone that you're coaching, is the most important thing," Harbaugh says. "It's no different here, at the professional level. Our guys, you could say they are big kids, so it's important to build confidence in them, too, and to build the understanding of accountability; to make them know that they are important; to make them know that they mean something to the team and their impact is going to have value on what the team does."

Coaches of kids should think about what their players are saying to others about their experiences. Are they enjoying the drills and the interaction with the coach? Are they gaining skills and progressing in a fun practice format? Do they anxiously greet their parents with non-stop stories of what unfolded at practice, or are the car rides home quiet because there isn't much to share? Coaches only get players for a few hours of practice time a week, so they should be aiming high and striving to provide sessions that aren't just interesting, but productive—ones kids will love sharing.

"You make sure that they all play and get reps and are a part of it and have a chance to make a difference," Harbaugh says. "And you find a way to get a win for every single child. There's got to be something that a child can win at, no matter what it is. Maybe they don't run as well, but they're the strongest; maybe they're not as coordinated, but they're the smartest; or whatever it might be. You find something that that child can win at. If you can do it every single day, if you can have a plan for every single kid every single day and get them a win, you've been successful."

Monique Henderson

Three-time Olympian ▪ Two-time Olympic Gold
Medalist ▪ Head women's track and field and
cross-country coach at Golden West College ▪
Four-year letter winner in track and field at UCLA

Young athletes these days want results—and they want them fast. They want to stockpile those wins, and savor heavy volumes of success, and they don't want to be waiting around for it to be happening a month from now, or a week from now, or even later in a practice that day. They want it all, and they crave it all right *now*. Sure, patience is a virtue, but it's not usually carried around by young athletes to their games, practices, competitions, and meets. In the world they live in, where instant gratification abounds, words like *process* and *journey* and *goals* and *development* rarely show up in their vocabularies, their text messages, or their Instagram posts.

It's a difficult concept for many young athletes to get their arms around, and for coaches to teach—that the fast track to success is actually, dare we say it, *slow*. Now, we're not talking sloth-slow, just simply slower than they probably envision. The most efficient route to sustained success is a steady and consistent engagement in the process of setting and meeting short-term goals, which ultimately leads to those big dividends that simply can't be achieved in the blink of an eye. They evolve over the course of a season; or, in many instances, over several seasons. Interestingly, one of the world's fastest women on the track had to learn this very same lesson during her teen years, when she wasn't immune to coaching feedback that helped steer her in a golden direction that eventually included three Olympic Games, two Olympic gold medals, and one terrific philosophy for working with young athletes that we'll get to shortly.

Born and raised in San Diego, Monique Henderson produced some blazingly fast times as a high school athlete. She is the only four-time 400-meter champion in the history of California high school track and field; and at the age of seventeen, she set a high school national record in the 400 meters. In 2000, she also became the first high school athlete to make the United States Olympic Track and Field team in the past twenty-four years. Named the

Girls National High School Athlete of the Year by *Track and Field News*, her national and state records in the 400 meters still stand today. That's how good she was back then. She would later win gold in 2004 at the Summer Games in Athens and again in 2008 at the Summer Games in Beijing, where she ran on the 4 x 400-meter relay teams.

"When you line up on the track and you have eight other people there, only one of those nine people in the race is going to win," says Henderson, the head women's cross country and track and field coach at Golden West College in Huntington Beach, California, just ninety miles north from where she first made her mark as a young sprinter. "So you have to figure out and find out why you enjoy what you are doing, and then be motivated for yourself. You have to recognize that you might not win, but focus on what it is that you are trying to accomplish, because that's what it's really about."

That's the message Henderson's coaches delivered to her early on in her career, which helped carve the mindset she needed to blend with her natural ability and work ethic to produce the amazing results she achieved.

"When my coaches told me that, it kind of put things in perspective for me," she says. "It started back in middle school, and then continued into high school as I learned how to cope with those big-pressure competitions. So, it was about learning how to navigate through that at a younger age, and then just learning how to focus on myself."

Henderson got hooked on track early on, as she would watch her older sister run and waited until she was old enough to get out on the track, too. "I always just wanted to be a part of it, and I loved it from the beginning," she says. She found the individual aspects of the sport fascinating, as she had to rely on herself to perform during meets (and when she ran relays, to learn how to handle the teamwork element and added pressure with four runners working together). What she worked on in practice, and how devoted she was to that work, would reveal itself on race days.

"I just like the personal challenge," she says. "Track is so cool, because one hundred percent of what you put into it is what you get out of it. So seeing the progress that I was making by working hard just motivated me to continue to work hard; it made me buy into the program that my coaches were giving me; and it made goal-setting fun, because I knew if I chipped away at it every day, I would be that much closer to my goals. So, every season going in and setting goals and then seeing the progress toward that goal always kept me motivated."

As coaches of a sport like track, where athletes are competing against the clock, the daily judge of their performance and development, the art of motivation takes on even more significance. There are going to be days where athletes are fired up and ready to run, perhaps still energized from a strong performance they turned in during a previous meet; or maybe they had a poor outing the last time out and finished well back, and their energy and confidence levels are tapped out. Just like with any other sport, coaches must observe and react to their athletes and have the ability to adapt practices, or do things differently that day, to squeeze as much productivity as they possibly can out of the session.

"Young athletes are not robots," says Henderson, who won a pile of titles in the 200 and 400 meters during her medal-filled career, as well as an NCAA Championship in the 400 meters while competing for UCLA. "So sometimes they come out and they are just not feeling great about whatever circumstances they are dealing with, or they are lacking in motivation. So I try to draw that out of them. I just have to remind them that every day that they are out there is a positive day, and another day toward reaching their goals. Every day is a day of improvement. So when they think about it that way, and we break it down into smaller steps and smaller successes, they get motivated, and I can get them to buy into it."

To help make every practice productive, Henderson recalls how her coaches used a variety of approaches to grab interest and fuel desire to get moving around the track. One of the methods was time trials, where it's simply the athlete racing against the clock. "You're challenging yourself," Henderson says. "You're trying to beat the clock. You're not worried about your competitors, but you are just worried about what you can do. Other days, you would be racing against your teammates."

It's a similar approach Henderson takes with her collegiate athletes nowadays, serving up a practice platter of variety, so that her practices don't become stagnant and her athletes bored by the process. "Some days they're working on their own pace," she says. "And other days, they're working on feeling like they're in a race and learning how to stay relaxed and focused with somebody right next to them and the pressure is on."

Henderson is a strong proponent of keeping that fun element woven throughout practice at not only the younger-age levels, but even at her elite level of competition, too. "I started running when I was five, and I ran track every year of my life for twenty years because I found it fun," she recalls. "And a lot of that was because of my coaches growing up—they made it fun. Making it fun is teaching athletes how to challenge themselves and making them aware of the progress they are making every day, and giving them positive feedback."

During a track meet, or any athletic competition, there are a lot of thoughts that can wriggle into an athlete's mind, many of which are unhealthy or even destructive in nature. If runners are worried about others in the race when they settle their spikes into the starting block, their ability to perform at their best is going to be compromised and the likelihood that they will post a good time or be the first to the finish line vanishes. All of their focus needs to be directed on themselves and what they need to do to run their best race, not expending their valuable energy worrying about what others might be doing to run their best times. It's an interesting dynamic that coaches of individual sports like track, swimming, golf and tennis, among others, must address with their athletes.

"Track is a cool sport, because it is an individual sport, and I tell my athletes all the time to just stay within their lanes," Henderson says. "That means just focusing on yourself, and trying not to let the things that are out of your control affect you. I started learning that from my coaches in middle school through high school, college, and then at the elite level, too—to always try and focus on what it is that I am trying to execute, while blocking out the outside factors."

"Track is a cool sport because it is an individual sport, and I tell my athletes all the time to just stay within their lanes. That means just focusing on yourself, and trying not to let the things that are out of your control affect you."

Of course, even the most gifted and hardest-working of athletes isn't going to be first across the finish line every race. There will be days when a runner records a personal best to grab first place; or there will be those races where athletes just don't have it that day. There are so many factors that go into that journey around the track. Coaches must prepare athletes for the inevitable fact that they are going to experience a variety of outcomes throughout their involvement in the sport. How they handle these will be instrumental in their development—or demise.

"These are definitely important lessons," Henderson says. "In track and field, when you line up on the track, you have usually eight other competitors that you are going against, and one of them is going to be victorious while everyone else is scrambling. There is only going to be one winner, so when you do suffer a loss, you have to look back at your performance that day and search internally for your challenges and your goals. If your performance was where it was supposed to be and better than the previous competition, then that is still a win for you. I am always reminding my athletes of that. You never know who you are going to line up against, but you do know that you are in control of your own race and executing your own strategy. I say it to my athletes all the time: you are not going to win every race, but you definitely have to enjoy what you are doing, and know that you can still improve yourself for the next one."

During races, all sorts of things can happen: a poor start out of the blocks can be disastrous and difficult to overcome; an athlete may expend too much energy early on, so there's nothing left in the tank on the backstretch; Mother Nature may opt to cast some windy conditions; and so on. All those types of experiences comprise that learning curve, which isn't going to come as fast as most athletes desire. But, as Henderson has pointed out, when athletes are taught to see their steady progress from practice to practice or from meet to meet, that will help drive them to continue putting in the work required to keep that progress climbing like a hot stock.

"Every day doesn't have to be getting ready for high-pressure competition," Henderson says. "But every day can be a day that each athlete can get better and have a really fun sporting experience. So I would encourage coaches to focus on those things. It doesn't matter how talented they are, or what their skills are, everyone has an opportunity to improve. I just enjoy seeing their faces when they achieve something that they might not have believed they could achieve, but I could see that they could do it. It's that moment when they just see their time or see their performance, and they are so grateful and thankful and excited—that to me is just so rewarding and the reason why I'm in coaching."

Ken Hitchcock

Former NHL coach ■ Ranks third in NHL history
with 823 wins ■ 2012 NHL Coach of the Year
■ 1999 Stanley Cup Champion ■ Team Canada
assistant coach in five Olympic Games

No matter the sport, the ages of the young athletes, their experience level, the coach's background, the program type, or even the length of the season, this much is certain: there are going to be some losses, and maybe even some rough patches, encountered along the way. Your young athletes are going to have to learn some tough lessons on handling the emotions that accompany setbacks and working through those performances that don't measure up—and the same applies for the coaches, too. Yes, there are those teams that will enjoy good fortune all season long, stacking wins and carving up the competition in the process, but those types of runs are rare and certainly can't be counted on to happen on your watch with your team. So as you enter your season, regardless of the sport you are coaching, you've got to be prepared for the adversity that at some point during the season will come knocking on your front door.

Losses have the potential to carve doubt into players' minds where confidence once resided. Disappointment and sadness can't be allowed to linger around the team following a loss, zapping the team's energy, eroding cohesiveness, and casting an unwanted shadow over the remainder of the season. Regardless if the team was involved in a lopsided loss or nipped by a point or goal in a big game, what unfolds afterward can be lethal to a season if it's not handled correctly.

"I always say that any coach that dwells on a loss keeps his team in the swamp," says Ken Hitchcock, former NHL head coach of the Dallas Stars, St. Louis Blues, Columbus Blue Jackets, and Philadelphia Flyers. "Get them out of the swamp. Provide hope for the next competition or the next practice or the next event. Your job is to move them forward as quickly as you can. That is the key to coaching, because it's about the next march you are going to be on with your players, not what just transpired. It's what can we learn and how can we get better moving forward. Your job is not to dwell."

Keep in mind that young athletes take their cues from their coaches. If those in charge appear devastated by the loss, and post-game behavior features coaches with their heads bowed and shoulders slumped, guess what the mood of the team is going to be moving forward? Enthusiasm will flatline, morale will dissolve, and a team sulk-fest will begin. It's common knowledge that sports teach so many valuable life lessons for athletes. Well, guess what? They can teach some pretty powerful ones for leaders of teams, too.

Naturally, most coaches see their team's performance as a reflection of their coaching skills. If the team performs well and wins the game, the coach must be doing an exceptional job, or so the thinking goes with those overseeing a youth sports team. At the other end of the scoreboard, if the team is beaten, the coach may think he or she somehow failed the kids with a bad game day strategy or poor practice planning in the days leading up to the contest. Both scenarios are incorrect, but certainly easy for volunteer coaches to get tangled up in. Of course, egos are involved; coaches want their athletes to perform well because it is so satisfying and rewarding when it all comes together with them responsible for orchestrating the success, and there's not a thing wrong with that. There is nothing wrong with feeling disappointment after a loss, either, but the coach has to be able to move on from it before he can expect his team to as well.

> ## *"I always say that any coach that dwells on a loss keeps his team in the swamp. Get them out of the swamp. Provide hope for the next competition or the next practice or the next event."*

"It's all a read off of you," says Hitchcock, who guided Dallas to the 1999 Stanley Cup. "Everything is a read off of you. How you conduct yourself, how you handle a loss, how you handle a win, and how you handle adversity. Everybody is looking at you all the time."

So in those moments after sustaining a loss, coaches must keep both their emotions and blood pressure levels in check. One of the common themes woven throughout this book is using a process-based approach to coaching, not outcome-based. So keep in mind that even in a loss, the team may have shown great improvement in an area you had directed a lot of attention to in practice leading up to the game. Maybe your athletes really hustled, worked hard, and did everything they possibly could have, but just happened to bump into a better team that day. Or maybe your messages didn't sink in, or it turned out to be one of those days where the players simply weren't focused and engaged, and turned in a sloppy performance. Whatever the reason, Hitchcock warns that getting into a lengthy post-game discussion accomplishes little. That is particularly true if the coach goes on a tirade or speaks to the team as though they are seated in a funeral home.

"For most kids, all they remember is whether the coach was happy or mad, not what he said," Hitchcock says. "What I have found is that if you win, say little, and if you lose, say less." Instead, give the players room. Revisit their performance when they have had time to digest what happened and will be more receptive to your feedback.

"You need to get away from the competition so the message that you want them to receive is going to be absorbed," he advises. "More than anything, if you take time and get away from it and send the right message, the kids will absorb it."

To achieve maximum impact, coaches have other options at their disposal. Sending a team text or email is a productive way to outline your thoughts, but remember, keep the tone positive and uplifting. It's known that we read text messages in the tone of the mood we are in, so coaches must choose their words carefully—otherwise, they can easily be misinterpreted by young athletes who still may be in a sour mood from a game twenty-four hours old. Using the message to highlight those areas that you were pleased with helps set the tone for players putting the game in the rearview mirror and generating energy and excitement for the next practice. As Hitchcock says, you want to pull your players out of that murky swamp filled with trouble, not keep them muddling around in it going nowhere. If they sense genuine excitement and enthusiasm from you about getting back to work no matter what unfolded in the game, then they'll be more apt to match that. And that keeps your season on track.

"The players have to feel that you are having as much fun as they have," Hitchcock says. "They have to feel your enthusiasm for something they have done well, like you're as enthusiastic for their performance as they are for their own performance. That has to be genuine. To me, when you look at the best instructors in any sport, they're the instructors that know when it's time to congratulate the player. You can't look at young kids as professional athletes. They need your constant feedback; they need your constant enthusiasm; and they need your constant support. The more you give it, the more you're going to get a good performance."

"So what it really comes down to is this: Your number-one job is controlling hearts and minds," Hitchcock says. "It's not the technical information you supply. It's controlling the hearts and minds in a positive direction. Every day you're with young people, your job is to provide hope. You're selling something, and the sales job that you're providing is that position of hope. In other words, if you do *this*, it'll give you a chance to get better, and that's what kids want to hear."

Misty Hyman

Olympic gold medalist swimmer ▪ Won thirteen United
States national titles ▪ Won five NCAA titles swimming
at Stanford University ▪ Former Senior Assistant
Swimming Coach for Arizona State University

 The blueprint for orchestrating one of the greatest upsets in Olympic swimming history originated under the blazing Arizona sun decades ago. It was there that Misty Hyman, a young and talented swimmer with the Arizona Desert Fox Swim Team, competed under the direction of legendary coach Bob Gillette.

"Besides my parents, he was one of the most important people in my life," Hyman says. Gillette was a teacher, leader, motivator, encourager, and renowned innovator. He spent a lifetime on a never-ending quest of helping swimmers find new ways, and better ways, to get across the water as efficiently—and as fast—as possible. And the man's impact has never been forgotten by Hyman. Not only did their work together produce a coveted gold medal for the young Olympian in that goose bump-raising 200-meter butterfly final at the 2000 Olympic Games (more on that race shortly), but now as a coach herself these days, she's applying many of the wonderful lessons she learned from him, along with incorporating plenty of her own ideas and philosophies, as she coaches and influences a whole new generation of up-and-coming swimmers.

"The biggest thing that he taught me was the idea that there is always something you can change to get better," she says. "That was a theme throughout our time working together that really has stuck with me throughout the rest of my life." Gillette began using heart-rate monitoring on Hyman at the age of fourteen to track workloads, intensity, and stress levels; and he even used food coloring in the pool to closely examine her kicking motion in order to maximize her power beneath the surface of the water, among other innovations.

"He was very much a pioneer in the sport of swimming," Hyman says. "He used math and science to help look for ways we could improve. So every time we went to the pool, it wasn't just going back and forth, and it wasn't just training hard for the sake of training hard, which of course is important. It was always very specific training with very good intentions of, 'This is why we are training so hard, so that we can change this specific variable in order to be faster.'"

In a sport like swimming, where the scenery never changes and the length of the pool isn't adjustable, finding ways to make sure one practice after another doesn't just blend into monotony is a challenge for swim coaches. When the emphasis is on creativity accompanied by purpose, and young athletes are continually being presented with fresh ideas and new challenges, that leads to energetic and productive sessions. And faster times, too.

"That kept the sport exciting for me, and helped me realize that that's true in everything that we do," Hyman says. "There are always little things we can change to get better if we are just willing to look, and maybe sometimes we have to look in different places than the usual. He was always thinking outside of the box, and trying different ways and different things to make us faster."

Hyman's path to the pool originated in a most unlikely spot: a doctor's office. Diagnosed with asthma at a young age, her doctor informed her mom that swimming was the best sport for kids with asthma. So they signed her up for the summer swim program through the local parks and recreation department.

"At first it was tough, because I wasn't very strong and I wasn't very healthy," Hyman recalls. "But I stuck it out and got healthier and stronger, and I started to realize that I really loved being in the water. After a couple of summers, there was just something about being in a pool that made me feel like I could defy gravity and fly like Peter Pan or Wonder Woman, and I have loved it ever since."

A fantastic junior swimmer, she won numerous national titles and in 1996 found herself competing at the United States Swimming Trials for a spot on the United States swim team that would compete in the Summer Olympics in Atlanta. It's here that she missed out on a spot by *three one-hundredths* of a second.

"I was devastated," she says. "It was pretty much a fingernail that made the difference. I spent some time feeling sorry for myself, and then I had to reevaluate, because for so long I had my big dream of being an Olympic champion, and I wanted so badly to make it big in swimming."

After a lot of reflection, she realized that at the heart of it all, she simply loved the sport. "I loved being in the water," she says. "I loved the way it felt going over my skin and I loved the way the water sounded when it rushed past my ears."

So when Hyman talks to young swimmers about adversity, she knows what it's like as well as anyone; and though the lessons can be heart-wrenching, it's crucial that coaches help young athletes think about why they are involved in the sport to begin with. If they harbor that same joy and passion that Hyman has, then coaches can have a powerful influence over athletes to accept that encountering disappointment is part of the process, but that it's only one part of a much larger journey.

"My advice to young swimmers is adversity happens, and there are always opportunities to grow and get better," she says. "Even if it's hard to see at the time."

She stayed with the sport and competed at Stanford under coach Richard Quick. "His biggest contribution to my career was the idea of belief, and the importance of belief in yourself," she says. "He was a great motivator, and he had a way of helping his swimmers give themselves permission to be great and to believe in themselves. Sometimes we don't realize how important that is. If the athlete has done all the work and shows up, but they don't believe in themselves or believe what they are trying to do is possible, then it just never happens. I really experienced that as I went through some challenges. There was a change of rules (regarding the length swimmers could use the underwater dolphin kick coming out of turns) that actually affected what Coach Gillette and I had worked on and innovated, and that had made me successful. There was part of me that got stuck and didn't believe that I could overcome that, and Richard really helped me to change my heart and change my mind. It was amazing that I can almost pinpoint the exact moment that I did and everything shifted for me and started to fall together, and that was just before the Sydney Olympics."

Hyman not only made the United States team for those 2000 Olympic Games in Sydney, Australia, but she qualified for the 200-meter final in the butterfly. For that race, she was in Lane 6. Two lanes away from her, in Lane 4, was none other than Australia's Susie O'Neill—"Madame Butterfly"—who, for the six years leading up to this event, was the best in the world. She was the reigning Olympic champion in this event. In this same pool several months earlier, she had broken the world record, and the majority of the fans in the stands for this race were pulling for her. But on this night, Hyman turned in the performance of her life, holding off a charging O'Neill over the final fifty meters of the race to win gold and set an American record in the event. (Check out the fantastic performance on YouTube, as the call of the race by NBC's Dan Hicks and Rowdy Gaines will deliver chills.)

How did she manage to slay a swimming giant with a performance of a lifetime that night, amid the crushing pressure of an Olympic final with millions watching? After all, young athletes in all sports become overwhelmed by pressure in all its many forms at some point.

"I tell the swimmers that I coach that that is a skill that you learn, very much like you learn a flip turn or you learn a start," Hyman says. "You learn how to manage your nerves. You learn how to let go and get out of your own way. The biggest challenge for most young athletes is that we get so wrapped up in the pressure and expectations, that we don't allow our bodies and our minds to do what they already know how to do. We actually have to get out of our way and allow ourselves to do what we love and what we've been practicing. It seems so simple, but it is very much a challenge, and the more times that you are able to do that, the easier it gets."

"I may have an idea of what I can help that swimmer with, but I really want to hear what she's feeling and thinking about and get her input on what she wants to work on."

So when athletes are affected by pressure, talk to them about it at the next practice. Inform them that each time they go through it, it becomes easier to handle the next time. Share with them stories of great athletes, like Hyman and so many others, who learned from their experiences and later performed at their best when the lights were brightest and the pressure was the most intense. Young athletes shouldn't fear pressure—teach them to welcome the opportunity to meet it head-on and deliver the best they've got. It's one of the countless ways a coach can influence a young athlete's life.

"What I enjoy most is the change," Hyman says of coaching these days. "I love to be able to affect change just like my coach Bob Gillette taught me, that there is always something you can change in order to get better. I really enjoy working with each swimmer individually, and I think of coaching as a dialogue. It's a two-way street. I may have an idea of what I can help that swimmer with, but I really want to hear what she's feeling and thinking about and get her input on what she wants to work on. And so it ends up being this beautiful dance between the athlete and the coach, working through it together to get to somewhere new. Every time, it's very organic and it's very unique—and it's always very rewarding, especially when you get to a place where you discover something that you didn't know you were going to discover that day. And so it's the idea of being open and letting go of my own ego and expectations for that athlete, and helping her discover what she is there to learn and to change to get better."

Hyman connects with her athletes by stressing the fun factor, but along with that, letting them know that fun comes in a variety of forms, too. "It's empowering the athletes to learn and to grow themselves," she explains. "For a lot of young athletes, if they care about what they are doing, and they enjoy what they are doing, that part is fun. Sometimes that's a byproduct of getting into that dialogue and that dance and for them to discover what they are capable of, but I do put a priority on making sure that what we are doing is fun. It's not meant to be torture."

Hyman also makes a point of teaching young swimmers how to gracefully accept challenge. "Sometimes we have to do things that are difficult and challenging in order to get where we want to go, but I try to help them learn to embrace that," she explains. "There is a fun in working hard and being uncomfortable, and there is a certain kind of fun that comes from working so hard that you are exhausted at the end. There is a fun in focusing on a technical change that you try over and over again, and it takes you hundreds of tries to get it right, but you eventually do. I attempt to pass on the joy of that process to them, that even though it's not playing sharks and minnows in the pool, there is a satisfaction that comes out of working toward a goal and learning about yourself."

Misty Hyman learned a ton about herself thanks in large part to some incredibly caring and influential coaches in her life. Now she's giving back to countless others who swim under her watchful eye and are soaking up her wisdom gained from a lifetime of competing and learning.

Kara Lynn Joyce

Three-time Olympic swimmer (2004, 2008, and 2012) ▪
Four-time Olympic medalist ▪ Eighteen-time NCAA champion
at the University of Georgia ▪ Personal swimming coach

A young athlete's mind can be a canyon of self-doubt; a place where negative thoughts flow freely, fears reside, and pressure and anxiety put the squeeze on performing. Coaches of all sports, and at all levels, must figure out ways to help their athletes navigate this treacherous terrain between the ears, because what goes on in this precious space can be an athlete's greatest weapon or their biggest nemesis. If a basketball player steps to the free-throw line thinking about the last couple shots she missed, it doesn't take a Vegas oddsmaker to predict the likelihood of the next shot clanking off the rim; and if a swimmer is in the starting blocks with fears swirling in his head about his ability to post a fast time, he is likely destined to not be the first to touch the wall while also posting a time that fails to meet what he has been producing during practices. When athletes get caught up in the mental clutter, they become bogged down by useless, negative thoughts that fester and multiply, which makes executing during games, races, and matches incredibly difficult. And oh-so frustrating.

Kara Lynn Joyce is familiar with the pressures that accompany competing at the highest levels of sport, as she has swum in the mega pressure cooker that pops up on our calendars every four years: the Olympics. A three-time Olympian—she swam in the Athens, Beijing, and London Games—Joyce learned how to sweep away the negative thoughts that can gather, attack, and ruin a performance. She had no choice, she had to in order to compete and flourish during a standout career featuring countless podium finishes. And as a coach herself these days in Denver, Colorado—where she works with everyone from youth swimmers as young as six to high-level college athletes, Olympic hopefuls, and even Masters swimmers pushing seventy—the mental side can be just as important, if not more so, than the technical side of the sport.

Joyce is a big proponent of reflection, and jotting those positive thoughts and accomplishments down on paper so they can be referred to throughout the season and before meets. "When athletes reflect on things that they did really well, that's a big step," she says. "I tell kids all the time that if you have a good practice, or if you did something well, then write it down. If it's something you should be proud of, write it down so you remember it. And at the end of the season, you can look back on all the things that you did. Maybe you swam with a senior group in practice that you have never been able to train with before. Or maybe you hit new intervals that you never thought you'd be able to do in a practice. Or you started eating even healthier and swapped out crackers for fruit every time you were hungry, or you're better at being hydrated throughout the day. Write down all the positive things that you do throughout the season, and when it's go time, when it's race time, look back at those things. Look at all of the things that you were able to accomplish, all of those small things. Those are all the right things. And remember that. That should help you stand with your chest a little bit higher and your chin up and know that, 'yes, I put in the work, I did a lot of great things, and I'm ready to go.'"

Clearly, this approach has enormous implications for any sport and can be applied by coaches with their respective teams. For example, if a basketball player is writing down all season long the shots they made, the great passes they delivered, or even how they have elevated their conditioning level which enables them to play harder and more actively for longer periods of time, consider how much more confidently they will approach game day. They will be free of some of those negative thoughts that lurk in the recesses of their brains, threatening to compromise performances.

"I work with athletes from all over," Joyce says. "I get to talk to them not only about their technique, but about the mental side and how they can prepare themselves. Having those relationships and those one-on-one interactions is something I really love and I'm really passionate about."

An athlete's past, if they have competed in sports for any period of time, will be ripe with both positive and negative images dangling in front of them. These memories and events—the good ones—can be plucked, written down, and used as valuable reminders for constructing a powerfully positive mindset that cultivates a confident and well-prepared athlete.

"Looking back on the things they have done helps give athletes their self-confidence," Joyce says. "It's easy to think about, or let negative thoughts creep in, but if you look back and think, 'wait a minute, I did study really hard for this class. I showed up every day for this class ready to learn. I am ready to take this test.' That is something that I am a big fan of."

Coaches can make it a team ritual: have every athlete keep a journal of the things they have done well, as Joyce says. Then, on a practice the day before a big game or meet, remind athletes to review what they have written before going to bed, as it will infuse positive thoughts and energy that can be transferred over the next day during competition. Or, have the athletes bring their journal to practice and at the conclusion of the session, have each share one positive they have written down. Besides bolstering the kids' confidence, it can also deliver a surge of confidence throughout the entire team as athletes listen to how good their teammates feel.

"I'm big on taking all of the things that you can control and controlling those things," Joyce says. "That's going to be how much sleep you are getting; that's going to be packing warm clothes for your meet and making sure when your event is coming up that you know your heat, and your lane, and staying hydrated and having snacks. Some things, like the pool being colder than anticipated or the official starting the race not being used to their cadence, those are things that swimmers can't control. But all things that swimmers have control over, they have already taken care of, so when something gets thrown their way, they know how to handle it."

"Look at all of the things that you were able to accomplish, all of those small things. Those are all the right things. And remember that."

Even as coaches work with their young athletes on controlling those controllables, nervousness is going to be common. It's simply a part of sports at every level. Those butterflies fluttering in one's stomach indicate that athletes are excited and want to do well, and that's certainly normal. But if their stomach is flipping like they are riding a roller coaster, then those nerves become detrimental to the athletes' performances and handcuff their abilities to execute like they are capable of doing.

"I have kids that I work with that are Division I college athletes or Olympic trial participants, so these are some of the best competitors in the country," Joyce says. "So when they tell me how nervous they get I always go back to, 'why do you think your parents put you in sports in the first place? Why do you think your mom signed you up for the swim team when you were six?' They always say, 'To have fun, to do a sport, to be fit, and to make friends.' Then I say, 'yes, and how many of those things still apply today?' And they will pause for a moment and look at me and say 'all of them.' And that's absolutely right. They are still doing it for the same reason. So, I tell them not to forget the reason that they even started this in the first place. Because all that applies today. So the light bulb goes off. It really shouldn't be something that scares them—it's a great and beautiful thing that we get the opportunity and privilege to do, and it should be enjoyed."

Remember, Joyce has competed in three Olympics, so she knows pressure, the suffocating variety, just about as well as anyone. After all, few people know or can even relate to the stress that accompanies standing on the starting blocks with the world watching and success and failure often measured in the blink of an eye. So, as she works with young athletes, she shares her tricks for silencing those pre-race nerves before they have a chance to strike and do collateral damage.

"There are a lot of different things that can go into the mentality of having all that pressure," Joyce says. "Some athletes react by having their bodies lock up when they are competing, or they feel so sick to their stomach before the racing starts or before the game begins. But something that's great about youth sports is the team aspect. Even in a sport like swimming, where it's an individual sport, there is still a big team aspect to it."

Joyce explains that she fosters that team camaraderie by telling the young swimmers she works with, "'Hey, you're with your friends; you are surrounded by your friends. You know what you should do? You should not only write your own events and heat race on your hand, but write their events and heat race on your hand, too, so you can make sure that you can cheer for them. You can get behind them and get really excited for their races, and for them to have you supporting them, they are going to get so excited they're going to swim even faster. And it works the same way for you. They're going to turn around and start cheering you on in your race. So, the more athletes can take pressure off of themselves and get involved in what their teammates are doing, what other people are doing, then their race is going to come around and they're going to be like, 'oh, it's time for me to swim now.' And they are going to be so much more relaxed."

And when they perform well, that will be more positive material to jot down on their journey to becoming athletes that are able to perform to the best of their abilities, no matter the pressure or circumstances surrounding the competition.

Karch Kiraly

Head coach of the United States Women's National
Volleyball Team ▪ Three-time Olympic Gold
Medalist ▪ Three-time national champion at UCLA
▪ 2001 Volleyball Hall of Fame inductee

On a mid-January Friday morning in Southern California, the greatest volleyball player on the planet climbs into his car to drive to the American Sports Center in Anaheim, the training base for the United States Women's Olympic volleyball team. The year is 2016, and Karch Kiraly, winner of three Olympic gold medals, 147 beach tournaments, and named best volleyball player of the twentieth century by the sport's international governing body, is 231 days out from leading the United States women's team in Rio at the Summer Olympic Games.

Naturally, there is a lot on the mind of Kiraly, who was handed the reins of the women's national team in 2012 and who will be coaching the squad that takes the floor for the 2020 Olympics in Tokyo, too. First and foremost, it's leading the Red, White, and Blue to the top perch of the medal podium, a coveted spot the American women's team has never reached in Olympic volleyball history. So, while these weighty expectations have been plopped on his tanned 6-foot-3 frame, on this particular morning, Kiraly isn't talking about how to attack the Brazilians or defend the Chinese. Instead, he is enthusiastically talking about something that genuinely grabs his heart and means so much to him—and that's coaching young athletes the right way. For thirty-two fascinating minutes as he navigates Orange County streets, he's dispensing golden knowledge and insight collected both from playing—and dominating—the sport for years around the globe.

An interesting detour occurs—not on the road but in the conversation—when Kiraly serves up a unique approach to learning. "As coaches, we've got to promote with our teams a mindset of learning and embracing mistakes and chaos," Kiraly says. "If we're operating at the edge of our abilities, there are going to be lots of mistakes, and we should be celebrating those—not punishing them. We need to get our kids to celebrate mistakes and maybe stop once in a while and point out how awesome it was that we were trying something and didn't get it right, because if we're never making mistakes, we're not learning fast enough."

Years ago, when Kiraly's sons entered high school at St. Margaret's Episcopal, a small private school in San Juan Capistrano, California, they endured a miserable season on the volleyball court. They lost every game—of every match. And they played thirty-one matches that season. With the urging of his wife, Kiraly became a co-coach. The following season they won a game; and then they went on to win a match. The next season, they advanced to the small-school title game, and the following year, they won the whole thing. So Kiraly knows volleyball as well as anyone.

He urges today's coaches of young athletes to embrace the mentality of celebrating mistakes, which actually puts players on the fast track to success. It's an approach that has proven effective, whether it's employed with youngsters unfamiliar with the sport, or world class players with pulverizing kill shots and crazy high vertical jumping ability. Since Kiraly's ascension to the top coaching post for the United States national team, this approach has been woven into its practice sessions.

"We try to do that in our gym, too," he says. "We have time set aside every day just for making mistakes. We call it 'School Time.' In School Time, we make the activities as much like a game as possible so that they are more prepared when we actually play a game."

During his playing days, Kiraly was a dominating force, equally comfortable competing in team volleyball contested on an indoor court as he was under the blazing sun on the sand in the fast-paced world of two-man beach volleyball. He is the only player (man or woman) to have won Olympic gold medals in both indoor and beach competition. These days, he's well-versed in the nuances of coaching and taking full advantage of the time allotted with young athletes. Every second is valuable. Kiraly can't afford to waste time during his practices, and that is also true at the youth sports level. Often, volunteer coaches only get a couple hours a week to work with their teams, so capitalizing on those moments are crucial. The more kids are forced to stand around, or put through senseless drills, the greater chances the season will veer off course and the players' zest for competing will fizzle.

"A lot of what we do on the sports field or court is what scientists would call motor activity," he says. "We have to move, we have to see, we have to meet a ball. That's what kids do all the time—in youth sports, they are learning to do it a little better. Our goal in training is to make every second of that training time count—to make it transfer. To waste as few of those minutes as possible. The more we can make it transfer and apply it to helping our team do what they need to do when they put their uniforms on, the better."

Now here's where a tricky part wedges into the picture that coaches must be aware of as they maneuver through their seasons: if the drills they are running their players through aren't really the best approach for skill development, then the practice sessions aren't productive, learning opportunities grow stagnant, and skill development stalls.

"So there's this idea of specificity," Kiraly explains. "If we're doing things in training that won't happen in the game, then we just wasted some of our time. Where we can get a real advantage is in making as many of those minutes count as possible. So, for example, in youth volleyball, I've watched the game for over fifty years and I've never seen a coach serve in a volleyball match. And I've never seen a coach stand on a table and hit a ball over the net to the defense in a real game or competition of volleyball. So the more those things are happening in our gym at the lowest levels, the more the science of motor learning tells us that we're falling behind other teams that do less of that. The less transfer we're going to get, then the less specificity we have."

"We need to get our kids to celebrate mistakes and maybe stop once in a while and point out how awesome it was that we were trying something and didn't get it right, because if we're never making mistakes, we're not learning fast enough."

Now, if you've ever seen a youth soccer game at the beginning levels of play, you know how those games go. At the start of the game, everyone is in their proper position, but once the ball is kicked, everyone chases after it, and all game long, you find a group of kids hovering around the ball. But volleyball is an entirely different sport and poses far more challenges for kids starting out.

"Volleyball is a tough sport," Kiraly says. "It's alien in a sense that most sports that are popular among Americans are ones where we get to hold on to the ball. We get to catch it in football and hold onto and run with it; we get to catch it and hold onto it in basketball; in soccer, we can receive it and hold onto it; in baseball, we catch it. But in volleyball, we don't get to hold onto it, so that in itself is really difficult. Soccer is a lot easier for five-year-olds to play than volleyball, since the ball is always in play on the ground. So when kids are learning a very difficult game, it means that a lot of the stuff we do is going to look really ugly, and we have to embrace that ugly instead of avoid it. And it's going to be really chaotic when you have ten-year-olds trying to play volleyball, but if we can celebrate that and expose them to the ugly and the random and the chaotic earlier, then they are going to be ready when you get to the weekend tournament and all the ugly comes out, anyway. All the random and all the chaos—they're just going to be embracing it and excited about it and excited to test themselves and test their learning."

So coaches need to enthusiastically applaud young players for their effort when they end up sending the ball flying all over the gym, because they are giving it their best effort; and they need to encourage kids to keep at it when their serves are deposited in the bottom of the net. It's all part of the process of learning and developing through the sport. Sure, it's going to have plenty of hard and challenging moments, but that's what makes coaching young athletes so incredibly rewarding—the opportunity to guide them on a life-changing journey while using a sport to achieve it.

"We need to celebrate that process, rather than punish it or dumb it down or control it in a way where we just deliver the ball right to them and they didn't have to move at all," Kiraly says. "And then they get to make a nice touch and it all feels good and looks good, but on the weekends nobody is spoon feeding the ball to anybody—the ball is flying all over the gym. So whoever embraces that more is going to learn faster and improve faster."

As Kiraly's drive comes to an end and he reaches his destination, he's asked what his message would be to those venturing out to coach young athletes for the first time. "If there's one valuable lesson that those coaches could teach their kids is to teach them to be learners," he says. "To learn how to learn and what that means, because that's going to help them in everything they do in life—in school, in sports, with their families, with their future careers. The people who learn fastest have the most successful careers. If I'm a faster learner, I'm probably going to have a successful marriage, I'm going to learn how my wife and I can be a better team. So that's an incredibly important skill. If they could just teach their kids to embrace and help them celebrate all the struggles that go along with learning and help promote life-long learning in them, that would be a hugely valuable service to them. Make it fun while you are celebrating the process, and then just getting kids to celebrate each other's successes and failures as they struggle and work their way through the quicksand and mud of the challenge of the learning process."

Jim Larranaga

University of Miami basketball coach ▪
2013 Naismith College Coach of the Year ▪
Two-time Atlantic Coast Conference Coach of the Year

In the deliciously rich and buzzer-beating history of the NCAA basketball tournament, Jim Larranaga is known for orchestrating one of the most phenomenal runs ever as the head coach at George Mason University. Flashback to 2006, when the Patriots bludgeoned the East Region—and busted the nation's brackets in the process—by disposing of perennial heavyweights Michigan State and North Carolina within the span of forty-eight hours on the opening weekend of the tournament. And they were just getting started on their improbable run. A week later, they knocked off Wichita State and top-seeded Connecticut in an overtime thriller to advance to the school's first-ever Final Four. And forever stamped Larranaga's name into tournament lore.

The beginnings of this most unlikely of runs can be traced all the way back to the start of practice in mid-October on the George Mason campus in Fairfax, Virginia, where Larranaga invited a sports psychologist to speak to the team. It was an individual Larranaga first met on a court—a *tennis* court. During his days as an assistant coach at the University of Virginia, Larranaga was playing a match at the Charlottesville Sports Club. At an adjacent court, a kids' lesson was being held. Larranaga was so intrigued by what he was hearing that he went over and introduced himself to the instructor. He wasn't in search of backhand tips or serving pointers that day. What grabbed his attention were the instructor's words encouraging the youngsters to visualize their strokes and to see their rackets moving in slow motion as they connected with the ball. That youth tennis instructor turned out to be Bob Rotella—yes, *that* Bob Rotella, before he became famous for authoring best-selling golf books filled with the power of visualizing what you want to achieve.

So, when that George Mason team gathered in the locker room before the dawn of its 2005-2006 season, they listened to Rotella's words as he told them to close their eyes and visualize what they wanted to unfold that season. And senior guard Lamar Butler told the team he saw them reaching the Final Four in Indianapolis. They saw it in their minds, they believed it, and they somehow made it happen in the face of outlandish odds during the crushing pressure of March Madness while slaying some high-seeded heavyweight programs in the process.

If that incredible run by George Mason hadn't taken place, perhaps this sit-down interview with the likeable Larranaga in the basketball building at the University of Miami on a steamy summer morning talking coaching, basketball, and kids would never have happened. You see, the charismatic Larranaga with the brilliant basketball mind parlayed his success at George Mason into taking over the Hurricane basketball program in 2011, where he now competes in the talent-rich, mega tough Atlantic Coast Conference—a conference where he has twice been named its Coach of the Year.

Visualization is an intriguing tool. Can it be taught to young players? Can it help squeeze the most out of their abilities, combat fear and pressure, and enable them to perform at high levels on game days, which every athlete is chasing?

"Ask your players to close their eyes and dream," says Larranaga. "Tell them to dream about how they want to play. The mind is a very mysterious organ, and it can help you prepare to execute something during a game, and all you ever did was picture it in your own mind as to how it should happen." Larranaga's players use visualization everywhere: in their hotel rooms the night before road games, before practices, and even prior to tip off on game day. They apply it to everything: they picture themselves sinking big shots, making key defensive stops, and even imagining students storming the court after pulling off a big upset.

> ## "Ask your players to close their eyes and dream. Tell them to dream about how they want to play."

"A great example is free throw shooting in basketball," Larranaga explains. "Before you ever go to the foul line, you should have visualized yourself being successful over and over again—actually creating the emotion you feel when you go to the foul line. See yourself relaxed, cool, calm, and collected, with a lot of composure going to the foul line and having a routine that you follow.

And then you make the free throw and you see that over and over again. That's why kids playing in the park or in their driveway will oftentimes use the end of a game and say '5...4...3...2...' and just as they say '1,' launch the shot. That's visualization, because they are seeing themselves dreaming about being in a game where they have to take the game-winning shot and make it."

Coaches can use it with their players before practice. Set aside a minute or two for players to close their eyes and imagine making shots or grabbing rebounds. Or, encourage them when they go to bed the night before a game to picture themselves performing well, whether it's sinking shots or playing great defense. It's applicable for coaches, too.

"Visualization is a very important part of being successful in any business," Larranaga says. "If you are an architect or a builder, you don't just start building a house. First, you have to have architectural drawings; you have to envision what you are building before you ever put pen to paper. As a basketball coach, or a coach of any sport, visualizing what you want your team to accomplish and what the players should play like helps them learn how to visualize themselves shooting, dribbling, defending, and rebounding the basketball."

The art of visualization can be tied to goal setting, which Larranaga is a huge proponent of coaches using at any level. Each offseason, he writes down his list of goals for the team for the upcoming season. Based on the age and experience level of the kids on your team, you can help kids map out short- and long-term goals for their seasons, too.

"We believe goals are very, very important, both short-range and long-range," Larranaga says. "With our long-range goals, we often use the expression, 'Begin with the end in mind.' So when we begin a season, we want to think and plan for where we want to be and how good we need to be by the end of the season. Short-range goals are the goals we set each and every day, each and every week and each and every month to eventually reach that goal at the end of the season. And so, we have goals for our shooting, ball handling, rebounding, all the fundamentals. And when athletes sees themselves improving in the fundamentals they enjoy, it encourages them, it motivates them, it inspires them to do more to get better and better. It's up to the coach to motivate and inspire the athletes so that they feel good about themselves. You're trying to build self-esteem and confidence so that they are doing things that they feel good about."

Making that happen requires establishing an environment in which young players feel appreciated for their efforts and valued for their contributions.

"The most important thing to create the right culture is to create a positive atmosphere," Larranaga advises. "We use a five-step teaching method to help our players. The first step is *explanation,* the second step is *demonstration,* the third step is *imitation,* the fourth step is *correction,* and the fifth step is *repetition.* But the most important thing in all of those categories is to stay positive. When we say 'correction,' we're not talking about criticism, we're talking about very, very helpful advice, and it's important for kids to receive that information in a constructive way so they stay positive."

While disseminating information to young athletes, particularly those at the younger and generally more inexperienced levels, it's advisable to stay away from complicated strategy and jumping too quickly to advanced skills before players have a chance to get comfortable with the fundamental elements of the sport that require constant work.

"I would tell volunteer coaches a couple of things," he says. "Number one: keep it very, very simple. Don't try to make it too complicated and don't try to be the master coach. If you're just introducing a child to the sport, even if it's a youth team where kids have played for four or five years, you still have to remember to keep things pretty simple. And secondly, to make it fun for them. Allow them to be themselves, to work on improving and not just trying to win the game. I have a lot of friends who are in teaching, and it drives them nuts that they have to teach to the test, a standardized test that the kids have to pass. The difference between true teaching and teaching for the test is like a coach: if you're just teaching to help the kids win, you're missing the big picture. It's all about helping them enjoy themselves and enjoy the process and continuing to improve."

Thomas Lott

Three-year starting quarterback for Oklahoma
University ■ Won three Big Eight Conference
championships ■ Texas High School Football Hall
of Fame inductee ■ Coach of several youth sports

 To be a member of the John Jay High School football team in the 1970s, one had to complete a running test that challenged players' fitness—and their heart for competing. Those who succeeded had the privilege of suiting up for the San Antonio public school to play on Friday nights, a huge deal considering that in the state of Texas, football reigns. Meanwhile, those teens who failed to meet the time limit imposed by the coach saw their dreams evaporate in the simmering summer heat.

On this particular day decades ago, a young player by the name of Thomas Lott—the one that legendary Oklahoma football coach Barry Switzer would later call "the greatest wishbone quarterback in Oklahoma history"—was struggling to complete the run in the required time.

"I remember in high school, we used to have this test where we had to run so many laps in a certain amount of time, and I was struggling a little bit to make the time, and it was one of the requirements to be a part of the team," Lott says. "I had run it two times that day, and didn't make it."

With his hopes of playing a game he loved teetering on the ledge, something special happened. And he's never forgotten it. As he began his third attempt at the punishing laps around the field, words of encouragement began filling the air. Teammates, sensing the predicament Lott was in, were urging him on, motivating and inspiring him. They showed they cared, and it meant all the difference in the world.

"That third time, my whole team cheered me on," he says. "And some of the players were right there running alongside me, giving me that extra strength." Those heartfelt words of encouragement pushed Lott to run hard and fight through the burning in his lungs and the pain radiating in his legs to complete the laps in the required amount of time and help ensure that he got to play a sport he loved for his school. And play it incredibly well too, as he rushed for consecutive 1,000-yard seasons in his two years as a starter.

Stories like these only happen when teammates care for each other and love each other like family. It's that type of atmosphere that coaches at all levels, and all sports, must strive to cultivate with their players. It's an afternoon that Lott remembers as clearly as if it had happened yesterday, and as he shares the story, one can hear in his voice how much it meant to him. So, no matter what sport he has coached through the years—football, baseball, basketball, and track among them—establishing that family-like atmosphere among his players has always ranked high on his list of priorities entering a season.

"It's one of those things you have to be constantly talking about with your players," Lott explains. "You have to constantly be talking about helping each other out. You constantly work on them being together, and you don't leave anybody behind. It's a journey. It's not something that you can talk about and expect them to get right away, because it's not going to happen that fast. That's part of the journey of developing into a close-knit team: it takes time."

It also requires more than just talking about it; it takes watching what is happening before, during, and after practices and games. "As a coach, you have to be very observant and always watching to see who's lagging behind," Lott says. "Who do we need to help? Who do we need to carry a little bit and get them to be a part of this? Everybody on the team has to feel like they are a part of it, and being a part of it is contributing. So you have to find things that they can contribute. Everybody is not going to be great at everything, but the thing you do is you watch and you observe what it is they *are* doing well. It may just be one drill that they are really good at, but you see the potential in them, and you work with them so that they do well at that one specific thing. And then use them as an example: 'Tom is really good at this drill, so Tom, come over here and show everybody how to do it. You lead this drill.' You give them opportunities to show what they can do, and be proud of it."

Of course, some athletes will be able to perform multiple skills at a high level, while others may be fortunate to be able to execute just one of them reasonably well. That's the nature of sports, particularly at the younger levels of competition, where young athletes are adjusting to their growing and developing bodies while also trying to learn new skills for their respective sports. Now, athletes will naturally compare themselves to others. For coaches, it's important to help each player focus on their skills, both recognizing what areas of the game they are excelling at and which aspects of the game they are having some difficulty with. When young athletes are worrying about how their teammates are performing, and how their skills stack up to others, it will detract from their level of play. It's that mindset that Lott used during his playing days, where he zeroed in on what he needed to do.

"Each time I challenged myself," he says. "You compete against yourself. You don't really compete against other people. You compete against yourself, and you try to outdo what you did the day before and the week before, but it's a process, it's a journey. It takes time for you to get better. You can't get discouraged because you're not like another kid, so don't try to compete against someone else. You just compete against yourself, and you work hard within yourself, and that's where self-confidence comes from."

"If you have a player who doesn't progress over the course of a season, that's not on that child—it's on you. You have to find a way to get him engaged and get him practicing."

Lott reminds coaches that they can't approach every athlete the same way, because there are so many different personalities involved, and athletes respond so differently to both praise and criticism. "As a coach, you have to look at each individual, because everybody is different," he says. "You can't coach everybody the same. You have to be alert and aware of each individual and what they are bringing to the table and what they need to work on. Every day, you try to find little things that each individual can accomplish. You look at what they are doing well and what you need to work on with them, and then you put them in position to do those things. It's important at every practice that every one of your players has some progress. If it's running track, and they have a time that is one second or even one-hundredth of a second lower, that's an accomplishment for them, and those are things that you chat up. And then you come back with, 'Okay, we accomplished something today, and that's progress. Every little thing is progress. So next week, let's try to get that down another second by working hard.'"

Coaching is also about helping every player on the team, not just the mega-talented ones who are easy to fixate on because they are fun to watch perform and exciting to coach because of their abilities. When Lott coaches, he cares about every player—and it shows. "Every year, I would have what I called 'my project,'" he says. "That would be the kid on the team with the least athletic ability who might not have even played sports up until that point. He needs more work than anybody on the team. I wanted to see how far my project had come by the end of the year, because I knew he needed more work than everyone else did."

When you're able to help the least talented player on the team learn and progress along with everyone else on the team, that's being a coach who genuinely cares about everyone. "Open your eyes, look at your guys and see what they are doing," Lott says. "See their temperament. Some guys you can get after a little more than others, and some guys you have to come at them from a different direction. But as a coach, your main job is to make sure everyone on that team at the end of the year is better than what they were when the year started. It's about improving each and every player. If you have a player who doesn't progress over the course of a season, that's not on that child—it's on you. You have to find a way to get him engaged and get him practicing. I would spend countless hours away from practice and away from the games thinking about, 'how can I get to him?' As a coach, you're learning just like they are. Don't ever think as a coach that you know everything, because you don't. And once a coach stops learning, he needs to get out of the game, because there's constant learning and adjustments that need to be made."

During his college football days in Norman, Lott played for Switzer, the school's all-time winningest coach who would later win a Super Bowl coaching the Dallas Cowboys, too. "The one thing that Coach Switzer always told us was you have to develop into a good citizen," Lott says. "We need to go out in society and be good citizens, so that's one thing I have always taken with me. Not only am I coaching, I'd be missing the boat if I didn't take some of those situations when we are practicing and in games and use them as material to teach kids something about life. Any coach that is not doing that is missing the boat—it's not all about winning. The winning will take care of itself if they are working hard and are sacrificing and committed. But it's those life lessons that you can equate to those situations, and that's something that I've always used when I've had an opportunity. I'll stop practice if I see an opportunity to teach them something about life. I'll gather them up and talk to them about how this is going to help them in life."

Prior to his outstanding collegiate career under Switzer, where he led the Oklahoma Sooners to three Big Eight titles and a sparkling 11-1 record and No. 3 ranking his senior season, he benefited from the influence of a number of outstanding coaches during his youth, too.

"I was so blessed to have the coaches that I had," Lott says. "All the coaches I played for throughout my youth taught me things about the sport, but they also taught me things that would equate in life. You can use these same lessons from playing sports—the hard work, the sacrifice, the commitment—as these are things that you can use in everyday life, too. Everybody is not going to play sports all the way to the pro level, but you take those lessons and you carry them over in life."

One of the many important themes woven throughout this book is the importance of coaches paying attention to all the details, because what may seem like the smallest ones can often have the biggest impact. Lott relays this story from coaching high school football, where he noticed that the team wasn't connected: "I noticed that the kids didn't seem to like each other as a group. I noticed that they were coming out to practice in pockets. There would be three or four players here, and three or four over there. They weren't together, and they weren't communicating with each other." So he did what good coaches do—he addressed the kids and began the work of getting them to care for each other, so they could support each other and play together as a unit.

"I brought them all together," he says. "You have to get them together and be able to notice if someone feels left out, if there's a pocket of people hanging out at practice. You have to constantly be talking about *we* as a family. We are a secondary family. We have to care about each other, and we have to help each other. When you see a guy that has fallen back in conditioning, you go help him, you help him make it to the finish line."

Lott's high school teammates helped him all those years ago, and under his watch as a coach these days – no matter the sport – he makes sure that no young athlete is ever overlooked or left behind. Follow his lead and make sure it doesn't happen on your team, too.

Joe Maddon

Manager of the Chicago Cubs ▪ 2016 World Series champion ▪ Three-time Manager of the Year ▪ Winner of more than 1,000 Major League games

During the Chicago Cubs' historical and long-awaited journey to winning the 2016 World Series, a fascinating ride that captivated the country, everything manager Joe Maddon said and did during that unforgettable postseason was dissected and analyzed along the way. His batting order, starting pitching rotations, when he chose to hit and run or give the go ahead to attempt stealing a base, when he elected to turn to his bullpen (or not use a reliever, for that matter), and more were all watched, examined, and talked about endlessly throughout the playoffs.

And guess what? Volunteer coaches in today's incredibly challenging, constantly shifting youth sports landscape face plenty of scrutiny, too. Of course, not quite to the degree of what Maddon endured during the pressure-packed playoffs, or what Major League managers face during the grind of the 162-game regular season. But, it does exist. There are plenty of eyes watching, judging, evaluating, and forming opinions. And it doesn't matter the sport or the age or experience level of the youngsters competing. It happens everywhere.

It starts with the young athletes. They've got eyes and ears, and they use them to soak in everything that happens during practices and games. A coach's words, reactions, and mannerisms are watched, often talked about, and most definitely filed away in the memories of the players. (And yes, their parents, too.) What happens will also be replayed and referenced all season long in conversations between teammates, and even at the family dinner table following practices and games.

"Understand one thing," says Maddon, seated near the visitor's dugout at Marlins Park a couple hours before a regular season game against the Miami Marlins. "The kids are smart and they don't miss anything. Kids will notice your good body language and your bad body language and any minor angry moment that you thought had maybe been overlooked. Your actions impact them way more than you ever thought they would."

That puts a premium on maintaining a calm demeanor at all times; speaking to kids in a positive manner; and really being aware of your body language and the verbal and non-verbal messages you are sending to your players. Verbal disappointment is an obvious one. When coaches yell at a youngster for misplaying a ball or committing a baserunning blunder, that criticism is heard by everyone—and it affects everyone to varying degrees. When players see a teammate criticized, for some, that will zap their aggressiveness moving forward. They'll be fearful of being called out for a miscue, as the coach's words will be dancing around in their subconscious. That often translates into youngsters playing less aggressively to minimize the chances of mistakes occurring, but which results in diminishing returns for the team in the process, as there will now be less opportunities for plays to be made, too.

Non-verbal cues are also picked up by kids and can have season-long consequences as well. When coaches shake their head, sigh, glare, kick the dirt, or raise their hands in exasperation following a play, those reactions don't go unnoticed by players. They see it and they feel the disappointment seep into their bones. Baseball is challenging enough as it is, and the more pressure that is applied by coaches, the more difficult the season will likely become for the players.

"If you talk about baseball for instance, you're going to have a lot of failure in this game and you have to be able to stay positive with your kids," Maddon says. "Even through those negative moments where they do fail a bit, so that they want to keep coming back for more. When it becomes too negative or oppressive, all of a sudden they're going to shy away from this and not want to practice or not want to show up, and they won't play with such verve. You keep it positive and keep the message positive and let them know that if they do stick with it, eventually they're going to come out on the positive side of things. For me it's an easy thing to do; for some people, it's more difficult to remain with that positive kind of an attitude. But at the end of the day, just be positive with your kids, and eventually they're going to come out on the right side."

Maddon is a big proponent of one-on-one conversations between coaches and players, no matter the level. "I'll tell you what we do, and I don't see why it wouldn't work on any level, and that's to have a meeting with each kid," he says. "Talk to him about what you perceive to be his strong points and what you like about him. And then explain, 'Here's what we think we need to work on,' and be very specific: 'We need to work on these particular items to help you get better.' Be specific, but not negative, and create a game plan for each kid."

Approach these meetings well-prepared, though. A positive meeting can energize players, helping them dial in and encouraging them to continue working hard. Be aware that using the wrong choice of words in these conversations can backfire, stinging kids and resulting in them feeling poorly about themselves or their role on the team.

"Be aware of what you are going to say in advance, and be careful," Maddon says. "Honesty without compassion really does equal cruelty at the end of the day. So know what you're saying and how you're saying it in advance, because the kids don't miss anything."

> ### "Understand one thing: the kids are smart and they don't miss anything. . . . Your actions impact them way more than you ever thought they would."

As coaches navigate their seasons, it's important to keep in mind that all communication with the team matters. Everything from the pre-game pep talks to mid-game strategy sessions to the post-game wrap up affects kids' perceptions of their skills, their confidence, and their interest in the sport. So those coaches who are able to keep a positive vibe running throughout their exchanges will see players who are more relaxed on the field, and those players will be more likely to be able to perform to the best of their ability.

"It's how you talk to them," says Maddon, one of only two active managers to guide teams to four straight ninety-plus win seasons. "If I want to talk to them in a stressful, uptight manner, the kids are going to reflect the same thing; and if I choose to not do it that way, they probably won't. The players should reflect the personality of your manager or coaching staff. If you have an uptight kid, a lot of times it's because of what either he gets at home or the message that's being brought to him by the coach. So lighten it up. Try to get this kid to relax, have fun with what he's doing, and believe that positive results are going to follow. Too many times when a kid does poorly, he's going to start anticipating that he'll continue playing poorly in the future, and that's a bad thing. You have to be able to talk kids through that moment, stay supportive, and keep them moving in a positive direction."

Part of keeping the season flowing in the right direction involves keeping everybody engaged in the process. When athletes feel a genuine connection to the team and appreciated for their efforts, it can be a special experience for all involved. But when players feel as though they are on the fringe, especially those recognizing that their skill level may not be comparable to others on the team, if coaches don't deliver the guidance that they need or connect with them, chances are they won't have a memorable experience and probably won't return to the sport.

"If you are going to go out and coach for the first time, absolutely keep it fun for everybody, there's no question about that," Maddon says. "And be aware of team building; be aware of having everybody involved. It's important for me that everybody plays and stays involved. When you have that concept going within the entire team, everybody embraces winning a lot more heartily and wholly, and it infiltrates the entire fabric of what you are doing. So keep it fun, keep everybody involved, be aware of team building, and be consistent in your approach on a daily basis. For me, every day I walk in the door I tell myself to be consistent, and especially when things aren't going well, because the players are going to feed off that. Consistency in your approach to the day is very important. If you just stay with those three tenets—involvement, team building, and consistency—things will work out well."

As a Major League manager who is paid to win games and deliver titles, Maddon is well-versed and accustomed to maneuvering through the mine-fields of pressure and stress. If he's not winning games, he'll be replaced. He's aware of that. It's the nature of the business he's been a part of much of his life. So he gets it. He wants to make sure that volunteer coaches don't treat their seasons like a Major League odyssey, though. Jobs aren't on the line in youth sports, but there is plenty at stake when it comes to building a youngster's interest in a sport and helping him or her develop both the confidence and interest to continue playing it for years to come.

"At the end of the day, everybody wants to win," Maddon says. "Don't misinterpret Vince Lombardi's message and all the great coaches that came before us. I need to win here as a Major League manager. As a Little League coach, winning isn't important—you've just got to make sure that you're making every player better."

Danny Manning

Wake Forest University basketball coach ▪ Most Outstanding
Player of the 1988 Final Four ▪ National Player of
the Year ▪ United States Olympic Basketball Team

College basketball coaches appreciate getting Teed up—technical fouls whistled by referees for disputing calls—about as much as losing a coveted recruit to a rival school. But in Winston-Salem, North Carolina, being Teed up carries an entirely different and much more profound meaning. Danny Manning, head coach of the Wake Forest University men's basketball team that resides there, chases a T every day his team gathers for practice at the 50,000-square foot Miller Center on the Demon Deacons campus. He wants his assistant coaches gunning for those T's with the zest of a Scrabble junkie, too; and he encourages youth coaches to make it part of their practice plan goals as well.

"Teach, encourage, emphasize," says Manning, seated on a second floor hotel balcony in South Florida. "On our staff, we call that being 'Teed up.' All of our coaches want to be Teed up every day at practice. We want to teach, encourage, emphasize. You want to applaud and recognize an action that you want to see repeated by one of your players. So, if someone does something as small as diving on the floor for a loose ball and gets that team an extra possession, you acknowledge that; you congratulate them for making that effort, and hopefully it will be a repeated action." Good habits that are cultivated through hard work and then repeated lead to that coveted skill development both players and coaches desperately crave.

"Teach, encourage, emphasize. On our staff, we call that being 'Teed up.'"

Manning's college basketball resume shines as bright as anyone's, as he is one of the most accomplished players in the history of the collegiate game. Among his achievements: leading Kansas to the 1988 NCAA championship;

consensus National Player of the Year; All-American; Olympian; and college basketball Hall of Famer, among so many others. And that was just the prelude to a fifteen year NBA career that began with being the league's number one overall draft pick; featured a couple of All-Star game appearances; and even a Sixth Man of the Year award. He likely never would have reached the pinnacle of the sport, where he was named the Most Outstanding Player of the '88 Final Four—where he led the Jayhawks, appropriately dubbed "Danny and the Miracles," to an 83-79 victory over Oklahoma—without having a laser focus on the fundamentals of the sport at an early age.

"I was very fortunate to play for my dad, he showed me the way," says Manning. "He, and the other coaches I had, taught me the fundamentals and helped me understand the ins and outs of the game. A lot of times parents volunteer their time, effort and energy, which is wonderful, but they have to make sure that the fundamentals are tackled properly each and every day to help kids continue to build and get better." Too often, once the games begin and the scoreboards are turned on, it's easy to get caught up in the excitement of the season and neglect other important aspects of coaching that directly impact the players' development. Fundamentals need to be a focal point all season long, and not lost amid efforts to introduce fancy or complex plays into the mix.

"At the end of the day, no one really cares if you win a championship at a tournament in July," Manning says. "The big picture is continuing to teach and develop and let the kids know that you have to work in order to get better. At each level that they move up, it becomes a little bit harder, and you have to have kids prepared for that. They have to be willing to handle criticism in a constructive way."

Blended with that criticism must come one of the key ingredients of being Teed up, and that's encouragement. When young players are fed those encouraging words, and receiving fist bumps and high-fives from coaches for their efforts, that crushes the banality of learning the fundamentals of the respective sport that can creep into a season sometimes. Plus, it pushes the enjoyment meter up a few notches for the kids who will begin arriving early to practice because they are anxious to learn and compete, rather than showing up at the last second as though they are about to take a test they have been dreading.

What kids must learn during the course of the season is that some days will go well, and other days won't. Some days they'll have the golden touch and everything they do will work well, and other days nothing will seemingly go right. When it comes to sports and skill development, there is a gigantic learning curve involved with lots of unexpected twists and turns.

"Sometimes the acquired taste of competition is something that's a journey," Manning says. "It's a process that you have to learn to get to, but so many kids get that competitive spirit, but they don't know how to handle it if it doesn't go their way. Sometimes you've got to say that, 'today wasn't my day. I've got to get better. Hopefully if I get better, there will be a different outcome next time I compete.' But the biggest part is making sure that your players can go out and put forth the maximum amount of effort that they can each day and that's the key. Maybe today they can go out and practice hard for thirty minutes, while the next day they want to go hard for thirty-two minutes, or thirty-three minutes."

That mentality of working and searching for improvement every day of practice must continually be fed and then carried into game day action. Even though scoreboards will be turned on and opposing players will be in the picture, the same facets apply. There are just more eyes in the process. Just like practices can be "wins" for the players on those days where shots are dropping, they're hustling and everything is in sync and working in perfect harmony to those lackluster days that can be filed in the "loss" folder due to poor concentration, awful execution, and zero indication of teamwork anywhere on the floor. It's about teaching kids how to respond to those practice victories as well as the setbacks.

"At the end of the day you've got to be able to say, 'hey, I did the best I could do, and maybe today it wasn't good enough, but I'll go back tomorrow and I'll practice and get better, and hopefully the next time we compete it's a different situation,'" Manning says. "But that's just a part of it. Every day you go out and you do the best that you can do, and that's all that any coach or any parent can ask for. My dad said all the time, go out and play hard, but some days are not going to be your day, and you've got to deal with it. It's part of life. Congratulate that person because that day they got the best of you, but you can also say, 'hey, I look forward to competing against you again.' And hopefully it's a different outcome next time if you do the work to change it."

Manning had the benefit of playing for a lot of great coaches throughout his collegiate and professional career. So naturally, he can grab ideas and approaches that worked and incorporate them into his teachings; as well as steering clear of those things that failed.

"I look at the different things that coaches did and said, 'hey, you know what, I like this,'" he says. "'I'm going to use this when I coach; or I didn't like this, I'm not going to use it. A lot of it is the type of kid you are working with in the sport you are playing, but the biggest deal is kids going out and putting it all on the line and knowing that they did the best they could that day and today we were successful, or we weren't as successful as we wanted to be and we have to work harder. If you have that mentality growing up, you're going to be successful in life because all the things we talk about in athletics and sports mirrors life: working hard, teamwork, being unselfish, going out and working hard for the greater good of the whole. All of these are things that you are going to have to use in your workplace when you get older and you're navigating life."

Every year when March Madness rolls around, footage of all the buzzer beating finishes and classic performances are replayed for basketball fans to soak in and relive. In the footage every year is a young, lean, and unstoppable figure with the number 25 jersey slashing to the hoop. Few players ever experience what Manning did during Kansas' magical run to glory during the 1988 tournament. But for Manning, it was being part of a team, learning to rely on one another, working for each other, and supporting each other. Those are the memories that resonate.

"You feel fortunate, you feel blessed, you know that you are part of a group that did something special and that's a memory that you always have that nobody can take away from you and that's probably the biggest deal," Manning says. "It's not being able to look at the championship ring or going back and looking at a video, it's knowing that you sacrificed for the greater good of the team and you were the last team standing. I was very fortunate to be on a team that it worked out for us like that."

As coaches, that's the ultimate: getting players to work together, pulling for one another, and having everything work out in the end. Every season is a wild ride, with new obstacles to conquer. How each season is going to end is a mystery, but a good starting point is getting Teed up, courtesy of Danny Manning.

Cuonzo Martin

University of Missouri men's basketball coach
▪ Former college basketball player at Purdue
University ▪ 2011 Missouri Valley Coach of the
Year ▪ 1995 First-Team All-Big Ten selection

Cuonzo Martin's final two seasons of high school basketball show-cased a glimpse of his greatness as both a player and leader: he guided his team to a pair of state championships, earned St. Louis (Ill.) Player of the Year honors during his senior season, and secured a scholar-ship to play at Purdue University. Those years at Lincoln High in East St. Louis also defined his toughness, as tales of him playing on a blown out left knee—against doctor's orders—the final two weeks of his senior season and never requesting to come out of the game for a break are legendary. And when he arrived on the Boilermakers' West Lafayette campus, the strength and grit of his character was revealed once again.

You see, Martin shredded high school defenses. He would knock down long-range shots over opponents or dip into his bag of moves and drive to the hoop for buckets. He was a nightmare to guard. But his first two seasons at Purdue under Hall of Fame coach Gene Keady didn't resemble the glory days at Lincoln. Instead, they were filled with hefty doses of disappointment and stats he wasn't accustomed to seeing next to his name. He averaged less than six points a game during his freshman season, and didn't sink a three-point shot during his first *two* seasons. It was a gigantic learning curve he may not have expected, but one that many athletes encounter when taking that giant step from high school star to Division One college sports.

Adversity had grabbed hold of him, and the young Martin had a decision to make. He could give into its forces and let it shove him down a path where he would be a role player, getting a few minutes of action here and there, or he could shake free of its grasp, not allow his confidence to waver, and be inspired by the challenge to become a player who would make a difference for his team. He chose the latter. He hit the weights. He ran the stairs. He worked on his shot until he was swimming in sweat. And then he shot some more.

So when Cuonzo Martin talks about facing adversity and helping young players break away from it, he's already walked in those shoes and slain those demons. The guy who didn't make a single three-point shot his first two seasons of college basketball made a school record, eight of them against Kansas during a pressure-filled tournament game during March Madness. For his Boilermaker career he made 179 of them, fourth most in school history, and he left with the highest career three-point shooting accuracy of any Boilermaker, at .451. And get this: during his senior season, he *led* the Big Ten Conference in three-point shooting and was fourth in scoring. He took that adversity and kicked it to the curb.

"Everybody goes through struggles," says Martin, the head men's basketball coach at the University of Missouri. "Whatever your sport is, everybody struggles and makes mistakes. Even the professional teams break down on plays and have struggles. Everybody goes through them." The long-time coach—he's been the leader at Missouri State, Tennessee, and California before arriving in Columbia to take over the Missouri program in 2017—recognizes that young athletes with fragile confidence often encounter difficulty processing a bad game, or even a stretch of just a few minutes in a game where shots aren't falling, or they are turning the ball over. Besides frustrating, these moments can be embarrassing to players who are relatively new to performing in front of strangers in the stands and not having the game go as they assumed it would when they arrived.

"As a young man or young lady, what happens when you have struggles is that you think everything is magnified and the whole world is looking at you," says Martin, a dad of three. "And that's the point you try to get them to overcome. It's a team sport, and everybody makes mistakes. Everybody has those nights. Even me as a coach, I have those struggles."

But coaches must be thinking what they can extract from these teachable moments to help players move on from them and learn from them, and not have their interest in the sport sabotaged simply by one bad performance or stretch of games in which shots weren't falling or the team suffered a string of losses.

"As coaches, you want kids getting up the next day and learning from those experiences and continuing to push forward," Martin says. "You can't let it break them where all of a sudden they are so mentally fatigued and stressed out and exhausted that they don't want to get out of bed. So that's the part as a coach you want to help them get through, because everybody goes through it. It's just a matter of when and at what level an athlete goes through it."

The younger the athlete, the more daunting the process will seem in their eyes. So those first encounters with struggles and setbacks will be crucial moments in their journey for coaches to talk about with them and explain that even the greatest athletes on the planet don't have every play or every game turn out in their favor. But when coaches can get kids dialed into being a consistent worker, willing to show up at practices and give everything they have, then over the course of time there will be improvements to celebrate and performances to appreciate. Yes, it can be a tough sell to many, especially these days where youngsters are accustomed to instant gratification in a lot of areas of their life.

"I just think as a coach, when you are dealing with youth, you have to help them understand that the purpose and the process is the biggest key in going through their learning," Martin says. "Because they are youth athletes, that means it's not their final destination. They will get older and they will get better and they will become more mature. Going through that process and purpose, there will be a tomorrow. So continue to point out how they will get better and encourage them to try to play as hard as they can play, and in the process, gain a level of mental and physical toughness."

"As a young man or young lady, what happens when you have struggles is that you think everything is magnified and the whole world is looking at you. And that's the point you try to get them to overcome."

That's exactly what Martin did at Purdue, and it was inspiring to see in action. And it didn't go unnoticed either. Keady, his coach there, calls Martin both the best leader and the mentally toughest player he ever coached—and he coached *a lot* of incredible players during more than fifty years on the sidelines.

"Talk to your team and encourage them to try to push past the hard part, because in the end, it will help you through life," Martin says. "Whether you are a professional or not, those things will help you through life, and that's the biggest thing." So explore ways that get players excited about learning, and trying to learn.

"The fun is in the process of knowing that the end result can be great," Martin says. "And you never want it to be a burden where you have a lot of worry, doubt, stress, and fear as a youth going through it."

When Martin glances back at his youth sports experiences growing up in East St. Louis, he remembers the coaches, their influence, and their guiding hands on his life. "Yes, they were coaching youth teams, but it was also about the relationships," Martin says. "It was more than just coaching, they were also trying to help me find my way and navigate through life along with my parents. So it was a combination of coach, teacher, and kind of a family member in a lot of ways."

Martin has been an influential and respected leader wherever he has been, and for today's coaches to impact young athletes in the same manner his influenced him requires honesty, but delivered in a way in which young athletes understand the areas they need to work on. Plus, that they are encouraged that they will reach that destination through practice and hard work.

"For me, it was having a good time, learning, growing, and trying to get better," Martin says. "But as you get older, you start to understand coaches who were honest and fair, and that put me in position to be successful, andn more than anything, just gave me a chance."

That's what is on his mind as he watches his kids participate in sports. Opportunity and fairness are what resonate with him. "What I always try to gauge is if you're being treated fair," he says. "And what I mean by that is, you have to earn everything you get. If you're doing battle in competition with someone else, you have to earn it. So my gauge as a coach as I'm watching another person coach my children, is if they are getting an opportunity to be successful. Now whether or not they're the first in line, the starter, or the last one in line, they have to compete for that. It's not my job as a parent to say, 'Okay, my kid should be this or that.' As long as they have an opportunity to be put in position to do that, then it's up to my kid to do that. So for me, because I've been in it for so long, I sit back and watch as a fan—I'm not sitting and judging and critiquing the coach, because I know what goes on behind the scenes, and it's not as easy as it looks."

Mike Matheny

Former Manager of the St. Louis Cardinals ▪ Played thirteen
seasons in the Major Leagues ▪ Four-time Gold Glove
winner ▪ Father of five ▪ Former youth baseball coach

On an evening back in 2009, former Major League catcher Mike Matheny settled into his seat for a flight home to St. Louis after making a guest appearance on the Major League Baseball Network in Secaucus, New Jersey. Like countless other travelers on the plane that night, he pulled out his laptop for the roughly two-hour trip. While his fellow passengers were busy writing reports, fine-tuning presentations, and firing off emails at 30,000 feet, he was immersed in his own project, tapping keys in a flurry as words raced across his screen.

You see, at that time Matheny was navigating unfamiliar territory. He was recently retired from a game he loved oh-so dearly and had played with every ounce of passion in his body for thirteen Major League seasons. He was also happily recovered from a concussion—set off when a foul ball rattled his mask near the end of his career—that had affected his vision and ability to engage in normal conversation for more than a year. So, as he was making the transition from the regimented schedule of a professional athlete to suddenly having the freedom to choose how to fill his hours, he was approached by some local parents in the community asking him to coach their youth baseball team.

The idea had traction. After all, Matheny loved the game more than Romeo loved Juliet. He was a product of youth baseball himself. Letting go of Major League Baseball was admittedly difficult, as it is with all those who play the game with the fervor Matheny did for all those years. Plus, the fact that his own ten-year-old son would be on the team provided another layer of intrigue. As he thought about it, he knew that if he was going to commit to the job, the season wasn't going to be wrapped around winning games, and parents weren't going to dictate batting orders, positions, and game day strategy. And they needed to know that before he agreed to take control of the team.

So, on that flight home, he typed a letter to the parents detailing his plan for how he would approach the season. It talked about respect, discipline, and humility; it stressed playing with class; and it clearly defined for parents that there would be no coaching, criticizing or interfering from the stands. The letter turned out to be five single-spaced pages—2,556 words poured from Matheny's heart. It was a letter, so it didn't have a title, but at some point it found its way onto the Internet and went viral. And somewhere along the way, it became known as the "Matheny Manifesto," and later a widely popular book of the same name. It was powerful.

The winner of four Gold Gloves during his career, Matheny had a firm grasp on how he was going to coach and lead; and as the holder of Major League Baseball's record for most consecutive games played without an error, he wasn't going to make mistakes with this impressionable group of ten-year-olds. After all, he was accustomed to performing and executing at a high level, and that certainly wasn't about to change simply because he had stepped into retirement.

By all accounts, he didn't fail either. In fact, his tenure was a resounding success. The season was packed with skill development, character building, life lessons, and a lot of fun. And arguably, the only downside to Matheny being named manager of the St. Louis Cardinals in 2012 is that he had to surrender his youth coaching duties. His time with those kids, and the impact he had on them, resonates in his heart all these years later. As it does for those who had the privilege of playing for him and learning from him, too.

"I don't believe it's a bad thing for a volunteer coach to go ahead and put out a legacy of what they want to be remembered for," says Matheny, seated outside the Cardinals spring training clubhouse on a sun-splashed Saturday afternoon in Jupiter, Florida. "Do you want to be remembered for being 12-0 in your eight-and-under youth league, or do you want to be remembered by those kids who you had an opportunity to impact that you made a difference? That you taught them something they're going to carry with them the rest of their life and go on and pass on to multiple others? To me, it's exciting to use a game that I love to impact people and that might be passed on for a long time."

Matheny is as competitive as they come. You don't play for as long as he did at the game's toughest position without those competitive juices flowing; and you certainly don't get a manager's job running one of the most prestigious franchises in the history of the game – and hold onto that position – if you're not winning games. But at the youth level, Matheny points out that if coaches are more concerned about the win-loss column than developing well-rounded kids with a mixture of baseball and life skills, they're wasting a special opportunity that they'll never get back.

"We're seeing the ball dropped by coaches who just have this lofty expectation that they're only successful by stacking up a lot of youth league trophies," he says. "And I'm not against winning, believe me; that's my job. But at the lower levels, we're trying to teach kids passion and give them a life-long love of the game, because most of them don't even understand it. So, you better start with fun and you better start with making sure that you're keeping them engaged. A successful day at the baseball field at the lowest levels is that the kids want to come back. Whatever you have to do—bubblegum, ice cream, whatever—make that happen. It's amazing how that just kind of keeps on growing if you keep on track. Let's let youth sports be about the kids. Let's not lose sight of the fact that it's our responsibility to pass on a passion and enjoyment of the game. There's so much we can do to help them enjoy it, but not to get our agenda, whether that of a coach or parent, in the way of truly making sports special for them. It doesn't have to go all the way to the big leagues for it to be successful."

How did Matheny make it all happen? How did he get parents to buy in to his approach and sit back and let him operate how he wanted? He employed multiple techniques—bathed in creativity and caring—all of which can be used by coaches of all sports to make the type of difference he did with his squad. For starters, kids got to play multiple positions. No one was sentenced to a season of boredom in right field, where opportunities to catch balls and make throws are pretty much non-existent at the younger levels of play. And get *this*. He actually spoke with the kids, asking them what positions they were interested in and what they wanted to try, rather than herding them out on game day to destinations unknown.

"We would throw a left-handed kid over at shortstop and just let him play there because he always wanted to know what playing shortstop was like," Matheny says. "We made sure everybody got to pitch as long as we made sure nobody was going to get hurt. We gave them the opportunity to experience some of these positions, because if you sanction a kid to right field, the likelihood of that kid wanting to come back isn't very high. So, we just wanted to continue to work hard to get them exposed to the entire game, and we put them in some spots they hadn't been in before, always asking them if there was something they wanted to work on. You are also going to have those games where it is a blowout one way or the other, and if you've got a kid who has always wanted to play a little bit of third base, it's a great time to throw him over there and see what he can do."

Secondly, practices were always moving, never stagnant. "I know when we run our spring training, the absolute worst thing that can happen is having anybody standing around where they're not doing something to get better," Matheny says. "We tried to run those same practices with the kids where we're moving and every minute somebody is doing something to help them improve in their game in some way. It's keeping them moving and keeping them engaged." Matheny also wasn't afraid to ditch the session and do something completely different, a great reminder for coaches to constantly track the pulse and mood of the team. If attention spans are wandering, and energy levels are fizzling, you better be prepared to try something else to salvage the session.

"Do you want to be remembered for being 12-0 in your eight-and-under youth league, or do you want to be remembered by those kids who you had an opportunity to impact that you made a difference?"

"When I noticed that we had lost our kids a little bit, we'd shut down and play Wiffle Ball," Matheny says. "You get the parents and coaches out of the way, you watch a kid who is maybe a little tentative, and he's running the bases and using his instincts, and all of a sudden they understand how to do a cutoff; they understand how to do a rundown. Sometimes it's just us getting out of the way and letting them play. We did it quite often, to be honest with you. It's fun to just initiate kids into that and see what they can do."

Matheny's practices weren't all about learning how to protect the plate with two strikes, running the bases properly, or making accurate throws, either. The life skills component was huge. He wanted kids taking away lessons that would help shape their character, mold their values, and help lead them into being respectable young members of the community. So he devised a plan for doing it and put it into action.

"It's pretty simple, first of all," he says. "You look and ask yourself, if I had a child, what kind of character qualities would I like to see developed in them? And then as a parent, what am I trying to develop in my kids right now? Take those ideas and brainstorm. Write a list out. And then take each of those once a week. You have to be intentional and deliberate if you truly want this to stick. If you truly want this to mean something instead of telling kids, 'hey, we believe you need to develop into young men,' you have to be backing it up with how you spend your time. Be willing to designate twenty or thirty minutes out of a practice and open up a topic like honesty, or to open up some tough topics like drug and alcohol abuse."

Matheny turned to a variety of interesting individuals in his community who he brought in to speak to the kids. Making that kind of effort, and using a portion of practice time, highlights to young players just how important these subjects are, and when done right, the impact can be ever-lasting.

"We went through how to treat a lady," Matheny says. "We'd get some parents involved and say 'you've been married for thirty years, give us some of your secrets.' We were just trying to get the kids to think at a higher level. We brought in some specialists, like police officers that would talk about alcohol and drug abuse. We'd bring in people that had dropped the ball and have a lot of remorse and have dealt with some terrible situations."

As a dad, Matheny also faced a delicate issue that most of today's youth coaches face: how to handle their own son or daughter. It's tricky, for sure, and Matheny urges those who are planning to coach to ask themselves some hard questions before they ever run a practice.

"It's tough because some people are wired for this and some aren't," he says. "Parent coaches just need to be real honest with themselves right from the top. First of all, can I keep my eyes off my own kid? Can I treat the rest of the kids with the kind of care that I want to treat my own with? A lot of parents have trouble with that. It's about being an honest evaluator and being able to realize there's probably more harm than good if this is going to be about me living vicariously through my child, hoping for their athletic success that maybe I didn't have, or me making sure that I'm showcasing my child so he can get to the next level. When those things start coming into play, it is so obvious that most of the time, the coaches believe they think they are hiding it. I do believe if that's the road you're going down, it's better that you find somebody else to do it."

If you can answer those tough questions, and step forward with Matheny's mindset of impacting the life of every single player on your roster, a memorable season can be delivered for every participant. "Being a coach is a trust," Matheny says. "You've been entrusted with a life. I feel the same way with this big league team. It's something that has been entrusted to me, and I don't want to waste it. Now there are stronger voices in their life and I realize that, but I also believe that I have to do my part, and I don't want to drop the ball on that. Thinking about some of the greatest coaches in history and the lifelong impact that they have had, when you ask these players later who really impacted them and they point out that coach, what a great compliment that they walked alongside what their parents were trying to teach and exemplified it during heated competition. To me, that's a successful coach."

When he sorts through all the practices and games that comprise a season; all the pre-game and post-game talks; the celebrated wins and stinging setbacks; all the conversations and humorous moments; how does one gauge whether he or she can label the season a success? From Matheny's view, it was simple to see, and even easier to evaluate.

"How you define success is really where it should come back to you as a youth team and you as a coach," Matheny says. "For us, it was trying to get these kids to have so much fun that they didn't want to stop the season. That was our goal."

That's a wonderful goal for your coaching journey, too.

Nikki McCray-Penson

Old Dominion University women's basketball coach ▪ Two-time Olympic Gold Medalist ▪ Three-time WNBA All-Star ▪ 2012 Women's Basketball Hall of Fame inductee

Nikki McCray-Penson's love of basketball was kindled on a Sunday afternoon in a Memphis suburb during her eighth-grade year. It's interesting to note that McCray-Penson, who just so happens to be one of the greatest women's college basketball players of all time, never had aspirations of becoming a dominant force on the court. Or even playing the game, for that matter. She did harbor some hefty athletic dreams, though they involved running track, a sport she loved as a youngster. As she sped around that oval during her youth, she had dreams of becoming the next Flo-Jo, following in the legendary—and very fast—footsteps of the great Olympic champion, Florence Griffith-Joyner.

The script for her life flipped that Sunday afternoon though, when the family gathered after church at her grandmother's house and the boys headed to the basketball hoop out back to play. The young McCray-Penson wandered out to the action, asked to join the game, and was met with a chorus of rejection.

"That didn't sit well with me," says McCray-Penson, who was named the head women's basketball coach at Old Dominion University in 2017. "So, I went into the house and told my Big Mama—we called my grandmother 'Big Mama'—that they wouldn't let me play, and she politely came out and said if I couldn't play, the game would be stopped. So, from then on I started playing, and basketball fell into my lap."

It certainly didn't take long to see that this was the sport that would drive her life. During her high school days she was unstoppable, averaging more than thirty-three points a game as a senior and finishing as the all-time leading scorer in the history of girls basketball in the state of Tennessee. She went on to star at the University of Tennessee under the legendary Pat Summitt, where she was twice named the Southeastern Conference Player of the Year and helped the Volunteers to two Southeastern Conference tournament titles and four NCAA tourney appearances. She also won gold medals with Team USA at the 1996

Summer Olympics in Atlanta and the 2000 Games in Sydney, Australia. She enjoyed a productive career in the WNBA, being named an all-star three times, and was inducted into the Women's Basketball Hall of Fame.

Big Mama got her on the court with a few timely and influential words decades ago, and that power of communication has come full circle now in her role as a Division One head basketball coach with the heavy responsibilities of leading one of the most storied programs in the history of women's college basketball. Big Mama's words that Sunday afternoon impacted a group of boys—and forever changed the life of a young girl. That story serves as a powerful reminder of how the words an adult uses in their role as a coach—both what is said and how they are delivered—can influence young lives.

"What you tell kids is going to stick," McCray-Penson says from her basketball office on the Old Dominion campus in Norfolk, Virginia. "So make sure that it is pure and that it is said with a lot of enthusiasm." Young athletes want constant feedback on how they're performing and how they can get better. They want coaches to know that they are doing their best and that their efforts are appreciated. And, they want to see that their coaches are, without question, all-in all the time on helping them every single practice get a little bit closer to where they want to be in their progression. Monotone deliveries, or speaking or teaching as though you are delivering a eulogy, will result in disastrous experiences for players.

"You let them hear your passion," McCray-Penson says of a coach's interactions with young players. "You give them little nuggets—like things that they can work on, or talking to them about their goals."

When dissecting the do's and don'ts of coaching, McCray-Penson routinely uses the phrase, "find a way." It's about teaching and encouraging players to find a way: whether it's being a better teammate, playing better defense, getting in better shape, competing with more energy, or creating a better scoring opportunity for a teammate. Whatever it is, *find a way.* That's a pretty potent mantra for coaches in any sport to tuck in their pockets as they embark on their seasons Find a way to make it fun for every player; find a way to teach skills that kids can relate to; find a way to build confidence in everyone; and so on.

"You start with the big picture," she says of how you approach getting everyone on board with the team-first mindset. "You have to get them to buy into little things like passing the ball, and you have to get them to buy into creating opportunities with their defense."

McCray-Penson had the privilege of playing for Summitt at Tennessee, who was a pure genius when it came to relationship building, motivating, and getting players to perform at high levels. She's never forgotten those lessons she learned while playing in Knoxville, either. When she landed the Old Dominion job, one of her first moves was meeting individually with each of the players, because a significant part of coaching involves connecting with players, and the more coaches understand about their players, the better equipped they are to make those bonds strong ones, and hopefully long-lasting, too.

"You start with the relationship," says McCray-Penson. "It's really communicating and building a relationship with them and then holding them accountable."

Naturally, coaches are wired to be on output mode, dispensing life lessons, teaching, correcting, motivating and uncovering what players are all about, what their goals are, and what motivates them. One of the many nuggets McCray-Penson pocketed from observing Summitt's interactions, both with her and with her teammates, was the value of turning the output dial off sometimes and being on input, too.

"Pat was a great teacher and motivator. She taught the game with unbelievable passion," she says. "But she was also a great listener. Coaches can learn so much from their players—as much as they are learning from you. When they come in and have conversations with you, and not just about basketball, you're building that relationship with them. When you build a relationship with a player and they trust you, they will go through a wall for you."

> ## "Coaches can learn so much from their players—as much as they are learning from you."

McCray-Penson felt that connection to Summitt. It was a powerful bond, one where she wanted to dive on the floor for a loose ball; she wanted to hustle back on defense; she wanted to corral that rebound. "I knew that she believed in me," McCray-Penson says. "So flat-out, I was going to do whatever it takes."

When coaches can generate that type of buy-in from their players, the doors swing open on learning as athletes, developing as people, and competing as a team. "When I teach, I want our kids to know that I am here for them," she says. "I'm a servant to them and they can come to me with anything. And when I'm out there teaching, they know that they are going to play hard, going for steals and rebounds and things like that, because that is what is going to lead to a win. I love to see our kids grow and wanting to get in the gym and get better."

Coaches who bring non-stop energy and enthusiasm to practices create a buzz throughout the team. Players will work harder and be more engaged. Plus, when those coach-player relationships are cultivated and genuine, the impact multiplies exponentially. "It's all about impacting lives every single day and watching them grow," McCray-Penson says. "I bring a lot of energy to the table. My advice for coaches working with kids is to get down on their level and keep it simple and have a lot of enthusiasm—and be consistent with that every single day."

That's a great message for all coaches to keep in mind, and certainly one Big Mama would approve of, too.

Archie Miller

Indiana University men's basketball coach ■ Played college basketball at North Carolina State University ■ Named the Atlantic 10 Conference Coach of the Year in 2017

Archie Miller, the head men's basketball coach at Indiana University, doesn't crave attention for himself. He's not egotistical or controversial; nor is he outlandish or boorish. He doesn't hunger for the bright lights of television interviews or thirst to see his name plastered on the front page of the nation's newspapers. But what he does care about—genuinely and passionately—are his players. Every single one of them. And what he most certainly wants is to be a leader and developer of young athletes; a teacher and motivator; a builder of high-character, hard-working teams who play together, with purpose and a relentless pursuit to be the best they can be every time they step on the floor. Turns out Miller's approach is a pretty good job description for coaches of young athletes in all sports.

"The athletes have to know that you care about them," Miller says, pausing for a half second before delivering this mega-important sentence that every coach in America, from the peewee levels of youth sports all the way up, must buy into if they truly want to be a high-quality coach who affects young lives: "More importantly, they have to know that it's not about *you*."

That's right, coaching athletics at any level can't be about trying to recapture lost moments from days long gone, or salvaging missed opportunities from your playing days. That journey is over. The door on those dreams is closed. This is your team's time to grow and shine, and you get a front row seat to orchestrate the journey. But you can't be in it for the pats on the back or to pad a resume in search of moving up in the coaching ranks. You've got to be all-in on the kids all the time. Yes, that will take some time. When athletes recognize that their coaches genuinely care for them as individuals, and that they are fully into developing them as players, wonderful opportunities for growth abounds.

"The players have to know that you're invested," Miller says. "And that takes time. They won't trust you right away, so you have to find ways to talk and communicate with them before or after practices, or while working out, and to me, all those little things will add up."

Looking back on Miller's career trajectory that landed him at a Big Ten school that oozes basketball history and tradition, there was little doubt that this is what he was destined to do, and do really well. Basketball was the family business. The Millers lived it and breathed it every day growing up, in season and out of season. Archie's father, John, was a legendary high school coach who won more than 650 games during a spectacular thirty-five-year coaching career that also produced four Pennsylvania state titles. Archie played for his dad at Beaver Falls Blackhawk High School in western Pennsylvania, where he learned valuable lessons in dedication, work ethic, preparation, and more. But it was all the powerful lessons that were dispensed at the dining table and car rides and during offseason workouts that were even more influential.

"At the time I probably didn't realize it, because he was very hard on us, and he was a very demanding coach," Miller says of his dad. "But he was really preparing us to do a lot of different things with our life once we were done with our high school basketball career. He made a lasting impression on me by showing how hard you had to work and how dedicated you had to be, and I thought that was the biggest thing."

Small in size, but the owner of a gigantic heart who outworked everyone in his path, Archie was a scrappy point guard at North Carolina State who produced on the floor. He ended his career among the school's leaders in free-throw percentage, three-point field goal percentage, and total three-pointers. He dove into coaching after his playing days concluded, and later had a wonderful six-year run at the University of Dayton, where he led the Flyers to four straight NCAA tournament appearances and one Elite Eight before being chosen to come to Bloomington and rebuild the storied Hoosier program.

While at Miller's level, the Indiana fan base will use the scoreboard as the determining factor in evaluating him as a coach, and he certainly knows that. At younger levels of athletics, he points out that coaches can't get too caught up in scores and lose sight of what their roles and responsibilities are all about.

"It's a new day and age, and you really have to understand when you're working with young people that it's not so much about winning and losing as it is improvement," he says. "You have to find ways to improve budding athletes and make them better, because if they feel like they are getting better, they're going to have fun and love what they're doing. If they're having fun and loving what they're doing because they can see that they're progressing, inevitably what is going to happen is you're going to have a philosophy of development, a culture of teammates growing up and improving together. As a youth coach or a person who is devoted to mentoring young people, it's about developing them at each incremental stage that they are at, and then making sure that they understand that they are getting better so they feel good about themselves. If you are that youth coach, the one thing you constantly have to keep in mind about youth sports is that winning and losing are not as important as the development aspect. It's about making these young guys and girls feel good about themselves so that they can keep on advancing; and if they do, they'll have a chance to continue to excel and play longer and longer and longer."

"The athletes have to know that you care about them. More importantly, they have to know that it's not about you."

Now, not only do coaches have to make sure their players are progressing and picking up skills, they also have to make sure that the young athletes themselves recognize and realize that they are developing and moving in the right direction. Improvement takes time and patience, and often doesn't reveal itself in the day-to-day work of practicing. When players are really making strides in their skills and development, but may not be aware of it, frustration and disappointment can settle in, resulting in progress stalling. Miller recognizes it's an issue that coaches have to have on their radar and be proactive in their approach, so everyone on the squad understands the process and sees for themselves that they are improving. Every step in the right direction, whether it's big or small, is worth noting.

"You have to find little ways to show the kids that they are improving," Miller says. "Whether that's strength and conditioning, skill development, or in their training, whatever it may be."

He suggests using numbers that players can relate to. "The biggest way that young people feel that they are getting better is data. Like someone is doing ten push-ups a day and eventually gets to fourteen, for example. To me, keeping records of improvement is the biggest thing," Miller explains. "If you are keeping track of the number of free throws an athlete is shooting every day, he will know that, at fifty free throws a day, he's making 72 percent of shots. As the summer continues, if he sees his percentage has gone up to 80, that keeps him motivated to continue to strive to be his best. Athletes want to break through barriers, so keeping charts, showing players data, and those types of things are something that are invaluable."

Keeping this type of data can also be a great resource for coaches in identifying those players who may be having some difficulty gaining traction in the skill development department. By reviewing the data they are collecting, coaches can spot trends and changes in efficiency levels. Maybe a player shooting those fifty free throws every day hasn't budged past a certain percentage mark in several weeks, which requires paying closer attention to his form to spot a flaw in his set-up or release, for example. Or maybe the young athlete has misinterpreted something a coach said and is going about the skill the wrong way all of a sudden, causing his performance to decline. When development has come to a standstill, before blaming players, take a closer look at your coaching and make adjustments there, first. Often that can turn out to be enough to rectify the problem.

"Everybody is different," Miller says. "I coach how I played and I coach how I trained, which is very intense. To me, I had to be that way in my mind to be a guy that overachieved. If I can bring what I did to overachieve as an athlete, as a player, and as a teammate to the immensely talented people that I am now coaching—athletes who have more gifts than I ever had—just imagine how special they can be."

That's powerful. As a coach, embrace your opportunity to propel athletes to heights you've never been to yourself. That makes for a special and memorable journey for both the coach and players.

"Your own experiences and your own life path really dictate how you operate," Miller says. "You have to be able to feed into your team who you are for them to believe in you, and for me it's been very simple—it's been very hands on, very one-on-one oriented. Training and communication and being able to look your players in the eye and they know that you've given them everything that you've got, and they'll respond by giving you everything back."

Because they see that it's not about you—it's all about them.

DeLisha Milton-Jones

Pepperdine University women's basketball coach ▪ Two-time
Olympic gold medalist ▪ Two-time WNBA champion

 DeLisha Milton-Jones' journey from the basketball courts of her youth in Riceboro, Georgia, to head women's basketball coach at Pepperdine University in Malibu, California, has been punctuated with success every dribble and jump shot along the way. During her playing days, she had more moves than Justin Timberlake, which she used to shake free of defenders and get to the hoop. Toss in a fierce work ethic that never wavered, and greatness was her destiny.

A dynamic high school performer, she was soon heading south with a scholarship in her pocket to play at the University of Florida. She led the Gators to four straight NCAA appearances and put an exclamation point on her illustrious collegiate career by being named the nation's top player. From there, she was a big contributor in helping Team USA capture gold in two Olympic Games—2008 in Beijing and 2000 in Sydney. Oh, by the way, she also had a seventeen year run in the WNBA, playing in more games than anyone in the history of the league while winning a pair of championships. She also appeared in three WNBA All-Star Games.

So naturally, what does the owner of a sparkling basketball resume that shines so bright—and goes on and on—like to talk about with players she is coaching or recruiting? Go ahead, and take a couple guesses, because you're going to need them. Milton-Jones likes to discuss—are you ready for this—her *failures*. That's right, this WNBA legend who closed out her career with the ninth most points in league history, as well as ranking fifth all time in steals and sixth all-time in rebounds, steers conversations to topics that most athletes would prefer to shove in the corner and forget. But it's the setbacks, struggles, and disappointments that Milton-Jones revisits, reflects on, and shares when working with athletes. Sure, she has to dig a little deeper than a lot of others to find them amid all her accolades. But they are there. And they have merit. She encourages today's coaches of young athletes to not avoid these topics with their players, but to drag them to the forefront to discuss, dissect, and develop from.

"I was recently talking to a recruit on the phone, and this is a subject matter that I speak on," Milton-Jones says from her basketball office on the Pepperdine campus. "I always start my speech off by saying, 'I'm the biggest loser you have ever seen in your life.' Everybody kind of takes a deep breath and is like, 'What is she talking about? She has gold medals and championships and this and that.' But I say that because I've learned so much more through my defeats than I have my victories."

As coaches of young athletes, it's easy to lean on the personal past glories enjoyed at the high school or, for some, even higher levels of play. The wins and noteworthy performances are fun to roll out and retell to wide-eyed kids eager to follow in the footsteps of a coach who has been there and done that. Yet, when coaches only turn to the positive results, it sends a distorted message to young players that everything is outcome-oriented and that losses or struggles don't warrant recollection. It's a foolish path to head down, one that will leave kids confused, disappointed, and disenchanted on those game days where they don't win and they're unable to match the level of only those success stories they've been hearing about from their coach.

Navigating both sides of the competitive street—with coaches blending in stories of those stellar performances from years ago with some of their not-so-pleasant days—provides a clearer and much more realistic picture of what competing in sports is all about. When kids understand that there are going to be some rocky days, because they've already heard about some of yours, they'll be better prepared to push past them, rather than get dragged down by them.

"I always try to portray to everyone that even in defeats, you can have victories because you learn so much valuable information about yourself, about the situation and circumstances of the game and your coaches," Milton-Jones says. "There's a plethora of ideas and information that's exploding there for you to grab if you allow yourself to be a dry sponge and soak all of that up. So yes, I've learned a tremendous amount from my losses."

Reflect back on some of your sub-par performances. Everyone has them filed away in their memory banks. How did those moments make you feel? How did you respond? What did you learn from those experiences? What would you have done differently? The answers to those types of questions can be important conversation starters with your players in the moments following a heart-breaking loss or disappointing performance. Or even following one of those games where nothing clicked, for whatever reason. When coaches pull from some of their experiences and share with their players how they felt and how they worked through it, it humanizes them. It shows players that everyone hits rough patches, and that it's all about the response to them that ultimately defines athletes, sculpts their character and shapes their season.

"I've learned so much more through my defeats than I have my victories."

These are life lessons, and they can be tough ones to digest, too. "Everyone tries to walk on eggshells now with how they coach and what they say. Kids are more sensitive these days, so they feel like they need to be more sensitive as a coach," Milton-Jones says. "And yes, you do to a certain extent. But you still need to keep the honesty, the transparency, and the accountability at high levels, too, because that's the only way you learn and get better and are able to withstand and grow from certain things. That's how you see that you're not perfect, and you're not supposed to be. You're supposed to make mistakes, and it's how you respond from those mistakes that matters. Coaches can use those moments as valuable teaching methods, but they kind of get overlooked, because a lot of times they don't want to upset parents or the child."

Athletic competition and the seasons coaches take their players through is an endlessly fascinating journey, one in which unexpected obstacles and even the sure-to-appear bumps along the way are precursors to building resiliency in young athletes. These are the types of moments that teach them how to respond to adversity by working harder, sticking together, supporting each other and helping pull each other along as a cohesive unit in the face of distress.

"When I look at my career, people think I'm the greatest because they see gold medals and championships," Milton-Jones says. "Well, it's the journey that has allowed me to be who I am." All the accolades, awards, and eye-popping numbers she posted during her playing days surpass impressive. But she's quick to point out that all the good that happens during games—and bad—is team oriented.

When coaches are having those talks with players, it's important to keep *team* as the central theme throughout. Some kids get more shots and score more points than others, but those shots are the result of others doing their jobs, such as making good passes or doing the unglamorous work of setting screens.

"You have to have an atmosphere where you are celebrating all the small things," she says. "Small victories could be the screen that was set that got the player the shot. What often happens is the end is celebrated; yes, that person is good because she can make the shots, but she's not as good if that person doesn't set that screen or the offense isn't run correctly and the timing isn't there. So celebrating all those small victories within whatever side of the ball we are playing on will create the type of atmosphere where everyone feels like they're a part of it and invested in it. They were crucial to that person hitting that basket."

Philip Montgomery

Coach of University of Tulsa football ▪ Father of two ▪
Played quarterback and free safety at Tarleton State

A good exit strategy comes in handy for navigating airport parking structures, wiggling out of a disastrous blind date, ditching a loathsome job, and yes, even wrapping up a youth sports practice, too. While the start of practice typically garners all the attention, with coaches looking to establish the energy and set the tone, how these sessions wrap up is equally important. Sometimes, even more so. What's said to young athletes during those final moments—or not said—marinates in their minds for often several days, until the next time they gather for another practice or game.

At the younger levels of sports, a coach may only see his or her team a couple times a week, with a Saturday morning game mixed in. So if young athletes are climbing into the family minivan with any unpleasant thoughts swirling in their head regarding what was said to them during the session, they're going to be lugging that around for days, which can corrode confidence and drag them into that murky territory where they may even begin to question their abilities and desire for continuing with the sport. At the older and more advanced levels of competitive athletics, where coaches see athletes daily, or at least several times a week, those practices that end on a sour note can still pose problems, leaving kids with an uneasy feeling that will likely linger as they crawl into bed that night.

It's why Philip Montgomery, the head football coach at the University of Tulsa, treats the end of his practices with a surgeon's care and attention. That's how important this period of time is to him, and it should be for any other coach of any sport, too. His players leave the facility in a positive frame of mind; he does everything he can to help ensure that by reminding his assistant coaches daily of their end-of-practice responsibilities.

"What I talk to our coaches about each and every day is making sure that as we're coaching them on the field, when they're leaving the field—especially the kid who you had to get on multiple times in practice—I want them to go put their arm around that kid's neck, and I want them to tell him something good that he did that day," Montgomery says. "So many times in sports, players are leaving with negative things in their heads, and I want to make sure that the last thing they remember as they walk off the field is something positive their coaches have said."

Now, these are young men competing in a Division I sport on Saturday afternoons in front of thousands, and countless more watching on television. So if Montgomery, a respected and successful coach who grew up in a sports-loving family, recognizes the value of planting a positive post-practice message in each of his players' minds, consider the impact such an approach can potentially have on younger players who crave attention and desperately want to please their coaches, too.

"You can find something positive every day to say to each and every kid," Montgomery says. He points out that the positive doesn't necessarily have to be performance-driven either. Sure, if a youngster put in great work, excelling with his route running in football, or boxing out on rebounds in basketball, of course that merits plenty of praise. But since this is sports, and these are younger players, there are going to be plenty of practices that fail to meet the coach's expectations, and plenty of kids who encounter all sorts of struggles and difficulties along the way. It's some of these moments that emerge as the most crucial—and also the most precious—during the season. Recognizing a player's effort can help their self-esteem blossom and instill in them the value of always working hard, regardless if they are achieving the desired results that particular day or not. It's all a part of the process, that journey to developing that has so many unexpected highs and lows along the way.

There are plenty of other opportunities to filter in praise too: kids who are genuine team players, urging and encouraging teammates, deserve praise for helping to bolster the team culture. So do those who compete with a positive attitude, where sulking and bad body language are foreign concepts to them. These are the ones who are quick to give a teammate who commits a miscue a pat on the back, or the ones applauding loudly when another player makes a great play.

Montgomery stresses the positive when talking to kids. "He may have had his worst practice ever, but you can tell him, 'Hey, I see that you are trying, I see that you are working hard and not loafing.' Find something positive to say about that kid. If you do that as you're trying to correct techniques and schematic things that he's doing wrong, he's going to be more apt to make those adjustments and become a better player quicker."

"You can find something positive every day to say to each and every kid. . . If you do that as you're trying to correct techniques and schematic things that he's doing wrong, he's going to be more apt to make those adjustments and become a better player quicker."

Now, the stronger a coach's relationship is with his players, the more receptive those young athletes will be to the words they are hearing from him. And the more they will mean to them. When kids don't fully respect their coaches, or feel a genuine connection to them, the messages that are delivered carry little meaning or significance.

"I've had a lot of good coaches that have been in my past, whether they coached me or I coached with them," Montgomery says. "And it's all about relationships and being able to take advice and take criticism, all those things. So it's so important for coaches to be sure that they have relationships with their players. As I look at our society today, there are so many kids growing up that don't have a prominent male figure in their life, so many times, coaches end up being that figure."

Striving to establish those all-important relationships with every player doesn't mean that coaching, teaching, critiquing, and correcting get shoved to the curb. Of course, a big part of a coach's role is helping athletes learn and develop skills, but along with that comes a sacred responsibility to make sure that young athletes are developing skills needed to lead successful lives. It's all about finding the proper balance for making it all work.

"Coaches have got to embrace that you have to work at it, and you've got to understand that it doesn't mean that you can't correct them," Montgomery says. "You just have to be sure that you are doing it in the right way. I tell our players all the time that we are going to coach them really hard, but we are going to love them really hard, too."

As much attention as Montgomery devotes to making sure practices conclude with good vibes and positive energy, it doesn't mean how they start carries any less significance. Again, he points the finger at himself and his staff to follow through on this: if they are fully engaged in the process, with a full tank of energy and enthusiasm to churn through practice, then they can expect the same output from their players.

"I put it more on us as coaches to make sure that we are bringing it every day," he says. "You have to show them that passion that you have for the sport and the passion that you have for coaching them, and you have to bring that energy to the practice field each and every day. If we are going to stand around and fold our arms, then that kid is not going to be excited to come out. We do different things at practice, including playing music, but it still goes back to the energy level that you bring as a coach, the excitement that you have for them as players and the sport, and you have to be consistent with that. You can't be on that roller coaster—you've got to step out from whatever is going on in your life at that time. When we step out on the practice field, everything is going into our players, into our kids, and we have to bring the energy if we want them to as well."

And don't forget to bring that good exit strategy along with you, too. Young athletes soak in what you say, or don't say, throughout practice, and the thoughts and mood they take home with them at its conclusion speaks volumes about how they feel about you, themselves, and the sport they are playing.

Porter Moser

Men's basketball coach at Loyola University Chicago
- 2018 Missouri Valley Conference Coach of the Year
- Played college basketball at Creighton University

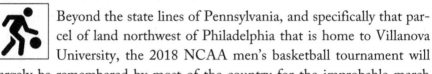 Beyond the state lines of Pennsylvania, and specifically that parcel of land northwest of Philadelphia that is home to Villanova University, the 2018 NCAA men's basketball tournament will largely be remembered by most of the country for the improbable march that Loyola University Chicago went on in jolting the college basketball landscape and reaching the Final Four. While Villanova took home the national championship, it was the Ramblers' run in busting the nation's brackets and captivating basketball fans with their selfless play that serves as a wonderful reminder of the endless possibilities when players work together, support each other, and genuinely could care less about who's getting the accolades in the process.

The 11th-seeded Ramblers blitzed the South Region, beating No. 6 seed Miami by two points and third-seeded Tennessee by one point during the opening weekend of play. Then they followed that up with a one-point victory against seventh-seeded Nevada and a 78-62 win against Kansas State in the regional final to earn that trip to the Final Four that all young basketball players dream about when lofting shots in their driveway as kids. While the University of Michigan ended the Ramblers' dream run at the Final Four, there is lots to be learned from Loyola coach Porter Moser, who engineered this run for the ages.

"If you want your team connected, you have to work at connectivity," he says. "You have to work at it. You have to work at getting them to know each other. We didn't just become this close team overnight."

Moser learned the value of a team-first culture, and players caring for each other, during his youth sports days in Naperville, Illinois, and those same philosophies were reinforced while he played college basketball at Creighton University. "I was very blessed with good coaches early on, and the impact they had on me was they always talked about the team first," he says. "They promoted team unity and doing things the right way on and off the floor, and my college coach at Creighton, Tony Barone, did the same thing."

That's exactly the culture Moser has created since taking over the Ramblers in 2011, too. And that's what was on full display for the nation to see during March Madness: his players working together, ruthlessly executing at both ends of the floor. There was the precision passing that created wonderful scoring opportunities on offense for teammates, and the non-stop communication defensively as they switched, rotated and helped each other that made scoring a big headache for opponents. They played as a team for every minute of every game, and it was spectacular to see.

"Having a shared vision is so important," Moser says. "We constantly talked about and emphasized and had this shared vision of what we wanted our team to be. When you get a shared vision, it trumps so many other individual goals. You start focusing on that vision, and then all the individual goals take care of themselves."

Young athletes want to play well, and of course be acknowledged for their skills, too. While every player on a basketball team can't be the leading scorer, or in football the team's leading pass catcher, for example, everyone can be fully invested in the process and enjoy the team's success when coaches are constantly highlighting the team, as Moser does. It's particularly interesting that he uses hockey as an example of how they recognize the efforts and importance of everyone at the offensive end of the floor, not just the player who sinks the basket and receives the fans' applause.

"We emphasize what we call the hockey assist," Moser says. "It's the pass that leads to the pass that leads to the basket. We really promote that unselfish play and promote not caring who gets the credit." Building that culture starts at the season's first practice, where players begin learning that everything they do is important to the team, no matter their role.

"You achieve what you emphasize," Moser says. "We show our players film of the unselfish plays that were made." Highlighting those hockey assist passes, or the player who dove for a loose ball, or the one who set the screen to free a shooter—those are those so-called little things that are actually huge elements of developing that team-first culture. When players identify with these aspects of the sport that coaches are genuinely emphasizing, teams have an opportunity to perform at a much higher level than those where players are more concerned about their statistics and recognition. It requires a season-long commitment to make happen, though.

"Like anything, it takes time," Moser says. "You can say it once: 'Hey, let's be an unselfish team,' but if you don't work at it and you don't spend time at it, you don't develop it."

The same applies to the fundamental elements of the sport. Most young athletes these days want that fast track to success and high-level performance. But there's not a shortcut for learning the basics of any sport. It's a process that requires focusing on the moment, rather than peeking months or years ahead.

"When we talked to our players at the start of the season, we didn't set out saying that we're going to the Final Four," Moser says. "We talked about focusing on the process and focusing on getting better." It's a never-ending journey, and not just for athletes but those who coach them, too. As coaches, we ask our players to embrace learning and striving to get better, and that's the same mindset that coaches in any sport, and at any level, should be excited to grab onto, as well.

"The learning process never ends," Moser says. "We tell our players that we want them to be life-long learners, because not everybody has that mentality. I am forty-nine years old and we just went to the Final Four, and I am obsessed with learning. I'm not obsessed with getting back to the Final Four, but I'm obsessed with learning more and getting better. For those youth who struggle, the harder you work, the luckier you get, so we have to teach young athletes to just keep grinding. There is no finish line with your work ethic."

There are countless attributes that go into being a complete player, and a productive one, regardless of the sport. If coaches aren't game planning for how they are going to impress upon players the importance of these components, or have strategies in place for helping players learn them, seasons can swerve into unproductive territory quickly. Moser gained an appreciation for the importance of fixating on the fundamentals while serving as an assistant coach on the staff of the late Rick Majerus at Saint Louis University. So, when he got the job at Loyola, he brought with him countless notes that he had jotted down while working with Majerus, and of course, he had plenty of his own philosophies and ideas on coaching that he was going to utilize when he stepped on the court, too.

While considering the best approach for helping players soak in all these valuable points, he came up with the idea of creating the Wall of Culture. Inside Gentile Arena on the Ramblers' campus is a wall—that was blank until Moser's arrival—that features painted words and phrases like VALUE

THE BALL; GET OUT OF THE MUD; FAKE A PASS TO MAKE A PASS; WHEN THE BALL MOVES, YOU MOVE; and TIME & SCORE. Those messages serve as daily reminders for players and teaching points for the coaching staff.

"Your culture is about your values and your belief system and what it is," he says. "It started with these little sayings and these little phrases, that were about habits. The accumulation of good habits and values and beliefs equals your culture. So I put them up on the wall and the players just embraced them. The accumulation of all these little victories, we call it, produces a big victory."

For example, GREAT DEFENSES ARE NOISY refers to the importance of players communicating with each other. "When you switch, you have to yell it," Moser says. "Great teammates talk to each other and they are noisy, yelling out *help, screen, shooter,* and those types of things. When we're playing our best defensively, everyone is chattering, and everybody is really noisy."

> *"The message I give to my camps and the young kids is to focus on the put-ups. Too many times people are putting each other down, giving put-downs at that young age, and that just chips away at your confidence."*

While many coaches of youth sports don't have access to a wall, consider how Moser's approach can be woven into your teachings. Simply using flash-cards or a dry erase board with some key terms or phrases can be a meaningful way to help players learn and be reminded of some important elements of their respective sport. Coaches can quiz kids about them just like Moser does with his players, as he randomly points to a phrase on the wall and has a player explain what it means. Coaches of young athletes can test their players before practices begin for a couple minutes, or make it part of the warm-up ritual. Remember, the more young athletes know about the sport and its many intricacies, the more enjoyment they will have playing it and pursuing improvement. And the more successful they will likely be, too. It's during that chase to get better, and perform at higher levels, that Moser stresses the importance of a positive tone being present at all times.

With nearly 700 kids attending his summer basketball camps, it's a message he delivers right away on the first day—and it continues throughout the week.

"I tell them that we all know what put-downs are," Moser says. "And I tell them that this camp is going to be about put-ups. We call them Porter's Put-ups. You want to create an environment of positivity at the young levels. The message I give to my camps and the young kids is to focus on the put-ups. Too many times people are putting each other down from a young age, and that just chips away at your confidence. And a put-up cements your confidence, it solidifies it so much. It should be all about put-ups; you should be picking each other up. We do that with our own team. That's one of the reasons how we got so connected. We're all about, 'hey, nice pass, nice screen, great job.' I talk to schools and youth about it all the time. The more you uplift each other and give put-ups, the more positive the environment and the more success you are going to have."

Loyola's 2018 run to the Final Four is certainly proof of that.

Eric Musselman

University of Nevada basketball coach ▪ 2018
Mountain West Conference Coach of the Year
▪ Former NBA head coach ▪ Played college
basketball at the University of San Diego

 When Eric Musselman was growing up, the conversations around the house had a tendency to drift toward one subject in particular: basketball. After all, when your dad happens to be a legendary coach who would spend nearly four decades coaching in the National Basketball Association, the American Basketball Association, and the Continental Basketball Association, topics like switching on screens, defending the low post, and getting out on fastbreaks could pop up at any time. And anywhere. Breakfast could be a bowl of cereal and a review of the previous evening's action by scouring the box scores buried in the back of the sports section. Afternoons could involve helping out by chasing and retrieving balls during team practices. Pre-bedtime talks could veer toward offensive and defensive schemes.

It was a special world that Eric had an all-access pass to, and he relished every second of it. The strategies and complexities of the game. Its ebbs and flows. The nuances of attacking and defending. The always-changing team dynamics and coach/player relationships. That beloved sound of balls bouncing on the court and dropping through the net. That symphony of squeaking, with players stopping and starting and spinning and pivoting, and the nonstop communication among players on the court, and from coaches relaying instructions on the sidelines. He had a front row seat to soak in all of these precious moments, and so many more.

It is impossible to gauge how much Eric learned during those years, but it no doubt would fill volumes of textbooks, not to mention what he gained along the way concerning work ethic, discipline, and dedication to your craft. So, it's little surprise that Eric would follow in his father Bill's steps, carving their names into the NBA history books as the first father/son combination to become head coaches in the league. Bill coached in Cleveland and Minnesota, while Eric coached Golden State and Sacramento.

The game, and its endless intricacies, had grabbed hold of Eric during his youth and never let go. It ignited an insatiable quest for more knowledge and more information to become the best coach he could be. It also spurred the relentless drive for helping his players be better than they were yesterday. It's a hunger that drives him now, as the head men's basketball coach at the University of Nevada, one that can benefit any coach in any sport, and at any level, too.

You see, Musselman is an enthusiastic learner, always exploring ways to enhance his skills and those of his players, and that's a mindset that serves any coach well. Of course, most coaches don't have access to the incredible insight that Musselman had in his own home. While his dad was a deep reservoir of basketball wisdom, Eric's voracious appetite for knowledge about all aspects of the game drove him to reach out and connect with countless coaches across the country. But there are plenty of wonderful examples for youth sports coaches to pull from and use to become a better coach and, in turn, have greater influence over their players, too. Musselman even does the same with his team nowadays.

"With my college athletes, we like to look at highlights of successful teams, like the San Antonio Spurs, and talk about their cultures," he says from the University of Nevada basketball offices in Reno. "Or we watch highlight tapes of the Golden State Warriors, where they make multiple pass after multiple pass and the ball ricochets around from teammate to teammate."

It's an approach that can work all the way down to the younger levels of play, too. Young athletes are paying attention; they know what is happening in the sports world. They watch games and dissect plays. They devour highlights. They know the best teams and best players. And coaches can use that to their advantage when working with their teams, just as Musselman does with his squad. They're called *teachable moments.* They can pop up at any time, and there are countless sources for them. It's simply up to observant coaches to be on the lookout for them; to recognize them; to grab them; and to insert them into their practices at the most beneficial times.

Both good and bad examples pack punch. For example, as Musselman points out with the Warriors' passing, kids who are watching games or following highlights on social media can relate. And when a coach brings up that impressive passing and asks players if they saw some of the great assists that were dished out in last night's game, they may be enthused to try replicating that execution with their teammates. Pose it as a challenge: how closely can you emulate that passing, always searching to get a better shot for a teammate?

All coaches crave teams that not only work well together, but who actually *want* to play as a cohesive group where no one cares who is scoring, just as long as somebody is getting the ball in the basket to help the team. So why not use examples of professional and college teams that are getting it done to spur on your young club?

Bad examples can also be highlighted to make strong points: maybe there was a three-on-one fastbreak in the big game last night where the ball handler didn't give it up to a wing player and failed to score when taking it to the basket himself. So you could reinforce that selfish plays reflect bad on the individual, and usually end up costing the team. Now, not everyone on a team may like the professional or collegiate team or players that a coach chooses to highlight, and that's okay. As athletes, they recognize that the team being referenced is having success, and that's the reason they are being talked about. (Coaches can encourage players to cite examples from games they have watched, or from specific teams that they follow and admire.)

> ## *"[Y]ou've got to have your team looking forward to something new to catch their antennae that makes the game fun and unique."*

"All those things are ways that you can develop and talk about teamwork," Musselman says. "The bottom line is, if it is a team sport, the only way to be successful is to utilize your teammates and make them feel good about one another."

These discussions can carry over to the court, field, and rink, too. A stale practice can be re-booted with a coach's challenge to replicate as closely as possible what players saw on television, or even YouTube. New challenges present new opportunities, exciting ones that can grab attention and produce outstanding effort. Also, delve into strategy discussions. Examine how a team effectively—or ineffectively—managed the clock in a two-minute drill in football, for example. Or, if the sport is basketball, how the team set up for the last-second shot at the end of the half or game.

Remember, there are countless opportunities for re-invigorating enthusiasm, spicing up practices, and explaining and teaching strategy. But always remember what you are striving to achieve. It's not about turning the team into a junior Golden State Warriors squad or operating at the efficiency level of the New England Patriots. It's about cultivating a team atmosphere where athletes are working hard, enjoying the process, playing together, and playing with confidence. Coaches can't lose sight that confidence is as fragile as porcelain, and can waver from day to day. Monitoring each athlete's level is imperative, and requires non-stop tinkering during practice sessions, regardless of how creative and innovative they are.

"There are a lot of factors when you are talking about practice and players having enthusiasm for practice," Musselman says. "Probably the number one thing is creativity and not allowing boredom to set in. Too often, whether it's an AAU practice, a high school practice, college practice, or even an NBA practice, you've got to have your team looking forward to something new to catch their antennae that makes the game fun and unique. When boredom sets in and it's a daily routine of the same thing over and over and over, nobody looks forward to it. The coaching staff doesn't look forward to it, and the players don't look forward to it. Whatever your philosophy is, one of the biggest things to focus on is figuring out how to continue to grab the players' attention. It's the excitement of walking into the gym or onto a baseball diamond. It's that anticipation of wondering what is coming next."

As drills are employed during practices, and references to examples on television are discussed, coaches can't lose sight of one of the most fundamental elements of working with young players: if they aren't seeing development in their skills and gaining that oh-so-important confidence to perform them in the heat of game day action, then methods have to be adjusted accordingly—and immediately—to ensure that future practice time is being put to good use to produce those desired results.

"Number one, if you want to have confident players at any age, they have to see themselves with success," Musselman says. "So in other words, if your Little League player is struggling with his batting average, you don't continue to put him in the batting cage and throw curveballs at him. He needs to hit off a batting tee so he sees success. If a player is struggling from the foul line, maybe you start him in two or three feet from the rim. You have to build confidence up through somebody seeing themselves be successful. At the collegiate level, when we have a player struggling, we'll bring him in and show him a highlight tape of when he had great success to make him feel good about himself as a player. So that's how you build young athletes up."

Ken Niumatalolo

Head football coach of the United States Naval
Academy ▪ Two-time American Athletic Conference
Coach of the Year ▪ All-time winningest coach in
Navy football history ▪ Former college quarterback

One of college football's greatest leaders—of one of the nation's grandest and most respected institutions—attacks every day with boundless energy and enthusiasm, and he navigates those hours with the utmost character, too. During the season, Ken Niumatalolo, the head football coach of the United States Naval Academy, is in his office well before the sun begins its climb, dissecting tape, planning practices, and plotting how to defeat that week's opponent. While that's a schedule that many of the nation's top, and mostly sleep-deprived, college football coaches keep during the fall season, Niumatalolo is equally passionate about teaching players the value of character and instilling it as he is driven to win football games.

As someone who exemplifies the qualities he aims to impart to his players, he encourages coaches of young athletes in all sports to take advantage of their positions to lead young athletes down that path where they want to be good citizens living their lives with good morals, and making smart decisions when adversity takes a seat on their doorstep. "At the youth level, it's got to be about more than just teaching the X's and O's. It has to be about more than wins and losses," Niumatalolo says from his Annapolis, Maryland football office. "It's about the development of character, hard work, teamwork, and selflessness."

During a busy youth sports season, often condensed down to a couple months, coaches naturally direct the bulk of their attention to teaching skills, plays, and strategies for their respective sport. But if those life skills Niumatalolo speaks of aren't on a coach's radar, and time isn't being carved out to talk about them during the season, wonderful opportunities to impact a group of impressionable athletes is being wasted. If young athletes are only taking away a shiny trophy that is on display on their bedroom dresser as the highlight of their experience, but they've gained nothing in the areas of respect and working together, that doesn't meet the standards of a successful season. In fact, it falls woefully short.

"Sometimes at that age, if it's more about wins and losses and trophies, kids lose sight of the fact of what's really important," Niumatalolo says. "And they start to focus on things that really don't matter in the long run."

How can today's coaches create a culture of character? Well, for starters, there are endless examples that can be pulled from what young athletes see on television, particularly when it comes to professional and college sports that they watch. Sometimes in big-game matchups, opposing teams get into shoving matches on the field during pre-game warm-ups; or on the way to the locker-room at halftime, players push or exchange trash talk with opposing players. Bring up these events during a warm-up session for a practice and ask your players what they thought of these incidents. How would they have responded if they found themselves in similar situations? Or how about games where coaches receive technical fouls, or are thrown out of games, for their words or actions directed at officials. What do your players think of that type of behavior? Do they find that disrespectful? How do they think a coach should handle instances where perhaps a call was missed without it turning into an attack on the official?

**"At the youth level, it's got to be about
more than just teaching the X's and O's.
It has to be about more than wins and losses.
It's about the development of character,
hard work, teamwork, and selflessness."**

While these incidents serve as a great platform for engaging players in important conversations about key life values, they are only relevant for making a difference in young lives if the coach models the good character he or she is stressing. Talking about it, but failing to live it every day, is an exercise in uselessness. Young athletes observe their coach's every move. So if a coach genuinely wants them to learn some powerful and life-long values, it all starts with how the leader of the team conducts himself or herself.

"A big part of it is your own life and the way you live," says Niumatalolo, who took over the Midshipmen in 2007. "If you're a guy who doesn't want your team to cheat, you have to do what's right yourself. Even at the youth level, the kids can see the way you conduct yourself and the way you are with the referees. If coaches are yelling at the referees, what are the kids supposed to think? So as a youth coach, first and foremost, teach off your example of who you are as a person."

During the 2014 college football season, Navy was preparing for a Saturday showdown with Temple University. Following a practice conducted in hot and humid conditions at the Philadelphia Eagles practice facility, the team's caravan of busses was headed out of the stadium parking lot. Niumatalolo stopped the busses so that water bottles could be handed out to the parking lot attendants working in the heat. He made that gesture because that's who he is: a man of character.

During the season, Niumatalolo and his coaching staff work long hours, waking up to alarm clocks buzzing at times when most are in the throes of REM sleep. But it's interesting to note that they don't work nights. Those hours are spent with families, as husbands and fathers. He's also been known to cut practices short when players need to study. So imagine how powerful Niumatalolo's words are when he talks to his team about character, decision-making, and the like. They see it from him every day. They know that's the way he lives his life, and that empowers them to want to take their lives in the same direction.

Character is a sign of strength, not weakness. Doing the right thing, regardless if someone is looking or not, is powerful. And when it's watched, learned, and picked up by players, it is incredibly rewarding for a coach to have that type of influence. Niumatalolo urges today's coaches to stay true to their values and impart wisdom and character-building guidance every chance they get. But always make sure those interactions with young athletes, when teaching and correcting, don't contradict the messages that have been shared about respect and appropriate behavior, among others.

"It can never be personal," Niumatalolo says. "You can always be demanding, but not demeaning. Especially at the youth level, because it's the first contact with sports for so many, and if it can be a positive one, it can be very influential for them. So tell kids the truth without doing it in a way that puts them down, continue to encourage them, and be positive in your feedback."

That's especially true as coaches fit players with those positions that are best-suited for the team, often to the disappointment of kids who had their heart set on playing somewhere else. "It's being able to find a role for everybody, and a big part of it is teaching that everybody on a team has different roles," Niumatalolo says. "Not everybody is going to make all the baskets in basketball, or score all the goals in soccer, or pitch in baseball or softball, but there are other roles that are just as important. It helps them learn life skills that not everybody is the president of the company. Everybody has different roles in life, and in coaching, if you do more than just teach the technical part of it by teaching more of the life values, that definitely helps young people."

Leah O'Brien-Amico

Three-time Olympic Softball Gold Medalist ▪ Three-time NCAA national champion ▪ Two-time world champion ▪ Named to the NCAA Division I Softball 25th Anniversary Team

Every four years, the Olympics rolls around, bringing with it mesmerizing performances and dream-crushing disappointments. Some of the world's greatest athletes earn coveted spots on the podium, receiving shiny medals and hearing anthems punctuating a lifetime of hard work and sacrifice. Others deal with the heartbreak of coming up short. Some find glorious contentment and a true sense of achievement by representing their country on the world's grandest athletic stage. With every game, event and heat that comprises the Games comes pressure—intense, unrelenting and capable of shredding confidence, crumbling focus and ruining performances. Leah O'Brien-Amico remembers that pressure that accompanied her as she took the field as a twenty-one-year-old right-fielder for Team USA at the 1996 Summer Games in Atlanta, Georgia.

"I'll never forget my very first game in the Olympics," she says. "My heart was beating out of my chest. You talk about butterflies—they were the biggest butterflies I've ever had. There was so much pressure, and all those months and years had led up to that moment."

Now, O'Brien-Amico could have been devoured by the magnitude of the situation, which certainly would have been understandable considering her age and the enormity of what was on the line; or she could take comfort and grab confidence from the fact that she and her teammates had done everything possible to fully prepare for these big-time games, where one error can result in a loss and derail golden hopes.

"For me, it all came down to, 'What did I do in the preparation?'" she says. "I will never forget Team USA pitcher Lisa Fernandez throwing that first pitch, and I had this peace and this calm come over me, and immediately, this thought went into my head: *This is the exact same game that I have played since I was six years old.* Yes, the stage is different, but don't focus on that. Focus on the game you've played forever. You know what you are doing."

It worked. O'Brien-Amico was prepared. She was ready. And she executed exactly like she had in all the practices and games leading up to the Olympics. "In that first inning, the ball was hit to me in right field and I threw the runner out at first base," she says. "And I said to myself, 'here we go.' Each Olympics was a little bit different—the pressure was always there—but the biggest thing was to go back to the little things in the game and keep it simple. And it helped to be with my teammates, cheering each other on and supporting one another."

O'Brien-Amico conducts coach and player clinics across the country, covering all aspects of the game. As a three-time Olympic gold medalist, she also speaks to numerous groups about motivation, being the best you can be, and how important possessing a positive mindset is for achieving success in the most pressure-filled of moments.

"Young athletes have to learn to constantly take ownership of what they are doing," she points out. "Sometimes what happens is that kids don't want to mess up; they're afraid to fail. And with that, they don't want to take responsibility. So as coaches, it's so important to teach kids from a young age that it's okay to fail, and that we need to own up to our mistakes and learn from them in order to grow and get better."

During her work with young athletes, she quickly recognized that many encountered great difficulty transferring their practice performances to game day. Suddenly, those smooth swings at the plate and accurate throws in the field during practice dissolved into ugly-looking swipes at pitches in games and errant throws with an opposing player sprinting down the base paths. Pressure can be a ferocious foe, turning muscle memory wobbly and wedging into the crevices of a young athlete's mind where confidence normally resides.

"For me, it's about putting pressure on in practice in terms of game-like situations," O'Brien-Amico says. "That's so important at the highest level, so why not start at a younger level? I found that I would work with a team and they would do well with throwing, and the next thing you know, I made it a competition and nobody could throw. So immediately it goes to the mindset of the players. It's so important to help players at a younger age create a positive mindset while taking responsibility for their actions, and learn how to translate that to game days."

It starts with sprinkling doses of pressure into the practice drills to gradually get players used to dealing with it. O'Brien-Amico explains that she loves to challenge kids at clinics, "Because what you find is some kids can learn the fundamentals, but the second pressure comes on them, they all of a sudden have a different mindset. So in our drills, I love to give them something that's like a test. When I work with outfielders, they have to hit a little cone with their throws, and it's hard to do. I love to see those players rise up to the challenge."

"It's so important to help players at a younger age create a positive mindset while taking responsibility for their actions, and learn how to translate that to game days."

But what those challenges build in players is persistence, resilience, and fortitude to keep at it, as well as gradually developing that all-important confidence to make that really tough throw from the outfield that may decide the outcome of a late-inning, one-run game. Put your players in some game-type scenarios in practice. Be creative. In a sport like softball, run scrimmages where each inning, a runner starts on second base and each hitter starts with one or two strikes in the count when they step to the plate. Besides working on handling pressure situations and late game strategy, it revs up the practice energy and helps keep young athletes engaged and focused by running them through different scenarios that likely will pop up during the season. And they will gradually become more comfortable performing during crunch time.

There are countless options for all sports. As the coach, you can make it happen. You've got to make that time count with your team. Creativity is great, as long as it results in productive practicing and beneficial exchanges of information between coaches and players. Creativity without purpose and progress is pointless.

"It's so important for us as coaches to strive for quality over quantity," O'Brien-Amico says. "Obviously, we need a lot of repetitions in order to be successful. But what I found in working with players is it's about the *quality* of what you are doing. If you go out and you're practicing something wrong over and over, or you're out there for hours and hours but you're just going through the motions, you're wasting your time and energy for nothing. But if you go out and make a conscious effort to do it the right way, you could get something accomplished in twenty minutes, rather than two hours. What is so important is what you choose to spend your time doing. We can all waste time, or we can make wise choices. In sports, it's doing the little things. It's having a purpose."

To achieve this key level of practice productivity—and maintain it—requires constant feedback from coaches. Young athletes of any skill level can lose focus during the course of a practice session, so it's constantly being in their ear encouraging and reminding them what they need to be trying to accomplish during this particular drill or exercise. If it's not continually talked about, it's easy for the practice to lose momentum and for productivity to fizzle.

O'Brien-Amico learned to really narrow down her focus to just the specifics when she was playing for the University of Arizona and being a big part of three—count 'em, three—national championship teams.

"For me, it was all about having a purpose," she says. "Anytime I stepped in to throw I asked myself, 'Okay, am I thinking about throwing or am I just throwing mindlessly? Okay, I'm only going to throw for five minutes, but right here I'm going to hit a spot. I'm going to have good mechanics, I'm going to look at my spin.'"

Translation: don't have players randomly throwing a bunch of pitches without any purpose attached to them. Have them work on hitting the upper corners, or lower corners. Give them game scenarios. Add pressure. Make every throw matter. O'Brien-Amico took the same mindset to the plate when she was working on her hitting, too.

"If I was hitting, I could just come and take a lot of cuts," she says. "Now, if I only take twenty cuts but I have a purpose with those twenty cuts, like I'm going to hit the inside part of the ball, or I'm going to stay through it and try to only hit line drives, then it took that aspect of keeping a purpose with everything we were doing."

That approach obviously worked because she swung a potent bat. Check out these sizzling numbers: .428 career batting average; and she holds the Women's College World Series Record for batting average in a single tournament at a mind boggling .750.

While running players through practices, she notes the importance of rotating them into different positions, too. Even if it's just for a few moments, it can make a big difference in a number of ways. Coaches may discover a player has a real knack for that position. It exposes kids to different nuances of the game, and prepares those youngsters who continue on with the sport in the coming years, when chances are pretty good that they aren't going to play the same position throughout their entire youth sports participation.

"That is so important," she says. "When they're starting out, I teach them a little bit of everything, because you never know where you are going to be needed. It's most important to just be athletic, to be versatile, to be flexible, and always willing to learn. I've seen players at the collegiate level in multiple positions, and it was because they were athletic and open to learning."

O'Brien-Amico reaped the benefits of that approach, as well. "I grew up as a pitcher and first baseman, and I didn't play outfield until college," she says. "But I'm thankful for those coaches when I was younger that did put me in the outfield for a little bit. Even though it wasn't my starting position, they would have me out there in practice and gave me a few opportunities that gave me some familiarity when I got to college."

And where did she play in her first Summer Olympics? The outfield. That's good coaching, and efficient use of practice time. And O'Brien-Amico has never forgotten it. She has also never forgotten how much fun she had playing and learning the game through the years.

"To the day I finished competing, I felt like it was always fun," she says. "There was always a purpose, for sure, but I loved what I was doing, and it was still fun to be at practice." As a coach of any sport, if you can ignite that same passion and love for participating that O'Brien-Amico had, you've done some good work with your team.

"At the heart of everything is keeping it fun," she says. "When girls love the game, they're going to go out and do their best. Coaches need to make every single girl feel like they're a part of that team, no matter what role they are playing. At the end of the day—even at the collegiate and Olympic level for me—what we took away and what so many girls will say is that we loved our coach because he not only made us better athletes, but better women. You need to stick to the heart of these girls, knowing your impact on them no matter what level they take the sport to. Some won't take it past high school, some may go to college, some may go internationally—but whatever level they take it to, you want them to walk away with memories that are lifelong in a positive way."

Cat Osterman

Assistant women's softball coach at Texas State
University ▪ Two-time Olympic medalist ▪ Three-time
National Player of the Year ▪ Four-time All-American

Cat Osterman's ascension from the softball fields of her youth to becoming one of the greatest pitchers the sport has ever seen was driven by pursuing what even she knew wasn't possible: perfection. Though all the hitters through the years who stepped into the batter's box and connected with nothing but air—and there were *a lot* of them—would probably admit that she got as close as anyone.

"I was always motivated by chasing perfection, even though I knew it wasn't possible," says Osterman, a two-time Olympian who won gold in Athens, Greece in 2004 and silver in Beijing in 2008, and these days is the assistant softball coach at Texas State University in San Marcos, Texas. "Accepting that I'd never be perfect, but trying to get as close to it as possible, is what really drove me."

And boy, did that thought process work. Check out this jaw-dropping list of accolades the former University of Texas standout collected, and the accompanying numbers that go along with her performances that would make a mathematician's head spin: she is second all-time in NCAA Division I career strikeouts with a whopping 2,265 of them; she was a three-time selection as Big 12 Conference Female Athlete of the Year; she still holds career records in victories (136), ERA (0.51), shutouts (85) and no-hitters (20) as a Longhorn; she holds the NCAA record for career strikeout ratio per seven innings (14.35); she finished her college career in Austin with a 136-25 record; and during her ten-year run pitching for Team USA she won fifty-nine games while losing just four and struck out a mind-boggling 832 batters in just 425 innings of work. How Osterman approached the sport, and how her coaches worked with her, proved to be the perfect formula for her. But it's not for everyone.

Now, when mega-talented athletes like Osterman emerge and stand out from their teammates, it often creates an intriguing team dynamic, as well as a significant coaching challenge. There will be athletes who understandably want to reach that level of the team's star, though there may be numerous factors working against them: they haven't played the sport for as long; they don't possess the natural athletic gifts; they lack the work ethic and true inner drive to want to be that good; or even their bodies at this juncture of their development haven't matured yet.

Of course, young athletes are going to be constantly comparing themselves to their teammates. They know who's the best player on the team. They also know where they fit in compared to everyone else on the squad. Some players will put added pressure on themselves to try to reach that next level where the best on the team reside. Plus, in many cases, parents who recognize that their youngster is behind on the talent scale of another on the team will push and prod to get their son or daughter there, which can create a toxic family atmosphere if the child begins to feel inferior and resent the pressure to meet new expectations. Osterman sees it all the time with young players who are casting an eye at their teammates, analyzing, evaluating, and judging.

"I give lessons to younger players and kids. At the ages of nine through eleven, they are at different talent levels," she says. "They're at various points in their pitching, because they are growing at different rates, so they have all kinds of body types. For coaches, it's about constantly encouraging them to see the process and to see their improvement, and not to try to be the same as their friend or teammate."

That means diligently monitoring the development and progress of every player on the roster, and not being mesmerized by the team's star while neglecting to recognize the other athletes' improvements, no matter how big or small they are. Everyone on the roster deserves a coach's feedback, and whenever coaches can sprinkle in those positive or encouraging words, or deliver a fist bump or pat on the back, the better.

"For coaches, it's seeing the bigger picture and really celebrating the process for the young kids," Osterman says. "If there's one kid that can only hit the ball once out of ten times, the first time she hits it three out of ten times, make sure it's celebrated and pointed out so the athlete knows that she is getting better."

What can sabotage coach-player relationships, and hamper a young athlete fulfilling his or her potential, is the tendency to direct more words on a negative, rather than shifting the attention to whatever the positive may be. "We live in a world of instant gratification and absolutes, and that's not how sports work," Osterman says. "The biggest thing is to put them in situations in practice where they can have both success and failure and make them learn through the failure, but make sure you point out their success. Especially at the young ages, everyone wants to teach the right fundamentals or teach the game the right way. Pointing out all the mistakes is great, but you also have to let them know when they *do* do something right. A lot of us focus on trying to make sure they do everything right and forget to point out, even if it's only one time, the one that they did correctly."

A native of Houston, Osterman has fond memories of her early years in softball. She played in an atmosphere that was fun and conducive to learning and developing skills, which really turned out to be the springboard for continuing on with the sport.

"The first team I was on was coached by three or four different dads of girls on the team," Osterman recalls. "They formed a coaching group and it was awesome. They tried as much as possible not to coach their own daughters, so we all got to hear from someone else, as opposed to our own dads. Growing up, all my coaches were encouraging, and the biggest thing is I've never had a coaching staff that was yelling, screaming, or punishing us for errors, or that kind of thing. I've always had coaches that were tough, but encouraging, in trying to help you get better and help you grow. So for me, I've never been in an atmosphere where it wasn't about trying to grow as both an athlete and a person."

> *"For coaches, it's about constantly encouraging them to see the process and to see their improvement, and not to try to be the same as their friend or teammate."*

These days, Osterman takes that same approach into her coaching, whether it's working with collegiate athletes or young pitchers just beginning to get a handle on some of the fundamentals and nuances of the position. "The big thing is we always put some competitions in there," she says. "Even when I give pitching lessons with groups of ten-year-olds, we do two sets of three pitches each, so they get six pitches and we see who can hit the most strikes out of them. It's always fun when you put a challenge out there, whether it's hit the glove three times or who can hit the most strikes, or something like that."

To keep these types of drills interesting, a fun "punishment" can be used for players who don't execute whatever the coach has set for the goal. Whenever doing this, just be sure to have kids of similar skills competing against each other. For example, if it's softball and you've got half a dozen kids who are relied on to pitch, break them into similar-skilled groups of three for the drill challenge, and the two athletes in each group who don't perform as well as the winner have to do the "punishment." Coaches can even have the players choose what that punishment is—just be sure to keep the focus of it on something fun that doesn't make players begin to associate running as something bad. Translation: boring laps around the field are a no-no.

"The group I work with has so much fun with this, they don't even have to come up with a quote-unquote punishment. They do it among themselves," Osterman says. "I watch them do burpees and frog jumps because that's what they choose to make their friends do." While you want the element of fun involved in what you are doing, coaches must make sure that players are still focused on executing the skill being worked on and that their attention doesn't wander.

"Every now and then, I give them a break and talk to them about, 'what are we focusing on?'" Osterman says. "I let them kind of take ownership of it and tell me what I said we were working on, what they think they can do better next time, and that kind of thing." Just remember, athletes will want to hit the fast forward button on the process of learning, anxious to keep advancing to new skills, when they need to dig into the process of working on a specific skill first and ironing out all the kinks in performing it before tackling something new.

"The biggest thing is all these youngsters want to try to throw five or six pitches early on in their career and that's not necessary," Osterman says. "You need to really master your fastball and then add a change-up and go from there. But sometimes kids get bored, and their parents get bored, too. They see some other eleven or twelve-year-old that has a drop ball and they think, 'oh my God, my daughter should have that.' But again, we're talking about different talent levels or just different skill levels depending on how long someone has been pitching. You can't rush it; they have to learn the mechanics and let the process happen. It takes a lot to be a really good pitcher, and a lot of kids just want to rush to have all the pitches, and it's not necessary. It's almost a detriment, because then they don't have any really good pitches once they get older. They'll have a bunch of average ones because they've been throwing four all their life instead of perfecting one pitch before moving on to the next."

So as coaches, it's about keeping players' focus on the task at hand, and away from worrying about where a teammate, friend, or another player is in their development. It's a process, one that takes time to go through and needs to be communicated to players while they are being recognized for the big and small improvements they are showing along the way. Chances are pretty good that you won't have the next Cat Osterman on your roster—after all, world-class athletes are rare—but you can have a young player who will grow and develop under your tutelage, who will look back some day and be thankful that you were that positive influence in her life, just like Osterman feels about her youth coaches.

"The biggest thing is try to make it a constructive but positive environment, and secondly, don't get ahead of yourself," Osterman says. "Teach them the fundamentals, because these basics are probably the one thing that are overlooked the most. Nowadays everyone wants to teach eight-year-olds how to turn a double play, but you can't turn a double play if you can't catch and throw properly. So don't overlook the fundamentals and how important those are day in and day out. The biggest thing is teach your players that coaching is positive and constructive—it's not meaning that they are not doing it right or that they're a failure. It's just that someone is trying to help them get better."

Sean Payton

Coach of the New Orleans Saints ▪ Super
Bowl XLIV champion ▪ 2006 AP Coach of
the Year ▪ Eastern Illinois Hall of Fame

During the 2012 football season, some of the plays called by Sean Payton, widely recognized as one of the NFL's greatest offensive minds, led to big chunks of yardage, trips to the end zone and celebratory hugs, high-fives, and back slaps along the sidelines. Other times botched assignments, turnovers, or penalties sabotaged the plays he dialed up and stalled drives. Yet, the Super Bowl winning coach of the New Orleans Saints—his team beat Peyton Manning and the Indianapolis Colts 31 to 17 in Super Bowl XLIV in Miami—didn't yell at referees or slam clipboards to the ground in disgust when his squad failed to move the ball downfield. His blood pressure didn't spike either, a frequent occurrence for all NFL coaches on the sidelines on Sunday afternoons, where one play can decide a game's outcome and even a coach's job.

You see, this particular season was different—much different. It was also special because it was far removed from the NFL world that Payton normally navigates. These games were contested on Saturday mornings—and the players were middle schoolers. Payton spent his NFL-mandated year of exile surrounding the Saints' bounty scandal on the sideline, running the offense for his son Connor's sixth-grade football team in the Dallas area. During this 2012 campaign, the former Associated Press Coach of the Year and member of the Eastern Illinois University Hall of Fame for putting up prolific numbers as a college quarterback put his free time to good use by teaching a game he loves to children.

Yes, as a life-long participant in sports, of course Payton wanted to win. That competitive fire is part of his DNA and has helped forge an incredibly successful NFL coaching career. And yes, he wanted his young players to execute plays, perform at a high level, and pile up touchdowns. But he also was well aware of the position he was in and the opportunities that accompany coaching a group of children. So while Payton wanted to help the kids win the league title, he also wanted to achieve so much more. He sought to make a real difference by leaving an imprint on his players in much more significant ways.

"For youth football coaches, it's awfully important that when that season ends, those children can't wait to play again next year," says Payton, seated on a second floor outdoor terrace in Boca Raton, Florida, during the NFL's annual league meeting. "That shows that you've done something well."

Payton brought with him the same terminology the high-octane Saints use to carve apart opposing defenses—though the playbook was chopped down to a dozen plays, instead of the hundreds at the disposal of prolific Saints quarterback, Drew Brees. Payton also brought something else to that Liberty Christian Warriors team: a relentless focus on all the kids and a passion for helping them learn skills, fill their confidence tanks, and inspire a love for playing the game for years to come.

To achieve that admirable goal of getting all the kids wanting to return to buckle up their chin straps and engage in contact again next year is a big task, filled with challenges along the way. A significant factor was that Payton made sure the kids were exposed to more than one position. Too often, volunteer coaches confine kids to one role for the duration of the season, giving them an incredibly limited experience of what the sport is all about. The likelihood that they won't return to play again next season if that one position doesn't grab their heart increases. Plus, kids who never get opportunities to try other positions may miss out discovering something they really enjoy, and coaches miss out on discovering a player who excels at a specific skill that could significantly help the team.

"It's important to have a mission statement," Payton says. That statement serves as a handy GPS to help coaches guide their teams where they want to take them; and how they plan to get them there without veering off on those all-too-common detours that can derail a season. For example, without that mission statement, coaches will be more likely to cave into parental pressure to play the most gifted athletes at the skill positions all season long, while all the other players are left wondering what it's like to play in those spots, too.

"Ask yourself, 'What are our goals?'" Payton says. "We said we were going to have multiple positions. The kids had an A position and a B position, so they were going to get a chance to play more than just one role." Consider how the excitement level ratchets up for a young player who is on the offensive line, for example, and gets the chance to run a handful of plays at tight end and maybe even have a pass sent his way. Does this approach disrupt the rhythm and timing of the offense or wreck momentum? Maybe. Does it provide a memorable moment for a young athlete? Most definitely. As a volunteer coach, it's important to think in a much broader perspective of what this season is truly all about and the position you are in to impact young lives.

It all goes back to what Payton said earlier about mission statements. Really take some time to define your goals, outline your plan, and communicate it to parents before the kids ever step on the field. If your reason for getting into coaching kids is to act like an NFL coach and only play the best players while allowing the lesser-skilled kids to languish on the bench, never to get a chance to catch a pass or make a tackle, then you're missing out on a great opportunity to be a real difference maker in young lives. Payton gets it: he didn't coach these youngsters like they were highly paid professionals. He coached them like the kids they were and focused on giving them all a rewarding experience that they will be able to reflect back on with a huge smile years from now.

"When players know how much you care about them, that empowers you, as the coach."

Look back on your initial experiences in youth sports. What stands out in your mind? Is it the win-loss record of your ten-and-under team? Or is it the memories of being a part of something special? Maybe that coach who took a genuine interest in you? Or the practices that you couldn't wait to roll around during the week because of how much fun they were. Or those Game Days when you got to put on the colorful uniform and get your crack at playing a position or two, or perhaps even three.

Giving children the opportunity to play different positions doesn't mean you're putting less emphasis on trying to win the game, or not having players compete hard and doing their best on every single snap of the ball. But it does send a clear signal that you care about all the kids and are dialed in to taking every single one of them on a season-long journey that they will recall for the rest of their lives. The kids will grin big when they think of you and their season of learning and playing their hearts out for you. As a youth coach, is there anything more special than that?

"A volunteer coach is no different than a teacher," Payton says. "When players know how much you care about them, that empowers you, as the coach. So, it can't be just check in, teach, check out. Part of it is knowing about their personal life and their family and their brothers and sisters. It's one of the great things about what we get a chance to do as coaches."

That season, Payton's team reached the title game, where they were beaten by several touchdowns. Afterward, a gracious Payton spoke to both teams, applauding the efforts of the winning team in a touching display that all coaches should take note of. Payton's players don't have a first-place trophy from that season sitting on a mantel or residing in a box stuffed in the attic. But you can bet they have memories—good ones—of playing for an NFL coach who really cared about them and their experience with the sport.

Payton beams when he says of that season: "We practiced on Tuesdays and Thursdays and played on Saturdays. I cut the oranges and mixed the Gatorade—it was fantastic." Of course, most volunteer coaches don't have an NFL background like Payton, and certainly not a Super Bowl victory next to their name. But if you coach with your heart, and you operate with a kids-first mission statement, you can reach kids and help ensure their memories playing for you fit into the fantastic category, too, just like Sean Payton. And that's pretty good coaching company.

Samantha Peszek

2008 Olympic gymnastics silver medalist ▪ 2015 NCAA All-Around co-champion ▪ 17-time All American ▪ USA Gymnastics Hall of Fame inductee

Samantha Peszek, Olympic silver medalist and NCAA gymnastics champion, knows all about fear and pressure. After all, when you're competing in a sport in which the tiniest wobble or the smallest of steps on a dismount can wreck scores and crush life-long dreams, you've got to find ways to fight through it. While the Olympics, and even trying to qualify for them, brings suffocating pressure and scrutiny that only the world's elite performers like Peszek understand and can relate to, when you pull back the curtain on sports at every level, all young athletes encounter fears, doubts, and worries at some point along the way. While some athletes are able to escape the grasp of those dark thoughts looming over contests and go on to perform and excel, for others, their confidence is threatened and their enjoyment and pursuit of development grinds to a standstill.

"I wish someone had told me when I was young that it's okay, people have fears," Peszek says. "And that it's fine to be nervous." Those fears can cover a lot of territory too—both physical and mental. There can be young baseball players afraid of getting struck by a fastball; soccer players reluctant to go full speed after enduring a painful tumble from an opposing player tripping them while battling for a ball; or a hockey player scared to block a shot after being struck by a puck on a previous play and still feeling the sting.

On the mental side, the fears are endless, too. It can be players who are afraid to strike out or miss free throws, or who can't sleep the night before games or function normally the day of games. It can even stretch to such debilitating extremes, where athletes are begging to be taken out of close games because the fear of performing in the high-pressure moments is crippling. These fears can originate from being self-imposed by athletes who so desperately want to achieve and succeed that they place incredibly high expectations on themselves; and it can come from outside sources—coaches and parents—whose words and actions result in young athletes feeling the heat to not just perform, but to perform well.

Now, keep in mind that athletes are taught to be tough and strong, confident and secure, resilient and focused. Revealing chinks in their emotional armor is seen as a big no-no. So Peszek, like most other athletes do, kept those fears tucked away in the privacy of her mind. Regardless of the sport, young athletes will usually do everything possible to keep any anxiety hidden from coaches and teammates for fear that divulging those thoughts and feelings indicates weakness and an inability to be a contributing team member. So a challenge coaches face is recognizing that this negative energy can filter into any athlete's psyche at any time. It struck Peszek, who reached the point when it came to the balance beam that she would wake up in the morning and hope that it had been removed from the rotation of apparatuses that female gymnasts competed on.

"I used to be afraid of skills, and even when I got to the elite level, I never told anybody because I was really embarrassed by it," she says. She was one of the lucky ones who figured it out, though. By working hard every day, she learned that she was adding layers of confidence and strengthening her resolve. It was that behind-the-scenes work that Peszek put in at the gym that enabled her to not allow the pressure that accompanied meets to sabotage her focus or belief in herself.

> *"So, at meets when you get this butterfly feeling in your stomach, you can either look at it as a negative and get caught up in the pressure, or see it in a positive way and say, 'I'm really excited; I have a lot of adrenaline.'"*

"The harder I worked, the more confidence that I got, which made me less nervous because I was so well prepared," she says. "So I was more excited to show everyone what I had been working on rather than thinking, 'I hope I do a really good job.'" It's an important point for coaches to keep in mind as they work with their athletes. By bolstering confidence during practice sessions, kids will go into those games and meets feeling more relaxed and ready to compete, with less chances of pressure situations compromising their ability to perform at the most intense moments; or fears of failure, injury or anything else ruining their performance.

"I used to channel all of the pressure as positive adrenaline," says Peszek, who won the NCAA all-around title in 2015 as a member of the UCLA gymnastics team. "So, at meets when you get this butterfly feeling in your stomach, you can either look at it as a negative and get caught up in the pressure, or see it in a positive way and say, 'I'm really excited; I have a lot of adrenaline.'"

And the 2013 USA Gymnastics Hall of Fame inductee's approach is one that young athletes in all sports can take with them to their games, meets and matches, too. Too many kids' performances are derailed by pressure: whether it's from coaches, parents, or even the athletes putting unnecessary burdens on themselves. So, learning how to manage the pressure, and not be consumed by it, is something athletes in all sports must be taught and work through. And that all starts with the messaging provided by coaches.

"For me, I always thrived on the pressure," says Peszek, who was part of the silver medal winning squad at the 2008 Summer Olympics in Beijing. "So, the more pressure that I had, the better that I tended to do."

But as a young athlete, there was a gigantic learning curve to reaching that point. Peszek fully recognizes that now. Her journey is remarkable; and the fears she conquered and the pressure she learned to embrace—rather than run from—to perform at an incredibly high level on the world stage is beyond impressive. She also knows that for many athletes, those demons cloaked in fear and self-doubt aren't so easily dismissed. And they can sledgehammer dreams when not handled the right way. Throughout her teen years, Peszek would help out at various gymnastics camps and would usually find herself working with young gymnasts on the balance beam, that four-inch wide and four-foot high plank of wood that can strike fear into the most talented and experienced of gymnasts. Once Peszek gained that coveted confidence to perform on the balance beam, it carried over into all the other events. And by the way, she won two NCAA titles on the balance beam, that same event that at one point she wished never even existed.

When it comes to the beam, building confidence in kids and helping them perform in pressure-filled moments, the creator of the Beam Queen Bootcamps is a pretty good source. Peszek conducts her camps around the country, where she talks to children about the fears of competing, the stress to succeed, and the pressure to perform. She has been there, done that, and emerged as one of the greats of the sport. What she shares matters, and it pertains to coaching all kids in all sports.

"Sometimes it was like my body was paralyzed, and I just couldn't perform like I wanted to. When I talk to kids about it, they all nod their heads and know exactly what I am talking about," she says. "But it's really hard to explain that feeling, because you have no idea why you are afraid, but your body just won't let you do the skill. Sometimes it's overthinking, and sometimes you think you forgot how to do it. When I talk to the kids, it's really reassuring for them to see that even if they are struggling with a skill, they can get over it and accomplish great things."

Peszek came up with the idea for the camps in the summer of 2016 and held the inaugural Beam Queen Bootcamp at the gym she trained at as a child in Indiana. Now, it has grown to a two-day camp that travels to interested gyms nationwide to help young gymnasts with the beam. Peszek's approach embodies what coaching young athletes is all about: staff bring tremendous energy to the camp, and they have fun busting fears and building confidence in kids.

The concepts employed by the Beam Queen Bootcamp staff are terrific, and coaches of all sports can use them with their young athletes, too. For example, they hand out an "Actually, You Can" award, which goes to a gymnast who overcomes a fear. Imagine doing something similar for a young hockey goalie or football player, where they get a boost of confidence by being recognized for conquering a fearful aspect of the sport. Or the "I Am The Storm" award that is presented to that gymnast who was fearless and excited to try new combinations and new skills. Coaches of other sports can create similar awards of their own that highlight athletes who aren't afraid to try new skills and, more importantly, don't allow the fear of failure to infringe on those efforts.

Peszek, and those who assist her at these camps, know that they are doing much more than simply helping young gymnasts improve their balance beam routines. They are building confidence, strengthening character, teaching resolve, and helping young athletes learn to stare adversity in the face and not blink. They're helping kids slay those inner monsters and emerge as stronger and confident performers, and individuals. The reality is that the overwhelming majority of these young gymnasts will never compete for the United States in the Olympics like Peszek did, but they will need the skills she is helping teach them to lead productive lives. And that's exactly what coaching is all about.

"I like sharing with young gymnasts that there are obstacles, and that's part of life, and part of overcoming them is to stay consistent and keep showing up and to keep reminding yourself why you do the sport," she says. "Gymnastics is a good sport, because it teaches you life lessons, and it teaches you listening skills, discipline, coordination, and flexibility." And how to handle pressure— which one of the greats of the sport certainly mastered.

"When I was their age, I had a lot of fear problems," she says. "I thought I was the only person in the world to ever be afraid of a skill, which is very silly. But now by sharing my experiences of being such a head case of a gymnast when I was younger, and a fearful athlete, kids can see that everyone has fears growing up. Everyone is scared of something at one point in their career—and a lot of gymnasts actually quit because of it. I almost quit, and it was a really traumatic time for me, actually, because I was so young."

Over time, and through hard work, she excelled. Nowadays, she can reflect back on those moments with a smile and genuine sense of accomplishment. Even if she never would have reached the Olympics, she knows the character she built and the life skills she learned through competing were worth it and serve her well in her daily life.

"I actually think that's what made me a mentally stronger gymnast in the long run," Peszek says. "Because I had to constantly work on my mind when I was a young kid." So, as you're working with your young athletes, be sure to devote time to managing their mindsets. It will pay dividends for a lifetime.

Tyrone Poole

Two-time Super Bowl champion ▪ Played fourteen
seasons in the NFL ▪ Selected in the first round of
the 1995 NFL Draft ▪ Division II Football Hall of
Fame inductee ▪ Volunteer youth sports coach

During his fourteen-year NFL career, cornerback Tyrone Poole played for some of the game's greatest coaches. There was Bill Belichick in New England, Mike Shanahan in Denver, and Dom Capers in Carolina, among others. Coaches well-known for being brilliant tacticians, motivators, and teachers. Coaches who won big games and got their players to execute at the highest levels, and in the biggest moments. Coaches routinely referred to as geniuses, labeled as masterminds, and, in the case of Belichick, destined to be a first-ballot NFL Hall of Fame inductee whenever he steps away from the game. Poole, a gifted and tenaciously hard-working athlete, won a pair of Super Bowl rings during his stay in Foxboro with the Patriots. He played one of the game's most difficult positions—where the smallest misstep could result in a touchdown for the opposition—at a high level, and for longer than most.

Through all the grueling training camps, practices, film sessions, conversations with coaches, big plays and missed plays, pressure-packed playoff games, and competing in Super Bowls with the world watching, the amount of knowledge he wrapped his arms around was enormous. Even more impressive than the career he had, and the glittery championship rings that are among the highlights, is what he is doing with those lessons learned and knowledge gained during all those hard-hitting Sunday afternoons. These days, he's putting that extensive database of knowledge to good use: impacting the young lives of those he now coaches in a variety of youth sports.

"I'm just out to try and bring the best out of the kids, whether it's eight-year-old third-graders or soon-to-be teenage girls," says Poole, who has coached boys and girls flag football, basketball, and baseball. "It's fun when you have that impact on people's lives. That's what it's all about at the end of the day."

Poole is aware of how influential an adult's words can be. Growing up in LaGrange, Georgia, he played every sport imaginable with his friends in the neighborhood. There was soccer, football, basketball, kickball and dodgeball. And sometimes, in order to play a sport, it required some creative thinking.

"We didn't have bats," Poole says. "So for baseball, we would break off a broom handle—our parents would get mad—and we would use any type of round ball we could find." Dreams of a professional sports career hadn't materialized at this point, as he simply loved playing games with his friends, and he wouldn't experience organized sports for the first time until the eighth grade, when he played basketball.

He first played organized football in the ninth grade. When he gathers with his youth sports teams—regardless if it's on fields or courts, or with boys or girls—he calls upon an enormous and impressive Rolodex of lessons learned from his NFL playing days to touch kids' lives. Following an All-American career at Fort Valley State in Georgia, the Carolina Panthers nabbed Poole in the first round (22nd overall) in the 1995 NFL Draft. He was the second draft choice in the history of the Carolina franchise (behind Kerry Collins) and the first defensive back taken in that year's draft. He also spent three years in Charlotte playing for Dom Capers, a former NFL Coach of the Year and Super Bowl champion.

"I began with Carolina and Dom Capers. He was a coach who was very detailed, and that's what I try to do with the young athletes that I work with," Poole says. "I try to help them understand all the details. For example, I coached my son's baseball team, and I tried to be detailed with them, and that's what the parents like. I never played baseball myself, but whatever it is I'm doing, I go and I study it. I look at videos and take the basic principles back to the kids. It's all details. It's all about checking your stance, making sure you can touch the outside of the plate with your bat, bringing your top thumb up toward your ear, having the bat lean back, knees bent, and waiting on that back foot. I tell them to go through that ritual every time they come up to the plate. I'm very detailed, and I learned that from Dom Capers."

Being detail-oriented applies to all skills, in all sports. As Poole says, it's all in the details. If coaches aren't honing in on the details of helping young athletes master the fundamental elements of basic skills, their journey in the sport is going to be filled with frustration and failure as they enter more competitive levels of play. Devoting practice time to those details that may seem small—like a youngster's grip on the bat—typically has big consequences later.

After spending three seasons anchoring the Carolina secondary Poole joined the Indianapolis Colts, where he played three seasons before ending up in Denver playing for Mike Shanahan, a three-time Super Bowl champion.

"Playing for Mike Shanahan, I learned to let players be who they are," says Poole. "I'm not going to change you; all I am going to do is put you in the best position to help the team win. I'm going to let you be you. I'm going to let you be you, as long as you are respectful to the team."

Translation: kids are going to show up with all sorts of different personalities, but as long as they are true team players and respectful to officials, opponents, and coaches, it's important for coaches to allow the uniqueness of each child to shine. Not every player is going to emerge as a vocal leader, for example. Some will lean toward the more reserved end of the spectrum, and that's fine. Coaches have to adjust to each player, and discover what works best for each. It's unfair, and unrealistic, to expect every child to behave the same way and respond to instruction and feedback the same way. It doesn't work, nor should you want to try and force that. Instead, invest in each child. Appreciate who they are, and show you genuinely care.

"You have to bring passion," Poole says. "Kids are some of the smartest people in this world who can recognize when you are there for them and when you are not. You have to come with real passion. If the kids see that you care about them, and that you are involved as much as they are, they engage better. I try to engage with them and make it fun."

> ## "Kids are some of the smartest people in this world who can recognize when you are there for them and when you are not. You have to come with real passion."

That critical fun factor can get nudged out of the picture when young athletes are being introduced to new skills and fighting through the frustrations that accompany all the difficulties of learning something different. So part of the process of making it a more productive, and enjoyable, experience for them is in the messaging of the coach. Too often young athletes will have unrealistic expectations of being able to perform new skills perfectly right away, when in reality it's going to take countless hours of practice to truly get a handle on it.

"I always tell kids I didn't just wake up knowing how to do this drill," Poole says. "So I tell them that I know they're going to struggle. That's the other part of this—as coaches, you have to understand that the kids are going to struggle, and you have to know when to pat them on the back. If you can understand those things, and paint those pictures for them, the kids will engage better and always want to be around you."

When Poole signed with the New England Patriots before the 2003 NFL season, he had played eight years in the league, but he never stopped learning. With the Patriots that year, he started at cornerback on a team that went 14-2 and defeated the Carolina Panthers—the team that drafted Poole—in Super Bowl XXXVIII. The Patriots' Belichick, widely regarded as one of the all-time coaching greats, is known for many things: beyond the monotone press conferences with the media, it's his almost supernatural ability to take a player, put him in a position to succeed, and then coach and work with him to get his best effort on game day.

"I learned from Bill Belichick how to motivate players and how to get the best out of them," Poole says. "How to put them in situations where they can be successful. Again, using the baseball team I coached as an example: they are third graders, and they allow a coach to be out there in the outfield with them. So, to help them be successful, where they can maximize their potential to make a play, I mark in the dirt where my outfielders should stand. I tell them, 'that's your mark, you stand right here. No matter what happens, you run back to this mark every time a new batter comes up to the plate.' I'm putting them in position where they won't forget where they need to be, so that they will be in the best position possible to make a play. I learned that from Bill Belichick: to put your players in a position where they can make a play."

This ties into Capers and being detailed. As a coach of young athletes, a big part of your job involves putting kids in position to make plays, but also explaining to them the *why* behind your motives. To fully comprehend what is going on, and to help gain an understanding of all the facets of the sport, letting kids know the *why* helps them learn how to eventually make adjustments on their own during games. When kids are able to identify for themselves certain in-game adjustments, without having to be told, that's when you know your players are truly engaged in the game, and are embracing your input.

For example, in youth basketball, most young players will drive to the basket with their dominant hand simply because it takes time, and lots of practice, to become comfortable handling the ball with both hands. So during games, if an opposing player is having a lot of success getting by a defender and getting close in opportunities to score or pass to a teammate, this is where those words echoed by Poole enter the picture. To help the defender, the coach can have him move a half step over toward the player's dominant hand while defending him, thus making it more difficult for him to slice into the lane to create scoring opportunities for himself or a teammate. Subtle moves like this enable the player to enjoy more success on the defensive end of the floor. Plus, they learn the importance of adapting to an opponent's strengths and being aware of those in-game adjustments that are needed to adapt to the flow of the game—regardless of the sport.

One doesn't have to have made more than 450 tackles during a long and successful NFL career, or had Super Bowl confetti rain down on them like Poole has had, to be a successful coach who changes young lives through sports. But the lessons Poole shares should be embraced and utilized, along with drawing on some of your own sports experiences that may also apply. For instance, just like Poole shares with his players that he didn't master drills the first several times going through them when he was playing, open up with your team on the difficulties you experienced learning skills that you are now teaching them. It connects you to the kids and shows that you share a common bond. Young athletes relate to that, and respond to it, too. It also humanizes you, which players appreciate. It helps them recognize that these difficulties and struggles are a part of sports and that everyone, regardless of skill level or experience, goes through. But by working hard, staying motivated, and bringing maximum effort to every practice, improvement and progress await.

"What I try to tell the kids that I coach is that if at the end of the day, you can say you gave your best effort, that's all that matters," Poole says. "If you give your best effort, you're going to win more than you're going to lose. Yes, you're going to lose some, but if you give your best effort and you keep coming back, then you are a winner."

Matt Rhule

Baylor University head football coach ▪ Led Temple University
to the 2016 American Athletic Conference title ▪ Coached
on Tom Coughlin's staff with the New York Giants

 During one of Matt Rhule's recent reclamation projects—resurrecting a Temple University football program that had detoured into hard times—you could often find him at the FDR Park in South Philly during the offseason, when the warmer temperatures emerged from winter hibernation. And a few of his staff members would accompany him. Now, there was plenty of good football for the group to digest, dissect, and most definitely savor, considering Rhule had done a masterful job in leading the Owls back to respectability with twenty wins during a two-year span. But their talks at the time had nothing to do with enhancing the Owls' Red Zone offense, boosting third down efficiency, or devising new defensive wrinkles to confuse opposing teams in the fall. Instead, it was all about organizing fun practices, teaching skills, setting line-ups, and making sure there were plenty of *snacks*.

You see, for most of the year, Rhule had the mega responsibility of overseeing more than 100 student-athletes at Temple, but during the off-season, he put his coaching skills to use coaching the Wizards, a youth baseball team of eleven and twelve-year-olds that included his son, Bryant. While the sports are dramatically different, and the skill levels of the Division 1 scholarship football players were of course significantly greater than those of the young ballplayers, there was also a lot of common ground as Rhule navigated the baseball season. For starters, coaching is about developing players, no matter the level. It simply has to be a part of every philosophy.

"Our focus is 100 percent on player development," says Rhule, who, after four seasons at Temple, took over as the head coach at Baylor University in Waco, Texas in 2017. "I want to win, don't get me wrong, but my job is to make sure that every coach that is here has what they need to help every player develop. If we can make each player as good as he can be, then the natural by-product will be winning."

"If we can make each player as good as he can be, then the natural by-product will be winning."

When coaches become too enamored with the scoreboard, and fixating on the team's win-loss numbers, skill development is going to take a big hit, and chances are many players will go through the season without seeing a whole lot of progress.

"If our only focus is on winning, we won't develop players in all areas of the game, both on the field and off the field," Rhule says.

So, when he worked with the Wizards, developing every player on the roster was the central theme. Yes, on game days, the team played as hard as it could, and of course played to win the game. If those wins came, that was great; but more importantly throughout the process, Rhule knew the entire team was learning all-important skills about the game, about the ups and downs of competing, and about themselves. And they were having a lot of fun doing so, too.

"So to me, it's no different at the youth level," Rhule says of coaching. "When I'm coaching my eleven-year-old son in baseball, the goal is for the players to be competitive, not for the coaches to be competitive. My job is to teach young athletes how to play the game, develop their skills, and develop their understanding of the game. In youth sports, if you have a complete and total focus on developing all your players, regardless of their ability levels, and try to make them the best that they can be, you'll usually naturally win, and the players will have a much better experience than if they played for somebody whose sole focus was on winning games."

The process of developing players is never a smooth Point A to Point B journey. It's part of what makes coaching young athletes so challenging, fascinating, and ultimately so rewarding. There are numerous ups and downs that await, and the season will be filled with unpredictability at every turn. But when it all starts to come together, and young players recognize what is happening and they're beginning to see the results of their work and your coaching, they'll get that bounce in their step and that look in their eye that makes it all worthwhile.

The starting point for getting players to this special juncture is handling the mistakes that will be made along the way. You can bet the young Wizards made a ton of them, and the same goes for those college athletes that have suited up for Rhule at Temple and now Baylor, too. That's certainly not a news flash. Mistakes occur at every level of play, and in every sport. It's about what the coach is able to do, and what message is being sent in the wake of them, that makes all the difference moving forward.

"One of the biggest things that prevents people from being successful is the anxiety that comes from worrying about what you did wrong, or what could possibly go wrong," Rhule says. "We have sort of a mantra here, which is very simply that whatever just happened, albeit good or bad or neutral, our focus immediately goes on to what the next thing is. It's about trying to be great at the next thing. It's an every down, every play thing. As a coach, you have to consistently and constantly coach it."

It can't be random messages; it's got to be hammered into young players and modeled by coaches for young athletes to buy into the philosophy and break free of the anxiety that often prevents many from performing at their best. "Whether it's on the practice field or in the meeting room, it's something we're talking about all the time," Rhule says. "It's constantly forgetting about what just happened, flushing what just happened, and moving on."

That tenuous attribute known as confidence comes and goes in the blink of an eye with young athletes. Don't expect to be able to simply tell an athlete to be confident and have those good vibes just naturally settle into their mind. It's going to require hard work, and it's not going to happen until an athlete achieves success, Rhule says.

"I don't believe that confidence comes from somewhere else," he explains. "I don't believe it's external, and I don't believe it comes from people telling you that you are doing a good job. Confidence to me comes from when you demonstrate that you can do something, and you know you can do it, and you know you are in control of the situation."

This is where coaches make their mark, taking an athlete through the steps needed to perform a particular skill, on a consistent basis, while opposing players are doing whatever they can to prevent it from happening. "We just try to keep coaching, teaching, and correcting, and making sure they understand that it's not personal," Rhule says. "All we're trying to do is get to the point where they can do it, and that's where true confidence comes from."

All athletes respond to coaching differently. Younger players relatively new to the competitive aspects of sports are likely to take feedback more personally than an elite level athlete who has been playing for years. It's tricky territory, for sure, but explaining to athletes from the season's outset what your role is can help alleviate some of those hurt feelings that arise with those players who are sensitive to feedback that is designed to help them correct mistakes or smooth out flaws in their execution of a particular skill.

"We try to make sure that they understand from the very beginning that it is the coach's job to find what you are doing right and what you are doing wrong, and to help you correct mistakes," Rhule says. "It is important that they understand that there is never anything personal. If we find something you did wrong, we're going to tell you that you did it wrong, make you do it right, and if you can get them to stay corrected, that's where confidence comes. It's not from pointing out what went wrong, but when that thing that's been going wrong eventually goes right, to me that's where true confidence comes from."

Rhule pulls it all together by making sure he and his staff hit on three key points—development, enjoyment, and competitiveness—which are valuable to keep in mind while working with young athletes in your chosen sport.

"Number one, make the consistent focus on development," he says. "Anytime where you are providing a plan where you are helping people get better and they're seeing themselves improve, that's fun. Number two, it's having relationships and making sure we enjoy the process with the things that we are saying and the way that we are coaching is important. And the third thing is, we try to make everything competition. A lot of people make the mistake where they practice, but they don't make it competitive. Whether it's one on one or seven on seven team drills, we try to make it a competitive entity where they're not just thinking about everything that they are doing, but instead they're playing the game, having fun, competing, winning some plays, losing some plays, and learning how to go out there and play just like they would on the playground."

Greg Schiano

Associate Head Football Coach at The Ohio
State University ▪ 2006 Eddie Robinson Coach
of the Year ▪ 2006 Big East Coach of the Year ▪
Played college football at Bucknell University

During the mid-2000s, a seismic shift rattled the college football landscape, creating chaos with the polls, startling the so-called experts, and grabbing the attention of fans nationwide, and it originated from the neighboring New Jersey cities of New Brunswick and Piscataway. It was there that a reclamation project of mammoth proportions was underway, led by a young coach by the name of Greg Schiano, who grew up in the state and played his high school football there.

Named the head coach of Rutgers University in 2000, the then thirty-four-year-old Schiano had the formidable, and unenviable, task of resuscitating a program that hadn't even made a bowl game *appearance* in nearly thirty years. His first two seasons didn't turn heads, as they replicated the decades of losing that the Scarlet Knights and their fans had become far too accustomed to, with just three wins total during that span. But gradually, Schiano began to build something special. Rutgers posted a winning record in 2005, then came back and won an astounding eleven games the following season, and even climbed to as high as number six in the national polls at one point. The team ended its bowl game drought in remarkable fashion by winning five straight bowl games.

Coaches don't orchestrate those type of massive turnarounds unless they possess fabulous teaching skills and recognize how to get those points across to athletes in myriad ways. As Schiano points out, coaching is not a one-way street of disseminating information. Athletes aren't robots; they don't digest instructions the same way or respond to feedback in an identical manner.

"To me, athletics is another type of intelligence," Schiano says. "Just like how some people learn math one way and others learn it another way, everyone has their own ways of learning athletics. So when you teach that intelligence, you have to keep using different methods to get through to all the kids. But there has to be a common denominator of what you are striving to achieve in your teaching, so there may be a different way to say it, but at the end of the day, everyone is learning the same critical skill."

As those lessons are being imparted by coaches to their young athletes, the man who gobbled up all the noteworthy coach of the year awards during the Scarlet Knights' remarkable run to prominence in 2006 reminds those working with youngsters to lean heavily on communicating in a positive fashion.

"Being positive is the biggest thing," Schiano says. "Nobody wants to have someone just downing them all the time, so find positives." Schiano's words are laced with passion and intensity fills the air as he speaks. "I often talk to leaders and coaches," he continues. "And I tell them that your words can be one of two things: They can be words of construction, or words of destruction. There's usually not an in-between. The words of construction keep building people up. It's easy to tear them down with those words of destruction."

Coaches enter that danger zone of destructive behavior when they are recognizing and correcting mistakes, and doing so with frustration in their eyes or venom in their body language or words. Attacking the player verbally isn't what good teaching is all about, and it certainly isn't a tactic that inspires young athletes to dig deeper or work harder. Good coaching is about finding the right way and the proper words and tone that fit that particular situation.

A player learning a new skill during the first week of practice will probably benefit from a lot of encouraging words and reminders from the coach that this is going to take awhile to grasp, so he can temper his expectations and not be overwhelmed by feelings of frustration. And when athletes run into difficulty later in the season—perhaps the quarterback has hit a slump where his passes are lacking velocity due to improper mechanics—the coach will have to identify the best way to help that young athlete return to his earlier season form. It may require talking about how well he threw earlier in the season, when he would follow through toward the target, or referencing how good his footwork was, or the way he positioned his body while dropping back in the pocket. Whatever it is, pinpoint it and go over it with the player in a manner and tone that encourages—not discourages—him.

"Tell your team what you want," Schiano says. "When a player doesn't do what you want him to do, make it clear, as his coach, what he needs to achieve. Keep building him up with, 'you can do this. Just keep working at it.' Now granted, I understand that people get frustrated, but especially in youth sports, no one is losing their job on the win or the loss at the end of the day, so let's make sure that the kids come back next time and play."

Following the Rutgers' resurgence, Schiano was lured to the NFL with the challenge of rebooting the Tampa Bay Buccaneers. At the end of Schiano's first season in Tampa, he gave all the players surveys, as his quest for knowledge and feedback on ways he can improve is never-ending. The players could fill them out anonymously or attach their name to them. As a coach who is constantly evaluating players and providing them with feedback, he turned the tables and asked his players to assess his coaching approach and indicate areas that he could improve upon, too.

Schiano's dismissal from Tampa following his second season never doused his passion for learning and discovering new and better ways to coach and impact athletes. He spent some of his newfound free time volunteering at the Tampa area high school, where his three sons played football. His official title was assistant defensive line coach. And he loved every minute of it. While his coaching credentials speak volumes, he advises coaches of young athletes who don't have those impressive coaching resumes to be consistent to gain players' respect.

"[Y]our words can be one of two things: They can be words of construction or words of destruction. There's usually not an in-between."

"All athletes want to know if they behave a certain way, they are going to get a certain response," he says. "If one day, the same behavior gets a different response, that makes people uncomfortable. What you are trying to do is find a comfort zone for any athlete at any level so they can go out and do their best. Consistent responses and consistent teaching is critical."

As athletes progress in sports to higher levels of competition, games will become more competitive. Along with that, athletes will put in more work, invest more emotionally into the contest, and consequently, take those setbacks hard. Helping players sort through those emotions is paramount for being able to draw something positive from the experience and put their attention on what game is next, rather than lingering on the loss for too long.

"We talk a lot about doing the best that you can do, and at the end of the day, if you tried your hardest, there really is nothing else that you could have done, right?" says Schiano, who is now the associate head football coach at

The Ohio State University. "So as the players get older and more serious about the game, did they do the best they could in their preparation leading up to the event and put their best foot forward on game day, or did they let an official's call or a bad play get them out of sorts and affect future plays? There's a lot of different things you can teach them, but at the end of the day, if they can honestly say they did the best they could, then win or lose, you really can't ask for any more than that."

As a coach, you want your team to play hard, play within the rules, play to win, and of course, do it all while displaying good sportsmanship. "I don't think there's anything wrong with competitiveness and showing your competitive nature," Schiano says. "It's just keeping it positive and within good sportsmanship. You don't want to act like it doesn't matter. There's a reason that competitive people do better in this world, so there's nothing wrong with having a competitive spirit. But that's what it has to be—a competitive spirit."

So naturally, coaches and their players will experience wins and losses along the way, and it's imperative that coaches don't overhype the wins or get sullen on the setbacks. Rather than riding a roller-coaster of emotions based on the scoreboard, learn to accept outcomes and move on from them.

"One of the things that I've always thought is when your income doesn't rely on the outcome of the game, don't take it too seriously," Schiano says. "I do this for a living, so if the outcome isn't right enough times, I don't get to keep doing it. But that's not the case in youth sports, so keep it in perspective."

David Shaw

Stanford University football coach ▪ Four-time Pac-12 Coach of the Year ▪ Former NFL assistant coach ▪ Played wide receiver during his collegiate playing days at Stanford

In the fall of 1993, a young wide receiver by the name of David Shaw was making his second career start for the Stanford Cardinal. Following a season-opening loss at twelfth ranked Washington the previous week, the Cardinal were facing San Jose State in their home opener. More than 47,000 fans, the vast majority sporting the Cardinal red and white, had gathered at Stanford Stadium that afternoon. During a tight battle, the inexperienced Shaw, who had a handful of catches to his credit at this early juncture in his collegiate career, believed he spotted a weakness in the San Jose State secondary that could be exploited. While he was on the sidelines, he informed his coach that he felt he could get behind the safeties for a big play.

The white-haired coach listened to his young receiver, trusted him, and eventually called a play that put the receiver's observations into action. The result? Moments later, Shaw had caught the first touchdown pass of his collegiate career and provided the first glimpse that he had the makings of being a football coach himself someday. Later in the contest, he would also snag the game-winning touchdown pass to help Stanford secure an exciting 31–28 victory. So, what's the relevance of that particular play? And that sideline conversation between a long-time coach and an inexperienced player?

Well, the head coach on the Stanford sideline that afternoon was Bill Walsh. Yes, *that* Bill Walsh, the iconic coach who won three Super Bowl championships with the San Francisco 49ers, was a two-time NFL Coach of the Year, and is a member of the Pro Football Hall of Fame. Walsh was in his second season of his second go-around with Stanford, having returned to the school following his Super Bowl titles and broadcasting career. The only way that sideline conversation takes place is because Walsh, besides his innovative genius with the West Coast offense, was a master at handling people, building genuine relationships, and getting players to perform at the peak of their abilities. Plus, he was a listener. He gave players his full attention, and they reciprocated with their best effort. It's a lesson Shaw not only has never forgotten, but that is in play every day for him, too, as he patrols the Stanford sideline as head coach and even occupies the same office that his beloved mentor once did.

If Shaw didn't feel comfortable speaking to his coach in the heat of the action that long-ago afternoon, that play may never have been called. And that game may have turned out differently. Walsh also could have showed up on Stanford's Palo Alto campus with a ballooning ego—which would have been understandable considering the incredible success he enjoyed following that trio of Super Bowl triumphs—and could have been uninterested in player feedback, or not find it necessary to establish relationships with everyone. It was all absorbed by Shaw, widely recognized today as not only one of the best coaches in football, but someone who genuinely cares about every single player on his roster.

"For me, it's constantly going back and forth between talking about football and talking about life," Shaw says of building and cementing relationships with players, the kinds that carry life-long impact, from the Stanford football office. "That comes from years of learning by being around Bill Walsh and Jon Gruden (head coach of the Oakland Raiders), and other people who have had a lot of success by making those connections." Meaningful relationships, the special ones that athletes both benefit from while playing and can reflect on and savor long after their athletic careers have faded, requires hard work. It's not something that materializes with sporadic effort during occasional practices. It needs to be at the forefront of every practice. It's why Shaw says it has to be on a coach's to-do list right out of the starting gates of the season.

"It goes unnoticed at times," Shaw says. "You've got to get to know the kids. What do they like? What don't they like? What are they good at? What are they not good at? How can I best communicate with this individual to get them to first, learn and understand; and then second, to perform at their best. To be able to say I know Jeffrey is different than Donald, and I need to develop an individual relationship with each of them in order to help them succeed. And it takes some skill to a certain degree to be able to do that across the team and not look like you're playing favorites. But saying, I need to have a relationship with each one of you guys, and I'm going to need to do and say whatever I need to get you to be at your best."

These relationships aren't established in the blink of an eye, or even over the course of a single practice session, or interactions during a week. It's going to take time, and a coach's full attention, to begin peeling back the layers on players' personalities, and discovering who they are, what they are about, how they respond to feedback, and what gets their juices flowing. As coaches begin to piece together how players relate and respond to coaching, they can formulate plans for teaching, encouraging, motivating, and inspiring them.

"If young players do enjoy football, there are going to be tough days, but we can make things competitive without making them combative," Shaw says. "During practices, at meetings, you can have some fun, play some music, and laugh with the players—and then turn back around and coach them. As a coach, as long as I have a relationship with the young man, I can raise my voice because he trusts me; he trusts me that I'm trying to make him better. I am not trying to belittle him, embarrass him, or hurt him in any way, shape, or form. I just want more out of him."

Shaw goes on, "And as long as that relationship is established, yes, I can raise my voice and ten minutes later crack a joke at him because he knows I still care a lot about him. But I'm not going to accept anything less than his best effort. And that's what's difficult sometimes at the youth levels—understanding that I'm going to tell you what to do and you're going to have to do it, and if you don't, there will be repercussions. But at the same time, I'm going to put my arm around you because I like you and I care about you and I want you to be successful both in this sport and in life."

"We're emphasizng hard work. We're emphasizing improvement. We're not necessarily emphasizing perfection."

From the outset, be precise in what you are striving to achieve with young athletes; be exacting with the atmosphere surrounding the team; and don't waver on how you're going to approach it. "A lot of it has to do with the environment that you set," Shaw says. "Young people follow the guidance of older people and experienced people. What are we emphasizing? We're emphasizing hard work, we're emphasizing improvement. We're not necessarily emphasizing perfection. 'Hey, you did it this way, so here's a way to do it better. Hey, you made a mistake, so let's learn from it. That's not going to work, but here's what is going to work.' That's what the best coaches and teachers have always done, which is to take something negative and make it a positive, as opposed to continuing to harp on the negative. So it's all in what you emphasize with young people."

Shaw soaked up every morsel of advice dispensed by Walsh and made countless mental notes of how the legendary coach interacted and motivated players. Walsh was well-known as a master at controlling the team's locker-room. Shaw can describe in remarkable detail how Walsh would use a joke to lighten the mood and then have that special touch to transition to a serious mode the next instant. It's a balancing act, for sure, but when coaches have connected with players, it creates incredible opportunities for controlling emotions while inspiring and helping young athletes perform to the best of their abilities.

"You always start with the fact that nobody is perfect," Shaw says. "Sometimes, for young coaches, it is hard to say to a player: 'Hey, you know what, I mess up periodically, too. I'm not perfect. So we need to go into this thing together and see how good we can be by learning from our mistakes. Mistakes happen, and we've got to learn from them and move past them so we don't repeat them.' So it's about the approach that you go into it, realizing that you can damage a young person and hurt them going forward both in the sport and out of the sport, by browbeating them on something that they didn't do intentionally."

Shaw continues, "I'll never forget that somebody told me a long time ago, early in coaching: 'Do you think these guys make mistakes on purpose? There's a reason why they're called mistakes, a reason why they're called accidents, why they're called learning experiences.' It's up to us to identify them and then solve the problem of them occurring so that they don't occur again."

Buck Showalter

Baltimore Orioles Manager ▪ Three-time American
League Manager of the Year ▪ Won more than 1,500
games ▪ All-American at Mississippi State University

Every March, when the Baltimore Orioles descend on Ed Smith Stadium in Sarasota, Florida—their spring training home since 2010—you can bet that longtime manager Buck Showalter has done his homework on all the players arriving for camp. A lot of it. Now, this particular research doesn't have anything to do with batting averages versus left-handers, on-base percentages or strikeout-to-walk ratios. Instead, the three-time American League Manager of the Year and winner of more than 1,500 big league games digs into the backgrounds of the players. Every single one of them.

So regardless if a player has a legitimate shot of making the Orioles' Opening Day roster and playing at famed Camden Yards against the likes of the Red Sox and Yankees, or if they're destined for another summer of long bus trips for games against the Rochester Red Wings, Charlotte Knights, and Louisville Bats, Showalter is going to learn something about them. Maybe it's where they went to high school; or how many brothers and sisters they grew up with; or how many kids they have of their own. It enables him to connect with them. Converse with them. And make them feel a real part of the team.

It's because Showalter exemplifies what coaching and managing—at any level—is all about. It's crafting those personal connections. It's forging bonds with players, finding conversation igniters, uncovering their passions and figuring out what their personalities are all about. He's been involved at all levels of the game, both as a player and leader of teams, so he understands the nuances and challenges that accompany overseeing a group—and the rewards that await when it's done well. You see, Showalter just so happens to be a big proponent of volunteers going about their coaching roles the right way. It's why he believes that what he does every spring with the players who come through his clubhouse doors is really no different from what youth coaches should be doing at the start of their season with their young players who are climbing out of minivans at their local baseball fields. It all starts with connecting with every single child.

"Well, there's a lot of comparisons, because I always try to look for the buttons with players," Showalter says, seated at the indoor batting cages at the Orioles' spring training complex amid buckets of baseballs, resin bags, and hitting tees. "I spend a lot of time looking at their bios. Where did they go to school? What country are they from? What state? You try to have some hook that gives you a personal in with them."

Showalter explains, "We have sixty players in camp. The first day you walk in, and there is some guy that nobody has ever seen, you have to walk by him and talk about his nickname from high school or his team colors, or learn his wife's name, or ask about a coach that he had. I can't tell you how much that means to them to have a personal connection right off the bat. It requires a little homework. Really watching and understanding what someone's button is so important. Why are they doing this? Is it because their parents are making them? Is it because they enjoy the game? Is it because one of their friends is playing? There are a lot of different reasons."

By asking the right questions, coaches can discover a player's reasons for being there. You can learn a little bit about their families, what their home life is like, and who their role models are. You can also find out what types of experiences they have had with the sport, who their favorite players are, and what position they have their eye on. And, as Showalter suggested, you may discover some insight that will enable you to be a better coach. For instance, if the child is passionate about the game and has been playing for awhile, he will likely be more receptive to your instruction and feedback; while those kids who are there because their parents have pushed them to the sport will have additional challenges in the areas of motivation, energy levels, and attention spans.

So consider Showalter's words and latch onto his approach. If it's proven to be an effective method in a Major League clubhouse for helping players genuinely feel more comfortable in their surroundings and cared for as more than just athletes, then it's certainly a worthy strategy to employ with kids—both newcomers to the sport as well as those highly skilled youngsters who have high school baseball careers in their futures. When players feel a connection to their coaches—whether it's T-ball, coach pitch, or even mega competitive travel team baseball—their love for the sport explodes.

Guess what else also happens? Their interest in working hard and their enthusiasm for pleasing their coach overflows. And that's the makings of a memorable season for everyone involved. Because when volunteer coaches are able to manufacture those types of results they have struck the coaching jackpot. Kids who are engaged, energized, and excited to be involved—because their coach cares about them as people more so than how effective they are at hitting with a 0-2 count or turning a double play—are going to carry lifelong lessons and memories with them. Plus, their chances of lacing up the spikes next season becomes more likely,

So, go ahead. Get to know your players. Just be sure to have a preseason parents meeting to introduce yourself, go over team rules, and outline your goals and expectations for the kids—and the moms and dads, too. This is also the perfect time to let parents know that you'll be engaging in conversations with their kids before, during, and after practices that at times will have nothing to do with the sport that you are coaching in an effort to get to know them a little bit better on a personal level. This alerts them that you're not prying for information behind their backs and you're not harboring any ill intentions; it's simply a courtesy extended to them that you are focused on connecting with everyone. You are establishing before the first pitch is ever thrown that you care about these kids for who they are, no matter how fast they can run the bases or how far they are capable of hitting a fastball.

> ### "Lighten up. Make it fun. Life's too short and childhood is too short. Would you want, as a kid, to play for you?"

Once those parameters are established and parents are aware of the importance being placed on knowing the young athletes, then coaches can dive into the process. "You're not just developing people for the next level," Showalter says of today's youth coaches. "You're developing people for the next level of life. I'm jealous; you have the chance to impact the heck out of kids, because they remember their coaches just like I remember all mine."

Just keep in mind that bonding with young athletes is just one piece of the coaching puzzle. If it's not tethered to other aspects, like practices that grab kids' attention and keep them moving, then all that time and effort that has been devoted to cultivating those relationships is going to get swept away in a forgettable season. Showalter has worked with young athletes and knows that, with so many activities and options pulling at their time these days, if baseball coaches don't infuse action and big doses of fun into their practices, then kids are going to chase other options in a heartbeat.

"My biggest challenge to youth coaches, and to those in high school, is to make it fun for the players," says Showalter, who was an All-American performer during his playing days at Mississippi State University. "One year I helped with my son's high school team, and the coach was asking me for pointers. I said, 'You have to make this fun.' I told him to look at the practice he ran yesterday. The kids sat around in the outfield for two hours shagging balls in batting practice. No wonder they're going to football and they're going to basketball and they're going to lacrosse. Why would they come do this? Let them play shortstop. Play intra-squad games. Start with 0-2 counts. Have movement. They want to run; they want to catch the ball; they want to throw it; they want to play different positions; have them put on the catching gear."

Translation: don't bore kids out of sports. Whether it's baseball or any other sport, if practices lack action and imagination and forces kids to stand in those dreaded lines, then chances are pretty good that they will begin not showing up at practices. And they probably won't be around the following season. As Showalter says point blank: "I always ask coaches, 'Would you want to come to your practice? Would you want to be part of your team? Is it fun? If I was in their shoes, why would I want to do this?'"

Showalter loves baseball. You can hear his passion for the game and see the fire in his eyes. He hates seeing kids being driven away from the game by coaches who fall short in their responsibilities. But, he knows there are a lot of great people who just need to be reminded that they have an incredible opportunity to infuse a love of the game in kids and connect with them if they simply take the time to approach it the right way.

"Lighten up," he says. "Make it fun. Life's too short and childhood is too short. Would you want, as a kid, to play for you?"

Audra Smith

South Carolina State women's basketball coach ▪
Played college basketball at the University of Virginia
▪ Participated in three Final Fours as a player ▪
Named Miss Basketball in Georgia in 1988

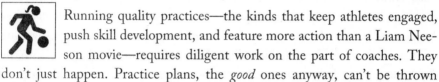 Running quality practices—the kinds that keep athletes engaged, push skill development, and feature more action than a Liam Neeson movie—requires diligent work on the part of coaches. They don't just happen. Practice plans, the *good* ones anyway, can't be thrown together at stoplights on the drive over. Or done on the fly during the actual practice, either.

A really solid plan takes time to put together: coaches must take into account the mood of the team, how it has been performing recently, and what they are looking to accomplish that week—and then figure out what course of action is going to make it happen. The best coaches carve out time in their schedules for constructing these plans, where they are outlining drills, devising innovative games and scrimmages, and even noting when to pause the action for water breaks throughout the session to help ensure that keeping players hydrated isn't overlooked, among other important aspects.

But guess what? Even after investing all that time and energy into putting together a wonderful plan, coaches must be ready to—are you ready for this—ditch it at a moment's notice. Everything. That's right, send the entire plan to the scrap pile.

"At every practice I'm excited and I'm ready to go," says Audra Smith, the head women's basketball coach at South Carolina State. "But sometimes our players will come in and I can tell that something is going on, that there must be a lot of assignments or projects due. So, we'll alter practice and do things a little bit differently. I may have wanted it to be a teaching day, like working on a new out-of-bounds play, but if looking at them you know it's not a teaching day, then it may be a day where we're going to need something that's fun and upbeat, like a lot of full-court drills, playing 3- to 4-minute scrimmage sessions, anything to try to create that positive atmosphere."

It is sometimes easy to forget that your players have lives outside of the sport they are playing for you. Other extracurricular activities, schoolwork, family gatherings, or even relationship issues with their boyfriend or girlfriend can monopolize their attention, infringe on their focus, and zap energy levels. Plus, how the season is unfolding can compromise attention levels, too. A disappointing loss days earlier may still be hovering over the team, clouding their concentration. Or maybe players endured a lot of difficulty during the previous practice and are expecting much of the same this go-around, too.

So, as players arrive for practice, observe their body language and gauge their enthusiasm levels as you greet them. If the sport is basketball, are they grabbing balls and getting right on the court to dribble and shoot because they are genuinely excited to get going, or are they lingering on the sidelines waiting for the coach to get the practice rolling? If it's soccer, are kids jogging onto the field and passing balls back and forth among themselves and taking shots on goal, or are they sitting on the bench with their heads buried in their phones?

Based on pre-practice observations, coaches must be ready to alter, or even ditch, their original plans. "Maybe you have had three straight hard practices and you can tell that they're thinking, 'oh no, we're going to have to do that ball handling drill that has a lot of running,'" Smith says. "So that's when you switch it up on them." Sometimes it can be tough to pull the trigger on that switch. After all, a lot of work was put into that practice plan. But a coach only has so many practices with their team throughout the course of a season. Wasting a 60- or 90-minute session sticking to a specific plan serves no purpose, other than to reveal a coach's stubbornness, or inability to adapt to the needs of his or her team that day.

"What happens is you have your mind set on, 'today we're going to work on a new offense or our 1-2-2 full-court pressure,'" Smith says. "And if you start out and your kids are just dragging through it, or they just can't seem to grasp it, it tends to frustrate you as a coach. The kids feed off of that and start to feel frustrated, too, so then they become more tense and more tight."

Whatever was planned for that day can be set aside and revisited at the next practice, when players may be more engaged and receptive to what the coach wants to teach. Practice time must be maximized, not minimized, and a lot can still be accomplished on those days when plans are changed. "A lot of times we're practicing and going over things and the kids are just not focused and not there, so we'll move on to something else," Smith says. "My whole philosophy is that practices need to be productive. If your players are not focused that day, you're not going to be able to drill anything in to them, so you need to wait and teach that offensive set at the next practice. Some days you have to do something where you don't have to think as much; where they can just run, catch, shoot, and play."

One of Smith's go-to drills are scrimmages in which different rules are in play for each team. "We'll do 3-minute segments where the orange team can only play zone defense the entire time," she says. "Even on missed shots, they have to get back into a zone. The purple team is in man-to-man defense the entire time." Adjusting the rules and giving players a different element to contend with adds sizzle. Rather than a basic scrimmage that players have competed in countless times, mixing things up on occasion grabs their attention, the intensity level rises, and production increases.

What Smith does has applications for any sport. For example, in a soccer scrimmage, a coach can have one team only attempt shots with their right foot and the opposing side just their left foot; in volleyball, one side only gets one touch of the ball to get it over the net while the other side gets two touches; in baseball, assign random counts to hitters as they step into the box, so some have a 3-0 count and others have to deal with being in the hole at 1-2, and so on.

"Coaches at the grassroots level are the most important, because they teach players the fundamentals and how to play the game."

Just like a Vegas gambler, athletes love action. They want opportunities to use their skills, and work on others. The more creative and interesting the setting the coach creates, the better for all involved. "Ultimately that's what they want to do—they want to play," Smith says. "And the biggest thing is kids need to learn how to play the game and play together. As they are playing, you can stop them and say, 'you need to run the sideline a little bit wider so you are on a proper angle going in for a lay-up' or 'you need to keep your head up while dribbling so you can see the whole floor.' So you can do teaching within these games."

Smith points out how important coaches are at the younger levels of play. She knows how important they were in her rise through the ranks, eventually playing college basketball at the University of Virginia. Even though the vast majority of athletes will never play a Division I sport like Smith, the lessons they learn through participation are bountiful. And, they will have a deep love for a game that can bring years of enjoyment both as a player and perhaps even as a coach someday, too.

"As a youth coach, it's important to understand that it's a game and you're trying to teach and help these young kids improve," Smith says. "These coaches at the grassroots level are the most important, because they teach players the fundamentals and how to play the game. Kids already have that added pressure. Coaches need to step back and not get so caught up in everything and understand that if they are relaxed, their team is going to be relaxed."

That pressure Smith references often comes from parents on game days. Whether they realize it or not, it's there. "I've been at games where kids are six and seven years old and parents are screaming from the stands 'you've got to make that shot' or 'what are you doing,'" Smith says. "So kids will hear that screaming from the stands and feel like they are not playing up to their potential and you, as the coach, say, 'you're fine. I have confidence in you. Yeah, you missed the last couple shots, but so what? Keep shooting, you're one of our best shooters.' Or if he missed a defensive assignment, just say 'relax, I know you're going to be able to defend because you're a great defender. Just go play hard. Just work hard and play to the best of your ability.' That's the biggest thing that I preach, even to my kids. I have three E's: Effort, Energy and Enthusiasm. You give me 100 percent effort, you play with a ton of energy, and you play with enthusiasm. We're here to have fun. If you have fun and you do those three things, you're going to be successful."

And it all starts with practices. Coaches must go in with a good plan to make it all happen, and be ready to dump it and move on whenever necessary.

Charlotte Smith

Elon University Women's Basketball Coach ▪ 2017 Colonial
Athletic Association Coach of the Year ▪ Most Outstanding
Player of the 1994 Final Four ▪ First Team All-American in
1995 ▪ Two-time ACC Tournament MVP (1994 and 1995)

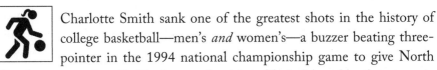 Charlotte Smith sank one of the greatest shots in the history of college basketball—men's *and* women's—a buzzer beating three-pointer in the 1994 national championship game to give North Carolina a stunning 60-59 win over Louisiana Tech. It's a shot that put several exclamation points on a truly special game that will forever be remembered, as well as ensured that those final moments will be re-watched on YouTube by basketball fans everywhere forever. What was less publicized though, and easily overlooked amid the euphoria that shook the Richmond, Virginia, Coliseum that evening, was this nifty nugget: Smith kept the statistician really busy by also yanking down an astounding twenty-three rebounds. So, it's no surprise that you-know-who was named the Final Four's Most Outstanding Player.

Smith was one of those special players that coaches dream about having on the roster, and that opponents dread facing, because she loved being a difference maker in all areas of the game. On the offensive end of the floor, she would knock down open shots and hit open teammates with passes; and defensively she would take charges, box out opposing players, and sprawl for any loose ball that was up for grabs. Now fast-forward a couple decades from those days, where her presence was felt all over the floor and that enthusiasm for embracing all facets of the game is as strong as ever. She has brought that same passion for the game to the Elon University women's basketball team, where she serves as head coach. The private liberal arts college sits less than forty miles from the Tar Heel campus in Chapel Hill, where she left her imprint on the game in so many areas beyond that championship-winning shot.

In today's youth sports culture, one that far too often is defined by a look-at-me mentality, where kids are hoisting shots every chance they get in the hopes of being noticed by travel team coaches or maneuvering themselves onto the radar screens of college coaches. So, important components of the game—things like rebounding, defending, and delivering passes to teammates for better opportunities to score—gets shoved to the side in the chase for that personal attention. It's one of the most pressing challenges coaches of all sports face these days: getting players to willingly forfeit the accolades that naturally get piled on the top scorer and exchange some of that attention for things like sacrificing a floor burn to grab a loose ball that generates another possession for the team and another opportunity to convert a basket; or absorbing some contact to set a screen that springs a teammate for an open shot.

It's those less-than-glamorous tasks that often are the most instrumental in swinging the momentum, and the game day results, in a team's favor. And that goes for any sport. If you're coaching basketball, of course you want players scrambling on the floor for loose balls with the same energy as if a $50 bill was laying there; if it's baseball or softball, you want players willing (and able) to lay down a well-placed bunt to move a baserunner over and gladly surrendering a chance to get on base because they want to do what is best for the team, rather than pad their personal stats; and if it's football you want (and need) guys who can block opponents and take satisfaction in creating the openings for the quarterback and running backs to maneuver.

So how does a coach make it happen? It's certainly doable, but it's not always easy. Plus, it's not enough for it to occur at random junctures throughout the season. It needs to happen every game, and that requires a concerted effort on the coach's part to cultivate a team mindset where everyone is working together in harmony for the overall benefit of the team.

"Players take what you emphasize to be what is important," says Smith, whose knowledge and coaching skills are so respected in basketball circles that she has served as an assistant coach on the USA Women's Under 18 National Team. "We try to emphasize a lot of the intangible things, a lot of the non-glamorous things." Because they really matter. They track stats like diving on the floor and taking charges. It's those non-glamorous and, at times, painful things players are willing to do that don't typically draw the attention that accompanies the player swishing a long-range shot, but that are integral to enjoying game day success and being a difficult team to play against.

Smith talks about this with her team a lot; it simply is just too important not to for any coach of any sport. But Smith actually does a lot more than simply talk about it with her troops. She backs it up, and her players are all-in on what it means to be an all-around player; a player that is willing to do more than loft shots to help the team.

"We grade a lot of different categories, and at the end of the game, whoever has the most points in terms of those statistics gets a stuffed animal that we present," Smith says. "For those non-glamorous things, we really emphasize just how important they are." So, what a great approach to take—and implement—with any team, in any sport, at any level. Coaches can follow Smith's lead and go the stuffed animal route, or get creative and come up with some other token that can easily be presented from game to game throughout the season that acknowledges players' efforts. Players will want to get their hands on these incentives, because the coach has made it clear they represent valuable contributions. It shifts noteworthy attention to a young athlete, and who doesn't love a reward for a job well done?

"I think the craft of teaching has been lost in the game, and there's a lot more criticizing and yelling than there is teaching nowadays. We have to understand that we have a great responsibility to the game that so many people love."

For example, it can be a hardhat with the team name and painted in the team colors, designating the player who worked the hardest. Or maybe it's a trophy that the recipient gets to take home and retains until the next game, or a basketball or football that the recipient signs, so as the season progresses players who captured the award will see their name displayed on it. There are endless possibilities. Coaches can even ask their players for input. You will be pleasantly surprised just how hard the players work and sacrifice to put themselves in contention for this special recognition, all while learning what teamwork is all about that will serve them well later in life while helping the team in the present.

There are significant benefits to approaching coaching in this manner. Of course, players learn about the obvious: teamwork and sacrifice. Consider the door that is opened for those players who may not be the strongest, tallest, quickest or the most athletically gifted at this point in their development, too. By recognizing, stressing, and applauding all aspects of the sport now, players have additional opportunities to excel and be appreciated for their efforts that unfortunately are not available on a lot of teams due to the mentality or philosophy in play.

So, by teaching all the details of the game, and acknowledging all contributions to these various aspects, you're creating opportunities. And memories. And those all-important team players that can carry that mindset into their future jobs and relationships where understanding how to work together for the greater good is in high demand, and sadly a diminishing commodity. In basketball, for example, every player can't go home and talk about how they were the leading scorer, but they can share how they led the team in charges taken or assists delivered. Just think how incredibly good that player who is presented the award for their efforts after the game will feel. You'll see it in their face and their body language. They'll certainly show up at the next practice with more confidence and more energy, too. In some instances that individual may not have made a single basket, or even had the chance to attempt a shot, but if they set some screens to free a teammate or made a couple of timely steals, they can feel really good about their efforts. And genuinely appreciated for them, too.

"I think the craft of teaching has been lost in the game, and there's a lot more criticizing and yelling than there is teaching nowaways. We have to understand that we have a great responsibility to the game that so many people love," Smith says. "We want to encourage people to participate in sports because there are so many benefits, and not discourage them. Coaches have to give players confidence and let them have fun. It's a beautiful game, and the kids should be enjoying it."

Smith takes those words to heart, literally and figuratively. Her team's Five Pillars of Success revolve around HEART: honesty, excellence, attitude, respect, and trust. "We talk about these things every day," she says. "One of the things that I learned from my college coach was the importance of emphasizing your standards and your vision for the team, so I just try to be a walking example of that which I expect of them."

She also works with her players to talk—to themselves—to help fill their hearts and minds with good vibes and positive energy. "Our thoughts are always talking to us, and we have to make sure that we're mastering our thought life," she says. "So on our team, we have what we call 'words of affirmation.' Those words affirm who we are as people and affirm who we are as a team. Everybody on the team has a word of affirmation, and every day, in our huddle at the end of practice, we say our words aloud. Mine this year was 'we are champions.' Others had 'we are powerful,' 'we are strong' and 'we have heart.'"

Rather than rest on her laurels of owning one of the greatest shots in college basketball history, she's capitalizing on her opportunities as a coach to impact young people's lives, both on the court and away from it. While none of us will ever experience the indescribable thrill of sinking a national championship-winning shot, we can follow in her footsteps and strive to teach kids to value and embrace all aspects of their respective sport—and acknowledge those contributions every chance possible. Teach these components from the heart, be passionate about them, and young athletes will respond accordingly.

Lisa Stockton

Head women's basketball coach at Tulane University ■
Two-time Conference USA Coach of the Year ■ Winner
of more than 550 games as a college basketball coach
■ Played college basketball at Wake Forest University

 During Lisa Stockton's basketball playing days at Wake Forest University, those in charge of keeping the team statistics knew they were in for a busy night. The four-sport high school standout—volleyball, softball, track and field, and yes, basketball—regularly filled in all the categories in the team scorebook with her all-round play. She oozed passion and energy at both ends of the floor, indicative of the numbers she posted: She became just the fourth player in team history to score 1,000 career points, and when her impressive four-year career came to a close, she left at the time as the school's leader in points, field goals made, minutes played, assists, and steals.

But for all the baskets made (she ranks fifth in team history) and consecutive games started (she ranks first all-time with 97), there's a category that means as much to her as all the others, and that's steals. (She had 206 of those during her career, by the way.) It's a statistic that doesn't get a lot of attention in youth sports these days, as *scoring average* is what tends to garner the most attention among young athletes in basketball, and even those coaching young players. While knocking down shots is understandably rewarding for young athletes, and imperative for winning games, there are so many other aspects of the sport that require a coach's full attention—and players willing to fill and embrace those roles. Securing buy in from players in these sometimes less-glamorous roles leads to stronger and more successful teams, but it takes a concerted effort from the coach.

"When you're talking in front of your team, how do you talk?" says Stockton, the long-time head women's basketball coach at Tulane University. "Do you talk about points, or do you talk about who set the best screens? Do you talk about who made the most passes?" Players will naturally devote their attention to those areas of the game that the coach tends to talk about the most. If you want players embracing good defense and wanting to make a difference at that end of the floor, then you do what Stockton does.

"We keep stats on players who tip balls on defense because we want to reward hustle," she says. "The things that you want to reward, it's important to give them something constructive that they can see." To help that defensive tenacity transition from practices to game day, stats can be kept during those practice sessions, which helps set the tone for how important a coach views them. Even if a coach doesn't have someone available to handle that, enthusiastically acknowledging whenever a player knocks away a pass or makes a steal sends a clear reminder to everyone of just how important those are in the coach's eyes.

"Embracing your role at any level of sports is so difficult to do," Stockton says of the challenges of getting young players to take on roles that may not have been high up on their list when the season began. "So positive reinforcement sends the message that this is the thing to do to help the team."

That type of attention to detail, and aspects of the game a coach chooses to emphasize, doesn't just happen during the course of a practice. It requires planning on the coach's part, much like a teacher prepares for that day's lessons. Otherwise, opportunities for recognizing specific plays or effort will slip by amid the action.

"At the youth sports level, I'm all about the fundamentals of the game," Stockton says. "You've got to teach those things, and it has to be a part of every practice, because otherwise you're basically just throwing the ball up and letting them go out and play. So are you really trying to make them better? And the other important thing is to be really organized. You know what you want to do, and you go into practice knowing how you want your groups set up. It's just like a lesson plan for a teacher."

Being a well-organized coach also sends positive messages to both your players and their parents, who recognize that you care enough to spend time plotting the best ways to help the young athletes learn and improve skills and function better as a team, too. "If you're really organized when you go in that, Number One, you have the respect of the parents," Stockton says. "And Number Two, the players stay more focused, because they know what they are doing. If you have to deviate from that plan, that's okay, but if you are showing up with enthusiasm and your practice plan, chances are they are going to have a great experience."

That parental respect Stockton references can be cultivated through continual communication, much like she does with the parents of her college players. She speaks with them often, especially heading into a season, which helps them get a clear understanding of what to expect. She suggests making time to connect with the young athletes' parents, who naturally are going to wonder about the coach and his or her experience in the sport, as well as what is in store for their child during the season.

"It's the same thing we do with our college parents," Stockton says. "Develop relationships with the parents so they know what your goals are and what your aspirations are for your team. Explain what you are in it for—that you're in it to try and make them better and make a positive experience for everyone. Sometimes describing those expectations might help you with the parents, so they know what you are trying to do."

As all the top coaches agree, being process-oriented, rather than out-come-focused, is important. During conversations with parents, that is an important topic to share with them and explain in greater detail. It likely will be unfamiliar to most moms and dads who sign their youngster up for sports and will use the scoreboard as their evaluating tool for how well the coach is doing and how the team is performing, because no one has told them any differently—though that's a disastrous view to take.

"When you're a positive person with positive energy and you show the players that you care about them, it has such a strong impact."

"At every level, you should be process-oriented," Stockton says. Now, that certainly doesn't mean trying to win games gets dumped in the backseat. It simply means that after a game—win or lose—coaches look at how the team performed the skills that they focused on during practice. Beating an inferior opponent while making a ton of mistakes and performing funda-mentals incorrectly during the game isn't worth celebrating; nor is losing a game to a superior opponent while executing skills well and showing improvement in all areas of the game a time to be disappointed and despon-dent over the outcome.

"Even in youth sports, if coaches are explaining that 'these are the things we did well, and these are the things we are going to work on for our next game,' then at least the players aren't about the outcome," Stockton says. "When you're just about the outcome, the players don't have the tools to change it. So I'm all about, especially at a young age, giving them the tools and the information to change what the next outcome will be."

During Stockton's youth, the junior high volleyball team she played on made sure the athletes learned the proper way to perform skills, so that when they did reach the high school level and stepped out on the court, they could perform them efficiently during match pressure.

"A great example of that is I played volleyball in junior high, and the junior high and the high school programs worked together," she says. "The high school program was very successful. The junior high coach didn't win as many games, but she really developed our skills. She didn't just say, 'get the ball back over the net.' We didn't always win, but when we got into high school, we were better players. If developmental programs can be that, and not be about the scoreboard, then you're putting kids in a better position so when they're older, they can use those skills to be more successful."

As players are working through a coach's practices, there are going to be plenty of hard days where struggles strike and frustration rises. As a coach, yelling and criticizing only fuels their despair, so it's crucial that coaches are operating with positive energy and enthusiasm to help them traverse these rocky patches in their development process. When they observe coaches engaged in their practices and thoroughly enjoying the process—even on those tough days where nothing seems to be going right—they will be more likely to adopt that same mindset.

"It's important in coaching that the kids know, whether at my level or the youth sports level, that you are looking out for their best interests and that you like what you do," Stockton says. "When you're a positive person with positive energy and you show the players that you care about them, it has such a strong impact. If you're yelling and screaming and all about the outcome, then it becomes a bad experience."

When coaches are operating with that process-based approach, it's imperative that post-game talks highlight many of the good things that happened, while also touching on those areas that need some additional work. "Help them understand that 'we played really hard and we played great defense, but we didn't pass very well,'" Stockton says as an example of balancing the conversation. "Be constructive and give them information to make the next game better."

John Tauer

University of St. Thomas basketball coach ▪ Winner
of 2016 Divison III National Championship ▪
University of St. Thomas Hall of Fame inductee ▪
Two-time Division III National Coach of the Year

 Much like a stand-up comedian's opening jokes set the tone for the routine, and the appetizer at a five-course dinner signals what's in store for the evening, how volunteer coaches kick off those crucial opening minutes of their practices can be the difference between a fun-filled session packed with laughter and learning and one that is spoiled by tedious, fun-crushing activities. When the men's basketball team at the University of St. Thomas, a Division III school of roughly 10,000 students, gathers for practice they know before they ever step inside the 180,000-square foot Anderson Athletic and Recreation Complex on their St. Paul, Minnesota, campus that a memorable, productive—and fun—practice awaits.

It starts at the top: When coaches are dialed in to the process and connected to what the kids need, blending enthusiasm and creativity, learning flourishes; while a lack of practice imagination that relies on recycling old drills or operating with a fear of trying anything new stalls development and puts the squeeze on running a great session. Coaches don't necessarily need to hit a home-run with the practice's opening activity, but striking out with a real dud establishes an atmosphere that is difficult to overcome the remainder of the session.

"A lot of it stems from if the coaches and leaders of the team are excited to be there," says John Tauer, who led St. Thomas to the 2016 national championship and is believed to have won more games in his first five seasons than any coach in Division III history. "Some of it is the way you plan and structure practice. Are there transitions? Are there competitions? Are there games? Are there light moments?"

Tauer *knows* basketball. He was an all-state performer and captain of the team in high school, and then starred at the college he now coaches and teaches at (more on the latter in a moment). A gifted all-around player, his name is still high up on the St. Thomas career lists for scoring, rebounding and three-pointers made, and he was inducted into the school's Hall of Fame in 2001. Along with his ability to both play and coach the game at a high level, he also understands the minds of those who step on the court to compete as well as anyone.

And by the way, you can call him *Coach* or *Doctor*—now *that's* a real double-double—as he earned a PhD in social psychology, in which he wrote his doctoral dissertation on intrinsic motivation. He teaches courses on campus dealing with everything from intrinsic motivation to competition, cooperation and goal-setting; and even authored a book on the psychology of parenting kids entitled *Why Less is More for WOSPs* (*Well-Intentioned, Overinvolved Sports Parents*): *How to Be the Best Sports Parent You Can Be.*

A few years ago, Tauer had a team that wasn't as vocal as his other teams had been, which posed some problems during games, where constant communication is essential for executing at the offensive end of the floor, and even more so on the defensive end where players need to be calling out switches on screens, for example. So during a meeting with his assistants, they were exploring ways they could ignite more communication among their players. During the course of the meeting, one of the assistant coaches didn't throw out trying a new drill, or introducing hand signals. He suggested *charades.* And it's an idea that can be filed in the Homerun Category because it made a tremendous impact, and has been a practice staple ever since.

"Part of why we did it is we had a quiet team and we wanted them to see how important communication was, and it just kind of stuck," Tauer says. "For us, it's become a very light-hearted way to start practice and get people in a good mood." Players gather, fun ensues, energy levels rise, and the players get dialed in to the day's work. "We start each day with two clues for charades, and it's become a really fun way to begin practice," he says. "We have a couple guys who don't play a lot, but they are unbelievable at charades, so they start off practice and they feel good and they're laughing. There are lots of ways to do it, and we did it to illustrate the point of communication, and it turned into a nice ritual to get practice going."

If it can work on the collegiate level, with a national title winning coach, it certainly has major applications at the younger levels of sports, too. Whether it's coaches in a similar predicament like Tauer with kids who are shy or quiet, or those in search of ways to rev practice energy and boost moods at the outset, charades or another fun game can turn out to be a real game-changer for the season. "If it's all business every day, every second, you can do that, but it's going to grind and wear on people," he says. "So it's coming in with a great attitude as coaches and being energetic, but also balancing fun and hard work and showing players that it's possible to strike a balance. In life, the people who are the most successful usually find a way to balance that, because if all you do is work really hard and there's no fun, that wears off; and if all you do is have fun and don't work hard, that's not good either. So we want our players to really learn that balance."

When players are treated to a cool practice experience, one that is entirely different from anything else other coaches have done, they get a real sense that they are a part of something pretty special. And that their coach really cares about them and puts in extra time and effort to make practice an event. When young athletes feel that way, and have genuine appreciation for how the coach is handling the season, their trust level rises and they become much more open and receptive to taking in feedback and embracing the journey to improvement.

"Focus on the process and really get kids interested in improvement and to trust that the process is going to lead them to be a better player," Tauer says. "If kids look at success and failure as sort of static places that they can't get out of, it's difficult to grow and develop. But if they look at it as, 'I'm trying to grow and improve a little bit each day,' kids who embrace that tend to grow and improve each day. And that's part of the challenge and fun of coaching. Sometimes it's our best athletes who are most afraid to do that because they may be trying to protect an image or they have never failed before. You certainly don't want failure, but you want to embrace it and learn from it when it does happen, because it always reflects something."

"If kids look at success and failure as sort of static places that they can't get out of, it's difficult to grow and develop."

It's important to note that running a fun practice, with a cool activity like charades to kick it off, only represents a portion of the season. If game day rolls around and the coach's mindset does a 180-degree spin, shifting to scoreboard watching and chasing wins at all costs, the season can spiral out of control. Plus, it sends distorted messages to the players, who see coaches behaving one way in practices during the week and in an entirely different manner on game days.

"Leading up to the game, we never talk about the score or trying to win," Tauer says. "It's much more about trying to be excellent and be the best we can be, and then after that, look back and see what happened."

Tauer recommends that coaches continually perform self-checks to ensure that they are attacking the season with the right approach. "The most important thing is to ask yourself repeatedly, 'what are our goals?'" he says. "Usually those are going to center around kids growing and developing, whether that's character development, leadership development, or even skill development. But if we keep that at the forefront, the idea that we're trying to help them develop and learn and grow, it becomes much easier to make the right decisions as a youth coach. When we get caught up in our emotions or what this means to us—and that's not to say that winning and losing can't be talked about, or even one of the goals—but it's keeping the big picture in mind. We all know how emotional sports can be, so that has to be a regular checkup. It might be the kind of thing that some coaches probably need before every practice and game, where they just look at an index card and it reminds them that this is why I'm doing this. I'm not doing this so my son can score twenty points a game; I'm not doing it so my daughter can get a scholarship to college; I'm doing this for 'blank,' and fill in the blank, because everybody has to have their own mission statement and stay true to that."

So, stock up on the index cards to make those notation reminders so you stay on track with your team and ensure your actions align with your goals. And while you're at it, go ahead and jot down some movie titles, television shows, or names of famous athletes and give charades a whirl at the start of your next practice. Your players will be glad you did.

Stephanie Wheeler

Head coach of 2016 U.S. women's wheelchair
basketball team ▪ Two-time Paralympic Wheelchair
Basketball Gold Medalist as a player ▪ Coach of
University of Illinois wheelchair basketball team

 Stephanie Wheeler loved sports from the beginning. There were gymnastics and T-ball in those early childhood days, and her voice drips with enthusiasm as she recalls winning all the field day events at her elementary school decades ago. "Sports were absolutely huge in my life," she says. "From a very early age, I was into sports."

When she was six years old, Wheeler was involved in a car accident that took away the use of her legs. But that accident couldn't steal her love for sports. It didn't douse her passion for competing. And it certainly never derailed the inner drive she possessed of wanting to learn, improve, and get better every single day, no matter how daunting the obstacles.

"After my accident, I didn't know anything about disability sports," she says. "So for about the next six years, I was aching and longing to be able to do something physical and figure out some way to play sports."

Wheeler, who led the United States women's wheelchair basketball team to a gold medal as head coach at the 2016 Paralympic Games in Rio, grew up in North Carolina, where basketball reigns. "If you are born and grow up there, basketball is in your blood," she says. "I love everything about the game. When a team is clicking, and everyone is in sync and working together as a group on the court, that's one of the most beautiful things that you can ever see."

Those initial years following the accident were difficult for a lot of reasons, one of them being that a game Wheeler dearly loved wasn't available to her. "When I found wheelchair basketball at twelve years old, it completely changed my life," she says. "It was absolutely huge to me as a child."

In their positions, coaches will come across all types of players who show up to participate: the athletically gifted and the clumsy; the shy and the outgoing; the lazy and the hardworking; team-first players and ego-driven look-at-me players; the incredibly focused and the woefully lackadaisical; as well as those dealing with physical and mental challenges. It's one of the challenges of coaching that makes it so rewarding in the end. All kids deserve a chance to play, and regardless of what type of program a youngster with a disability is competing in—whether it's wheelchair basketball or recreation basketball—they deserve to play for a coach who is all-in on teaching, encouraging, and motivating them just like they would any other athlete.

"For disability sports, the biggest thing is that coaches should have expectations," Wheeler says. "They should have the same expectations of the kids on their team that have disabilities as they would if they were coaching any other youth sports team. That's huge for kids with disabilities, because there are so many times where they don't have expectations put upon them because they are seen as not being able to do certain things that are physical, or they are seen as being fragile."

During those early years, Wheeler experienced the heartache of being relegated to the sidelines while her friends were engaged in athletic activity. "I know I experienced my own little bit of that as far as not being allowed to participate alongside my peers in sports and physical education because my teachers didn't know how," she says. "And because they just thought that I wouldn't be able to do it."

Wheeler discovered firsthand the power of expectations. It doesn't matter the age, sport, or skill level of the athletes involved—if expectations are never laid out for athletes at the start of a season, the journey is sure to be an unfulfilling one blanketed in chaos and confusion, and ultimately ending in complete disappointment.

"When I started playing basketball, the biggest difference was all of a sudden someone had expectations of me to be physically able to complete something," Wheeler says. "So it is absolutely huge that coaches have expectations of their players, and teach them to have expectations for themselves, too. Players should be able to do things, and if they can't do something one way, they need to be creative and courageous and figure out a different way to do it. That's the first piece of big advice I would give outside of any technical basketball advice—to have expectations for that child that you are coaching."

Wheeler excelled at wheelchair basketball. She was recruited to play at the University of Illinois and was a big part of leading the Fighting Illini to three straight national championships while earning All-American honors each of those seasons. She also enjoyed success on the international stage as a player, helping Team USA capture gold medals in women's wheelchair basketball at the 2008 Paralympic Games in Beijing and the 2004 Games in Athens. Her transition as a player to the coach of the United States national team to her current role as coach at the University of Illinois has certainly been aided by the fact that she has done everything she is now trying to help others do. And she's done it at an incredibly high level.

On the technical side, sports like wheelchair basketball certainly pose some different challenges regarding various offensive and defensive skills. But other aspects—such as helping athletes plow through adversity, work through difficult stretches, and focus on building confidence and improving their games—are inherent to all coaching. At all levels.

"For disability sports, the biggest thing is that coaches should have expectations. They should have the same expectations of the kids on their team that have disabilities as they would if they were coaching any other youth sports team."

"That's a battle that we face at all ages with sports," Wheeler says. "We talked a lot about that with the national team, and now with my team here at the University of Illinois. I teach my student athletes how to be life-long learners. One of the ways that we talk about that is by pretending that we are jungle tigers. We talk about what jungle tigers have to do to survive and how if they fail finding food or fail in whatever it might be, they keep working because it's what they need to do to survive; it's what they need to do to get better. That's one of the ways we like to change it—instead of looking at it as failure, we look at it as an opportunity for improving and getting better."

Despite owning a golden resume, Wheeler endured her share of disappointment along the way, too. These are experiences that haven't been discarded but rather treasured, for they have helped shape and define her, and turned her into one heck of an outstanding coach.

"I had to fail, and I failed a lot," she says. "I didn't make my first national team. Even once I made the national team, I failed a lot on the court. Having to work through those things and having to understand that while I didn't succeed here, this is how you turn it into something positive and this is how to be resilient and bounce back. I use that every single day at my job. I don't get things right all the time as a coach, and I have to bounce back and be able to do it better the next time. Just like my dedication to life-long learning—doing something every single day to make myself a better coach. As an athlete, I did something every single day to make myself the best athlete I could possibly be."

The pursuit of improvement and skill development will always be tricky territory to navigate, especially since young athletes naturally will always be comparing themselves to their teammates. Kids watch and observe, and they recognize who the best athlete on the team is. They are well aware who possesses the most skills, and who they dread facing in one-on-one drills. It's one of the areas Wheeler spends a lot of time on, because when players are so wrapped up in the skill level of a teammate, they are directing wasted energy and attention that they should be pouring into themselves.

"We try to keep the focus as much as we can on the athlete, but not in a comparison to somebody else," she says. "So it's tracking their individual progress throughout the course of time. It's a tough thing to do because we are a society driven on 'Have you won?' or "What achievements have you had lately?' So as much as we can keep the focus on the individual athlete having fun and working on their personal growth, that helps in keeping the attention off of other people, or off of achievement."

Wheeler's journey might never have occurred if she didn't discover wheelchair basketball all those years ago and have the opportunity to play for coaches who understood just how powerful sports are in a child's life, and how important it is not to waste a second working with young athletes—regardless if they are dealing with a disability or not.

"I remember the first practice that I went to. I just had all these amazing feelings that this is what I am supposed to do," Wheeler says of that first wheelchair basketball practice. "I love the sport, and at that moment I wasn't seen as the kid with the disability. I was included in a group, and I could get all that competitiveness out—that same competitiveness that drove me to win on field day back in the day—in an environment that was designed for me that I had never experienced before. It was amazingly life changing."

Monty Williams

Assistant coach for U.S. Men's Basketball Team at 2016 Summer Olympics ▪ Former coach of the New Orleans Pelicans ▪ First round selection in 1994 NBA Draft ▪ Recipient of 2017 Sager Strong Award ▪ Played college basketball at Notre Dame

 During *Hoosiers*—widely considered one of the greatest sports movies of all time—Gene Hackman delivers a riveting pre-game speech to a high school basketball team before they take the floor for a state championship game. One of the key scenes in the film, based around the improbable run of tiny Milan High School (with an enrollment of 161 students) to the 1954 state championship, shows him talking to his team about playing with effort and concentration and focusing on just being the best that they can be. In *Miracle,* the movie about the U.S. Hockey Team's stunning win over the Soviet Union at the 1980 Winter Olympics, Kurt Russell (playing the role of U.S. Coach Herb Brooks) tells his team before they take the ice against the Soviets in a goose bump-raising scene: "this is your time." And in *Friday Night Lights,* Billy Bob Thornton, playing a high school football coach, delivers a mesmerizing half-time speech where he tells his players that "being perfect is about being able to look your friends in the eye and know that you didn't let them down."

These are all iconic scenes, delivered with Hollywood glitz, flair, and drama. There are plenty of real-life examples of coaches firing up their squads before games, too. During March Madness, we're often treated to quick glimpses inside team locker-rooms with those coaches who have agreed to allow television cameras to capture portions of their pre-game speeches to their teams. So as coaches of young athletes, it's easy to get caught up in the whirlwind of a season and believe that every Saturday morning soccer game or mid-week basketball game requires getting up in front of the team and delivering a motivational speech infused with big words and loud volume that sends them charging out onto the field or court to play better than they have all season. But there's a time and a place for these types of speeches. The pre-game routine doesn't have to feature a fiery message every time.

"I don't think you always have to have a pre-game talk," says Monty Williams, an assistant coach on the 2016 U.S. men's Olympic basketball gold medal-winning team and is an assistant coach with the Philadelphia 76ers. "Sometimes coaches feel like they have to say something every single game."

Williams knows all about pre-game speeches: he listened to his share of them during a standout career as a high-scoring forward for the Notre Dame basketball team and as a nine-year NBA player, and he's delivered them during his days as an NBA coach, most recently with the New Orleans Pelicans. He advises coaches to gauge the team's mood and performance during the week before deciding whether they're going to need an extra boost before the game.

"It's important to read your group," he says. "If you've had a good week of practices, or if you had a good practice the day before the game, then sometimes that is the pre-game talk. Sometimes you may want to ask one of your leaders to say something. And then there are times where you've thought about it all day and you have something you saw on TV or read that you want to share, and that's great. But if you are fabricating it every single day, kids, players, and teams generally read right through that."

Williams, one of the NBA's most respected voices, makes several import-ant points. Consider, for example, that a team has had a great week of practice heading into a big game. By *not* delivering a lengthy pre-game speech, the coach is actually exuding confidence and letting players know that he is so pleased by the effort and progress that he knows the team is ready to play. There isn't a need for even attempting to stir up excitement, throw around motivational phrases, or employ a rah-rah type speech.

"It's important that coaches figure out when and when not to speak, and that can be motivating as well," Williams says. "Sometimes you just say, 'let's go' and everybody is ready. And sometimes you give a Knute Rockne speech to get the players ready to knock down a wall and that's great. But I don't think you have to do it every time. You have to do what's appropriate for that day." Communication: it's not just speaking the right words, but choosing the right time to deliver them, too.

When it comes to the game, and communicating about it, Williams has both those areas well covered. While playing for the Fighting Irish at Notre Dame—where he majored in communications/broadcast journalism—he led the team in scoring and rebounding his senior season on the way to earning Honorable Mention All-American honors. At the time of his graduation, he was the twelfth leading scorer in Notre Dame history. The New York Knicks grabbed him in the first round of the 1994 NBA Draft, and he played nine seasons in the league before eventually getting into coaching. As the father of five, he knows how important spending quality time with your kids is, and that also translates into coaching, too. No matter the sport, coaches can't lose track that every young athlete on the roster is an important individual deserving of the coach's attention and help.

"You make all the kids feel special when you spend time with everyone," Williams says. "Unfortunately, there are some teams in some places where kids with the most talent get preferential treatment. The best way to build confidence and to help a kid along is to make sure that you share an equal amount of time with every child, because kids understand when they are being pushed to the side." Young athletes who don't possess the same gifts as some of their more talented teammates, or who may be slower learners than others, still deserve to have their coaches speak to them in the same enthusiastic and caring tone as they communicate with the stars of the team. If these conversations aren't genuine, the kids will spot it, and coaches will lose them.

"There may be kids who don't have the same amount of talent that all the other kids have," Williams says. "But if you go over and talk to that kid the same way you talk to the kids with the higher talent, you never know what you can do for that child." That's one of the many beauties of coaching, how a conversation at practice can spark a love for competing, or create that extra layer of confidence that has been missing in a young person's life. It's these moments that can transform lives.

"It's important that coaches figure out when and when not to speak, and that can be motivating as well."

It all ties into establishing a team-first culture, where players recognize that everyone must work together and—equally important—*wants* to. Williams encourages coaches to use phrases that grab attention and that young athletes can relate to. "It takes a lot of work to teach teamwork," he says. "One of the things that I always talk about with players is 'if one of us isn't right, then all of us aren't right;' or 'if there's a weak link in the chain, the chain is going to break at some point;' and 'we never leave anyone behind.' I try to pound home these catch phrases with the hope that players will start to repeat them."

It's no secret who the best players are on any given team. The coaches know, and so do the players themselves. While some athletes will have more prominent roles than others, that doesn't detract from the importance of everyone contributing in their own way. "Even though there are some players on your team who have less talent, the bottom line is it's a team sport, and as much as you can talk about the team as a whole, the better," Williams says. "I always talk about the name on the front of the jersey as opposed to the name on the back of the jersey. That doesn't negate the ones who have great talent, but at the end of the day, if you don't have a team, you can't win."

Many coaches have played sports throughout their lives and have lots of experiences to call upon. While drawing from some of those positive ones can be beneficial at times, Williams advises not to get too caught up in the past, because this is a different generation of athletes, and the focus must be on meeting their expectations and their needs.

"It's important to be able to see things the way kids see them where they are right now," Williams says. "Not where we were when we were kids, because things have changed." What hasn't changed is the important role coaches occupy in young lives, and the incredible opportunities that are available all season long for teaching those all-important life skills.

"For any coach, it's important to be a positive role model, because you are an extension of a child's moral base," Williams says. "They get it at home, they get it in school with their teachers, and another good place to get it is in sports with their coaches. Whether you know it or not, kids are looking for structure and people to emulate. I know my youth coaches were great role models who set great examples for me. They were people that led me in the right direction. If you are a youth coach, you can't forget that the kids in America and around the world are looking for examples, and what greater way to be an extension of what they get at home than to do it in the sports field?"

Roy Williams

University of North Carolina men's basketball coach ▪ Three-time national champion ▪ Inducted into the Basketball Hall of Fame in 2007 ▪ Two-time Associated Press Coach of the Year

 Every summer, young basketball players of varying ages, abilities, and backgrounds descend on the University of North Carolina's picturesque campus in Chapel Hill. Dressed in colorful gear, these high-tops wearing, basketball-loving young athletes come from Asheville to Zebulon, and everywhere else across the state of North Carolina to participate in the week-long camp led by Roy Williams, the Tar Heels' Hall of Fame coach, three-time national champion, and one of the sport's most revered and respected coaches—ever. For most Division I coaches, basketball camps for children and teens have become as much a part of their summer itineraries as family vacations and golf outings.

The camp agenda at North Carolina features plenty of drills, skill stations, and fun-filled games that zero in on helping these young players, who dream of becoming the next Michael Jordan (the famous Tar Heel alum who led them to the 1982 national title) or Kobe or LeBron, improve their passing, dribbling, rebounding, and defensive skills.

This camp has a slightly different tone to it, though, operating under the radar of the participants. Yes, the youngsters are there to elevate their games, and spending a week under the watchful eye of a man who was inducted into the Basketball Hall of Fame more than a decade ago, that most certainly happens. But Williams has long recognized a greater purpose of camp week. He wants to achieve more than simply dialing up the kids' skills and sending them home with a cool souvenir camp t-shirt at the end of the week. His mission runs deeper. His goals are greater. And his outlook for the week is emblematic of what it means to work with kids in any sport, and at any level. He wants all participants, regardless if they are just learning the game or destined for high school stardom, to take home special experiences. We're talking about the life-changing variety that will be remembered and savored for years to come. This aspect means so much to him that he stresses it to his staff to help make it happen well before a camper dribbles a ball or lofts a shot.

"Everybody that volunteers to be a coach has to understand that kids are really going to take in and believe everything they say, so the influence they have is tremendous," Williams says. "I tell all my coaches at the summer basketball camp to try to be as positive as they can possibly be, because those kids are going to remember what they say, and it is going to have an influence. It did on me. It's all personal experience. It's something that I jokingly say, that that kid that you are really nice to in camp or on the team that you have volunteered to coach may end up someday being your pilot on an airplane. And when you get on that airplane and he sees you, you want to make sure that he dodges all the bumps that he can dodge."

Regardless of your frequent flier status, it's this mindset that Williams points to—using a humorous story to illustrate something deeply important to him—of genuinely caring for young players as people first, and athletes second. It's the mindset that volunteer coaches should be charging into their seasons with. Williams knows better than most just how influential and impactful coaches can be for kids. He lived it, experienced it, and benefited from it. Those coaches he played for on the basketball courts and baseball fields of his youth taught him the skills and fundamentals of the game. But they also served a greater purpose. They were father figures and role models for Williams during a childhood in which his father wasn't often present. These coaches spoke to him before and after practices. They encouraged and supported, applauded and inspired. They connected. It was life changing.

"When I was growing up playing Little League baseball and basketball and everything I could possibly play, my coaches were the most important role models to me," Williams says. "I had a very difficult home situation at times. My mom was the angel of the world, but those coaches really were people that made me feel very good and gave me confidence."

When Williams attended T.C. Roberson High School in Asheville, North Carolina, his basketball coach, Buddy Baldwin, changed the course of his life. "My high school coach made me feel good about things, made me feel that I had a tremendous opportunity, and gave me confidence," Williams says. "That made me feel so good. He's the reason I decided I wanted to be a coach. The influence that my Little League baseball coaches and my high school coaches had on me at that time is still a great influence today."

Think about *those* words. A half century later, they still resonate with Williams. They gave him direction and a purpose. They inspired and motivated him. And they changed his life. So, whenever he comes in contact with young athletes at his camps, or in daily interactions with his college players, those youth memories are never too far away.

"Everybody that volunteers to be a coach has to understand that kids are really going to take in and believe everything they say, so the influence they have is tremendous."

"There is nothing better than praise when you are dealing with young kids," Williams says. "I even feel there is nothing better than praise when you are dealing with older players, too." It starts during practice, where setting the proper tone can lead to plenty of wonderful opportunities for impacting a young life.

"Practice needs to be fun, but you also need to establish early on—whether you're a volunteer coach or the coach at North Carolina—what your goals and dreams are. If you do that, youngsters understand it more," Williams says. "A structured environment with a very organized practice that kids enjoy will keep them involved. I tell everybody who is a volunteer coach, whether it's Little League baseball, basketball, or whatever the sport is, that if they can make sure they make it fun, those kids will gain a lot from it."

Of course, game days present a smorgasbord of opportunities for life lessons to be taught. Everything from dealing with pressure and being a respectful young athlete to working through adversity and always putting forth the best effort possible, among so many more. Williams understands pressure as well as anyone, as his Tar Heels are annually one of the nation's top teams navigating big-time games during that cauldron of pressure known as March Madness. It's important that coaches address pressure with their young players, and explain that it's a part of competing, but that it can't overwhelm thinking.

"There is stress in big games, and you have to understand that you like a little nervous energy to help get you to the highest level," Williams says. "But you can't think about results. Your players should be thinking about process. In a golf swing, you should never say, 'gosh, I've got to hit this close.' You go through your routine and go through your process. A guy who goes to the free throw line should never say, 'boy, if I don't make this free throw, we are going to lose the game.' You go through your checkpoints: 'I've got to have full extension and a good follow through.' So you try to keep them focused on the process, as opposed to the result."

During those games where shots aren't falling, or the opposing team just happens to be playing better, coaches must pull their players through those rough patches where confidence can deteriorate, and youngsters can get down on themselves in a heartbeat. "There are going to be tough times in athletics," Williams says. "There are going to be times where the other guy gets the upper hand, and as a coach you've got to try to continue pushing your player that you are coaching. You've got to push him, but at the same time you have to put your arm around him and say, 'hey, don't be your own worst enemy. You've got to get through this, you're good enough to do it. Focus on what you've practiced.'"

And no matter what, don't look to blame officials when the game isn't going as hoped. Talk to your team. Explain to them that the officials are doing the best they can, just like the players are. Athletes make mistakes, and so do officials. It's all part of the game. Regardless of the experience level of the officials, or if they are teens or adults, they never deserve to be disrespected or blamed for a team's performance.

"Officials are a huge part of the game, whether it's the youth leagues or major college or the NBA, so you have to have respect for them and know it's a very difficult job and they are doing the best they can do," Williams says. "A lot of times, my players will use the officials as an excuse, and I don't like that. I say, 'Hey, you missed the shot, or we dribbled the ball off our foot out of bounds, or we let that guy score, so the official had nothing to do with that."

Roy Williams' youth coaches shaped and enhanced his life. As a youth coach, you can have that same influence on a child that Williams' coaches had on him. You never know when a child will silently crave a positive influence in his life and someone to help navigate a challenging childhood. It all begins with genuinely caring for the youngster.

"Understand that you are a role model, and the kids are going to pick up on what you do and how you act, so treat every kid like he or she was your own son or daughter," he says. "Treat that individual like you would want somebody else to treat your son or daughter, and if you do that, you are probably going to be okay there. But understand too, to set goals and dreams for improving. One important thing is for a youngster to feel like he's getting better, so through the course of a season, if that youngster can be coached and motivated and urged on every single day to get better, and he feels that he is getting better, then you are really doing some good things."

Christy Winters Scott

Four-year letter winner for the University of
Maryland women's basketball team ▪ University
of Maryland Hall of Fame inductee ▪ High school
girls basketball coach ▪ Television broadcaster

When the lights are on and the cameras are rolling, Christy Winters Scott delivers. Whether it's broadcasting a college basketball game, doing a studio show, or providing analysis for the NBA's Washington Wizards or the WNBA's Washington Mystics, she dishes out must-hear insight and observations with enthusiasm and a smile. It doesn't matter if she had a hectic morning with her three kids, dealt with a late-arriving flight the night before, or was stuck in snarling traffic within the shadows of the nation's capitol. No matter the magnitude of the game she is broadcasting, or the chaos surrounding the lead up to the telecast, she blocks it all out and performs in the clutch.

That pretty much sums up how she operated during her playing days, too. A four-year letter winner for the Terrapins at the University of Maryland during the late eighties, she averaged nearly eighteen points a game as a senior while earning All-Atlantic Coast Conference First Team honors. She finished her career as Maryland's second all-time leading scorer, as well as ranking fourth in rebounding, fifth in blocked shots, and eighth in field goal percentage on the school's all-time list. She's also one of only two players in school history to score more than 700 field goals.

Her trek to greatness began in the family driveway, when her dad put up a basketball hoop. After her family moved to Reston, Virginia, when she was eight years old, Winters Scott played in her first organized basketball league and didn't like it—she *loved* it. "That's when I truly fell in love with it and loved the team atmosphere," she says. "I was hooked."

She starred at South Lakes High School in Reston and led the team to an undefeated season and a state championship her senior year. Many years later, she was inducted into the school's first Hall of Fame class, along with seven-time NBA All-Star Grant Hill, who told the audience that he was glad to be known as "the male Christy Winters." She was *that* good. South Lakes was where she honed her game, where she became a real headache for opposing players to defend, and where she gained a true appreciation of the value and importance of everyone working together on the offensive and defensive ends of the floor to achieve success.

After college, she headed overseas to play professionally, since the WNBA didn't exist at that time. New cultures, time zones, and unfamiliar living conditions didn't affect her when she stepped on the court, as evidenced by the jaw-dropping thirty-seven points and twelve rebounds she averaged during her final season in Switzerland. Back in the states, she found herself with assistant coaching positions with several Division 1 schools—Georgetown, Maryland, and George Mason—before arriving back where it all began: coaching the girls varsity basketball team at South Lakes, which she has been doing for several years now.

"I love it because every day is different and every year is different," she says. "I always tell the players at the beginning of the year that it's not a mistake that we are here together. This is for a purpose."

Winters Scott played in high-pressure games at all levels throughout her career and went through the highs and lows of competing. So, she has a deep reservoir of insights and experiences to pull from and share with the teens that compete for the school that she once played for. She fully understands what her role is and the opportunities that she has every season to impact young lives beyond the sport.

"You want the best for them," she says. "The trick is to have them want the best for themselves. A lot of self-awareness is involved in that, and a lot of confidence is involved as well. Hopefully, as coaches, we're the bumpers on the bowling alley, just trying to make sure that they are headed in the right direction—not just for basketball—but in the big picture of life. We want to make sure that they are processing and thinking the right way and pushing forward when things don't go their way, and hopefully it's all-encompassing in that regard."

When adversity strikes for teams, and it certainly will, how players react and respond not only reveals their competitive spirit, it provides a peek at their character—and helping young athletes learn to face tough times with their heads up and their confidence intact is one of a coach's most important responsibilities. When games tilt in the opposing team's favor, or shots aren't going in, do players move onto the next possession, or are they stuck in the quicksand of negative thoughts? Even worse, are players hanging their heads in frustration, sulking, or displaying that negative body language we've all seen on athletes before? That is a huge no-no under Winters Scott's watch.

"That's a pet peeve," she says. "That, to me, is such a selfish thing. Body language speaks louder than any words, I don't care what volume. For me, in a team environment, to have that kind of reaction is unacceptable."

All great players bump into games where shots that normally find the bottom of the net bounce out. It's sports, and it happens. In the state title game during her senior season, where her team was undefeated and feeling the pressure of trying to complete an undefeated season, Winters Scott endured one of those shooting droughts during the first half.

"Personally, I was so tight and the shots that I would normally make were rimming out," she says. "It was so frustrating. I was upset that the shots weren't going in, but when I didn't see them falling, I decided to try to do some other things." There was no time for getting down; her high school career had mere minutes of playing time left. Her team needed her, and she recognized she had a responsibility to them. If she couldn't knock down a shot that most times would typically drop in for her, she was going to gather all her energy into contributing to the team in another way. It's a message she hammers home with her squad these days. It's a team game, and there are so many areas where players can make their presence felt beyond simply scoring.

"This is what I have told them before," she says. "You can be upset, but let that anger fuel you to do something to help the team. Box out harder, sprint faster to get back on defense, or set a better screen next time down the floor. Do something basketball-wise that will help us as a group. When you get so wrapped up in your own head that you can't perform to your capabilities anyway, you are already hurting the team."

Being a team-first type of player—the kind that coaches love working with and other athletes love playing with—requires helping kids figure out the maze of obstacles that can thwart productivity. So it's assisting players with addressing that inner self and squashing any negative displays threatening to escape.

"There are so many negative things that come from bad body language," Winters Scott says. "That's why I always say you have to compete with yourself before you can compete against an opponent. You have to win that game first against yourself, and when you do that, then you can step forward and have a chance to compete against everyone else."

Just like all skills, it must be continually worked on and honed during practices. There aren't any magical buttons to push or switches to flip to bring a mindset to game day in which bad body language will not make an appearance. It takes a concerted effort during practice and requires coaches addressing it with players when it does occur. The most minor head drops or exasperated sighs when shots aren't falling during a shooting drill can easily escalate to more demonstrative actions on game day when the shots mean more, and the stands are full of people watching those shots miss their mark. It's an element of coaching that Winters Scott never ignores.

"Even in practices, if you're not having a good day, if you don't feel well, or if your friend got mad at you at lunch, you can't be carrying that vibe into the gym," she says. "Within the lines, you have to be focused on the team. If you miss a shot, it can't be just about you, because the game isn't just about you, and the practice isn't just about you. I really think as a competitor, going back to my playing days, I was upset when I wasn't playing well, but I don't think you could tell from the outside. On the inside, I was screaming I was so mad, but on the outside, I didn't stop playing and drop my head down and trot back, because that would hurt the team as a whole."

When the entire group grabs onto that mentality, they can recognize when a teammate is struggling and offer those powerful words of encouragement to lift them up and keep them focused on the moment. When young athletes learn the value of looking out for each other and being there for one another during the rough patches, that's where team chemistry evolves and relationships flourish.

"It doesn't mean you don't have emotions," she says. "It just means that you are in control of them, and when you get angry, you can focus on how you can use that as fuel for creating something positive for the team."

There's a different mentality that many young athletes bring to the gym these days, one that requires some rewiring on a coach's part to help players understand that it's a team sport and no one player—no matter how talented she happens to be—is bigger than the group.

"That's a huge issue," Winters Scott says. "Especially these days, where players feel like they are entitled to do well. Just because you want to do well, doesn't mean it's going to happen. Going back to my state championship game, I wanted to do well, but I wasn't ready for the moment, and even though we won the game, I still feel like I left something on the table. When you are so caught up within yourself instead of letting the moment speak for itself in a team environment, that's where you go wrong. I've had those experiences, so I know what it feels like. So it's not like I'm telling players, 'Hey, you have to be a robot.' I'm not here for that, and I don't want them to be a robot, because I'm not. But there are ways to process through that and help the team, rather than hurt the team."

"There are so many negative things that come from bad body language. That's why I always say you have to compete with yourself before you can compete against an opponent."

Putting players in competitive game-like situations in practice helps them learn to manage their emotions and funnel their energy in the right direction. "I always tell them that the practices are the quizzes and the games are the exams," she says. "Every practice, you are going to be working toward something and preparing for the final exam. Twice a week, you have exams in these games. Our practices are mini tests to get you ready to compete, and different situations are going to happen that you have to be ready for, mentally more than anything, to execute. What I have found over the course of coaching at the collegiate level, as well as high school, is that players thrive in competitive atmospheres. The more you can keep things competitive, the better it is in the long run for them. If it's a mundane shooting drill and you're just taking shots, I found that that doesn't really help in the development of that competitive fire. For us, every single drill is competitive."

She creates all different types of situations in practice, employing different spins on ordinary drills to rev energy, create challenges, and force players to respond in game speed mode. "We do drills with all different types of rules," she explains. "Sometimes the offense can only score on pick and rolls, or it can only score on shots in the paint. So we change up the rules, and I have found that this brings out the best in our kids." It also is great at prepping them for when similar scenarios unfold during games.

"We'll do situations in practice where there are two minutes left and we're down six points, for example," Winters Scott says. "I remember in a timeout we had during one of our games, one of our kids said, 'This is just like the situation we had in practice.' It resonates with them, and they become more comfortable in those environments. When you develop that confidence in them, or when they develop it through those situations in practice, it comes out in the game. So when they see that happen in a game, they buy in to what we are doing every day in practice, and it's not just, 'We have these two hours and we're going to go through some drills.'"

Marissa Young

Duke University softball coach ■ Three-time
All-American pitcher at the University of Michigan
■ 2003 Big Ten Player of the Year

Marissa Young navigates motherhood much the same way she approaches her job as the Duke University softball coach: with never-ending love, care, and a gleam in her eye. The mom of three, who was one of college softball's most feared pitchers during her playing days in the early 2000s, knows—and fully appreciates—the unique personalities and characteristics of all youngsters, from the tykes to the teens.

"Being a parent has helped make me a better coach," says Young, who struck fear into the hearts of hitters, and struck *a lot* of them out too, during her dominating career at the University of Michigan. "My kids are so different, and they need and want such different things from me, and the same really goes for coaching, too."

Young never envisioned being a college softball coach, and certainly not one expected to build a Division I program from scratch at one of the country's most respected institutions, as Duke began playing softball for the first time in 2018. She thought after her award-filled career at Michigan—three-time All-American, 2003 Big Ten Player of the Year, 2002 Big Ten Pitcher of the Year, and the school's all-time strikeout leader—that she would slide into being a lawyer. But as she began the process of applying for law school, she was asked if she would be interested in working with softball players at an indoor academy in Michigan. She tried it, loved it, and now does her best work at the newly constructed Duke Softball Stadium on its campus in Durham, North Carolina, rather than in front of judges and juries. It all goes back to relating to people and getting a handle on what they are all about.

"It's really important to understand how fragile young people are, especially young women," Young says. "You have to reach each kid based on the way that they tick. Sometimes as coaches, we get the mindset that it's a one-size-fits-all approach, and that's definitely not the case." Different personalities present different challenges, and those require different approaches for connecting. The more coaches can learn about their players, the more successful they'll be at decoding what motivates and excites them, and the greater the chances they'll be able to steer them on the path to productive seasons.

"I encourage coaches to really get to know their players and understand them and their personalities," she says, "so that they can reach them and motivate them based on their personality type."

Young was a fierce competitor when she took the field; and she embraced and benefited from coaches who pushed and challenged her. "My coaches had a tremendous impact on me, and I'm thankful for how they really helped me grow and mature," says Young. In order for coaches to have that same type of impact on their players that Young remembers so well from her playing days growing up in Santa Ana, California, they must really commit to connecting with everyone on the roster. Forging young athletes' confidence is a must for creating those special coach-player relationships that last longer than the season.

"You have to continue to make the kids confident and believing in themselves," Young says. "I always say that you have to compliment before you challenge." Young is a huge proponent of coaches conducting practices that do exactly that: challenge and test players. She played the game at an extremely high level for a long time. Along with being a potent pitcher, she also swung a lethal bat, tying the Wolverines' single-season homerun record. She's been on the field for a lot of practices during her journey from youth athlete to Division I star, so she recognizes the value of practice time, and not wasting any of it on time-draining drills that fail to promote learning or skill development. It's important that practices serve a purpose and that coaches have a specific plan for the session. Drills that turn out to do nothing more than fill time will result in not only unproductive sessions, but disinterested players.

"Now more than ever, pitchers just go throw pitches and do a pitching workout, but they don't really practice as if they are preparing for the challenges that they are going to face in a game," Young says. "Coaches need to challenge them."

She even advises weaving some drills into your practices that will be out of the players' reach, but will serve to help them deal with difficult situations and adversity that can pop up unannounced during games.

"I would encourage coaches to simulate games, and also give players challenges that aren't attainable," she says. "Like being perfect on nine out of ten pitches. They know that's not realistic, but you want to see how the pitchers respond and how they are going to handle the failure. The more often they are challenged that way, the better they become at overcoming it."

Coaches can alert players to those drills that have the increased difficulty, even explaining the purpose of them. Young athletes will appreciate hearing the insight into the process their coach is using to raise their game day skills. Plus, most will take comfort knowing that a plan is in place to help take them where they want to go.

"It's really important to have a plan and outline for them: 'Here's where you are now; here's where we want to get you to; and here's how we're going to do it,'" Young says. "Kids really latch onto that, when they feel like their coach has a plan for them and is going to get them where they want to be."

Before coaches get those drills going, it's crucial to establish a practice environment where kids understand that making mistakes is okay—it's all part of the journey to improving and developing.

"The kids have to know that they are in a safe environment where, even if they make a mistake, it's okay as long as they are giving max effort and working to make adjustments."

"The kids have to know that they are in a safe environment where, even if they make a mistake, it's okay as long as they are giving max effort and working to make adjustments. They know the coach is going to help them get better and isn't passing judgment on them," Young says. "Because right now, their identity of learning who they are and who they want to become is really shaped by the adults that they come in contact with, so for us as coaches, it's very important that we reward the process, not just results."

Of course, in a sport like softball, players want to crush home runs and be mobbed in the dugout with high-fives from their teammates, be the one that delivers that game-winning hit in the clutch that generates cheers from the stands, or be the center of attention mowing down hitters from the pitching circle.

"Softball is a team sport, and as much as players love getting up there and hitting that home run, sometimes their job is to put the ball on the ground to the right side to move that runner along," Young says. "When coaches are able to make their players think more about what they can do to make their team better, instead of what they can do to make themselves look good—that's when it becomes a fun environment."

A lot of attention naturally gets directed at the pitcher during a game, but Young urges coaches to help their pitchers understand that softball is a team sport. And the pitcher can be a tone setter for being a great teammate.

"More than ever in the game of softball, teach pitchers not to be the princess in the circle," says Young, who finished her career at Michigan second in wins, with 88 total. "Coaches need to really get their pitchers to focus more on their team and how to be a better teammate, how to encourage their teammates, and how to appreciate them and get excited when they make great plays behind them." After all, while pitching is a big part of softball, it's still a team game that requires plays to be made in the field.

"As much as a team counts on a pitcher, they can't win the game all by themselves," she says. "So as coaches, we need to encourage them during the week in practice to work as though the team is depending solely on them, but on Game Day, it is totally about the team and enjoying the journey together."

Conclusion

Coaching sports is hard, and the challenges that accompany the task are never-ending—and often unexpected, too. It doesn't matter the age, sport, or experience level of the participants, either. Every season, and every team, is different. But each, with its assorted personalities and diverse skill levels, will present its own unique array of challenges for you as the season unfolds. How prepared you are, as a coach, to respond to these as they occur, and lead your players through them, determines just how enjoyable and rewarding their journey will be with you—and how you will be remembered for the rest of their lives.

After reading this book, I hope you are aware of how important your role is, one that can never be taken lightly at any moment. The more well-versed you are in the basics of coaching, the stronger the foundation you will have in place to serve as the springboard for a terrific season of fun and learning for everyone involved. This includes everything from planning those practices and motivating athletes to propel themselves to levels they never thought possible, to correcting mistakes without crushing confidence and forging those all-important team-first attitudes. You also learned that you have the opportunity to be incredibly influential in so many areas of a young athlete's life, many that may not have even been on your radar when you stepped forward to coach. You now know that coaching young players is a huge responsibility, and that every interaction has the potential to lift or beat down a child's confidence, self-esteem, and enthusiasm for the sport.

As Chicago Cubs manager Joe Maddon pointed out, kids see, soak in, and evaluate everything. Whether it's your words or body language, they see it all. Every moment matters; every interaction has significance. So you have a responsibility to make every one of those moments as positive and meaningful as possible. You also recognize that every practice session represents so much more than simply an hour of running players through a series of drills. Yes, your practices are a wonderful opportunity for teaching skills and elevating performance levels, and that of course is a huge component of being a successful coach and great leader. But it's also the chance to impart some positive or encouraging words that make kids feel good about themselves, and that they can take home and share with family and friends.

Remember, as Super Bowl champion John Harbaugh said, strive to give every young athlete something that they can feel really good about and enjoy retelling at the dinner table. Youth sports can be a great memory maker, and those memories don't have to all revolve around scoring a touchdown or delivering the game-winning base hit, either. Those moments are fleeting—and not every athlete will have the luxury of enjoying one. But every athlete can be applauded by her coach for hustling, for being a great practice performer who energizes the squad with his enthusiasm, or even for executing a particular skill well in the practice that day that she can proudly share afterward with family or friends. Plus, those practice sessions are the chance to help young athletes dig into the process of working hard and really finding joy in that exertion and overcoming struggles along the way. And just think how powerful those lessons will be as they deal with work projects and other struggles later in life—they'll remember they have the ability to work through it and the confidence to not give up.

You have also learned that those practices are valuable hours devoted to coming together as a team, and genuinely pulling for and encouraging each other in the chase for something much more important than personal accolades—and that's team unity and success. Seeing players working in harmony, not worried about who is scoring the basket or catching the touchdown pass, is incredibly rewarding to watch and a wonderful reflection on a coach when his or her athletes care more about the team than individual attention.

As you've seen in these pages, game days, road trips, and extracurricular activities all represent terrific opportunities for you to teach, mold, and develop young athletes, and instill in them wonderful characteristics and life skills that they will carry with them into adulthood. And who knows, maybe some of these young athletes you are working with will choose to get into coaching too, later on, because of the impact that you have had on them that they can pass on to the next generation. So, consider yourself lucky: you have an amazing opportunity in front of you. You've got a front row seat for watching your team develop and evolve, and for your young players heading down that path of becoming wonderful citizens and future community leaders. You can take great pride in being a part of helping make it all happen.

Now, as you have read through these pages, there were probably many aspects of coaching that you might not have been aware of, or perhaps hadn't given a lot of thought to with your attention understandably being pulled in so many different directions. There is no need to be overwhelmed, or doubt for one second your ability to coach, and to coach well. Just like you want your players stepping on fields, courts, and rinks with a positive and confident mindset, the same goes for you, too. The more confident you are in your abilities, the more likely that your players will follow your lead.

As was mentioned by several of the coaches featured in this book, they have reached the highest levels and had the greatest impact because they embrace life-long learning. Every day they aren't just striving to help their players perform better, they're searching for any ways they can improve their skills, too. That's one of the helpful features of this book. You're not expected to digest all this incredible information and use every piece with your team all at once. But be a learner and embracer of knowledge like these outstanding coaches. Grab those nuggets that stood out to you and apply one each time you gather with your team, or at whatever pace you are most comfortable taking.

Hopefully the insights from these coaches has shined some light on ways you can improve your practices and make them more appealing, or enable you to become a better communicator, or help you approach teaching a difficult skill in a different manner, and so on. Also, maybe something one of them said will spark your own ideas for connecting with or encouraging players. So no matter if you are prepping for your first season on the sidelines, or if you have been a long-time and beloved coach for years, by navigating your seasons with an insatiable thirst for learning and improving, you'll position yourself as one of those coaches that youngsters love playing for and learning from.

The National Alliance for Youth Sports applauds you for taking on the role of coaching young athletes and thanks you for your passion in wanting to be the best coach possible. As Baltimore Orioles manager Buck Showalter said earlier in this book, all coaches of young athletes should ask themselves this question: If you were a kid on a sports team, would you want to play for you, as the coach? By using the many wonderful ideas, techniques, approaches, and philosophies presented in this book—courtesy of some of the most respected and successful coaches in the country, who were kind enough to share their secrets—you can be on your way to making sure the answer to that all-important question is a resounding yes!

National Alliance for Youth Sports

The National Alliance for Youth Sports (NAYS) educates, equips, and empowers youth sports leaders, volunteers, and parents so all children can enjoy the lifelong benefits of sports.

NAYS programs are provided at the local level through dynamic partnerships with more than 3,000 community-based organizations, which include parks and recreation departments, Boys and Girls Clubs, Police Athletic Leagues, YMCAs/YWCAs, and other independent youth service groups throughout the country. NAYS also has a strong presence on U.S. military installations worldwide, including every Air Force and Army base. NAYS offers several membership programs:

- **NAYS Coach Training & Membership**, a training program for volunteer coaches.

- **NAYS Officials Training & Membership**, a training program for officials.

- **NAYS Parent Orientation**, a sportsmanship training program for parents.

- **NAYS League Director Training & Membership**, a training program for volunteer administrators.

- **Academy for Youth Sports Administrators**, a certification program for professional administrators.

NAYS has also created several youth development programs that are utilized by recreation departments, military bases, and youth organizations across the country:

- **Start Smart Sports Development Programs** help children as young as three years old learn and develop basic motor skills needed for a fun and successful experience in organized sports.

- **Hook A Kid On Golf** is a comprehensive program that introduces youngsters to the game of golf and provides opportunities for them to continue playing the sport.

- **Ready, Set, RUN!** prepares children ages eight to thirteen to participate in a 5k run.

www.nays.org • nays@nays.org • (800) 729-2057 • (561) 684-1141

BETTER SPORTS FOR KIDS, BETTER KIDS FOR LIFE

Your First Coaching Book

A Practical Guide for Volunteer Coaches

The National Alliance For Youth Sports

As a youth sports volunteer, you should get used to wearing many hats, for you'll be not just a coach, but also a teacher, friend, and confidant. Coaching can be rewarding, but if you venture into the season unprepared, the role can be a frustrating one. Enter *Your First Coaching Book*. Created by the National Alliance for Youth Sports, it provides valuable tips on how to encourage fun and good sportsmanship, maximize basic skill development, deal with inappropriate behavior from players and parents, and prevent injuries by maintaining high safety standards.

$5.95 US • 80 pages • 4 x 7-inch paperback • ISBN 978-0-7570-0200-7

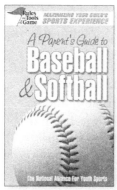

A Parent's Guide to Baseball & Softball

Maximizing Your Child's Sports Experience

The National Alliance For Youth Sports

Millions of kids participate in organized youth baseball and softball programs each year. It's an exciting world of colorful uniforms, post-game ice cream treats, and smiling faces. It's also one in which you as a parent can make a positive difference in helping your youngster grow and make the most of this experience. *A Parent's Guide to Baseball & Softball* lends a hand by offering advice to help your child set and meet season goals, develop the necessary skills for the sport, gain self-confidence and self-esteem, develop good sportsmanship, deal with challenges, and have a safe and rewarding season.

$4.95 US • 64 pages • 4 x 7-inch paperback • ISBN 978-0-7570-0201-4

Why Johnny Hates Sports

Why Organized Youth Sports
Are Failing Our Children and
What We Can Do About It

Fred Engh

All across this country, a
growing number of children
are dropping out of organized
sports—not because they don't
like to play, but because the
system they play in is failing
them. Written by one of this
country's leading advocates
of youth sports, *Why Johnny
Hates Sports* is the first book
to look at the growing problems
inherent in the way we introduce
our children to sports.

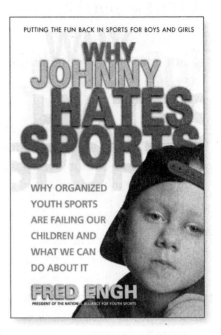

In this timely book, Fred Engh explains why many of the original
goals of youth leagues have been affected by today's win-at-all-
costs attitude. He then documents the negative physical and
psychological impact that parents, coaches, and administrators
can have on children, while providing effective solutions to each
of the problems covered.

Why Johnny Hates Sports is both an exposé of abuses and
a call to arms. It clearly illustrates a serious problem that has
been going on too long—a problem that, until now, has been
tolerated by most, with little concern for its effect on our
children. Most importantly, it provides practical answers that
can alter the destructive course that youth sports has taken.

$14.95 US • 224 pages • 6 x 9-inch quality paperback •
ISBN 978-0-7570-0041-6

For more information about our books,
visit our website at www.squareonepublishers.com